COME,
LET US ADORE HIM

By

Denver C. Snuffer, Jr.

Mill Creek Press
Salt Lake City, Utah

Published in the United States by Mill Creek Press.

ISBN: 978-0-9798455-3-6

Printed in the United States of America on acid-free paper
Mill Creek Press website address: www.millcreekpress.com
pfb32975

First Edition

Cover design by Arisman Studios, Exeter, MA
Cover drawing by Leonardo DaVinci

"Behold the Lamb of God,
which taketh away the sin of the world."
John 1: 29

Table of Contents:

SUMMARY OF ABBREVIATIONS USED:

The following abbreviations will be used for the authorities frequently cited in this work:

History of the Church of Jesus Christ of Latter-day Saints, 7 Volumes, published by the Church of Jesus Christ of Latter-day Saints; will be cited as *"DHC"* followed by volume number and page (i.e., *DHC* 6: 23).

Teachings of the Prophet Joseph Smith, arranged by Joseph Fielding Smith, published by Deseret Book Company; will be cited as *"TPJS"* followed by the page number (i.e., *TPJS,* p. 23).

The Journal of Discourses, 26 volumes, will be cited as *"JD"* followed by the volume and page number (i.e., *JD* 6: 23).

Lectures on Faith, compiled by N.B. Lundwall, published by Bookcraft; will be cited as *"Lectures"* followed by Lecture Number, paragraph and page number (i.e., *Lectures, Fourth Lecture,* paragraphs 50-54, pp. 90-91).

The Second Comforter: Conversing With the Lord Through the Veil, Denver C. Snuffer, Jr., published by Mill Creek Press, Salt Lake City, 2006; will be cited as *The Second Comforter.*

Nephi's Isaiah, Denver C. Snuffer, Jr., published by Mill Creek Press, Salt Lake City, 2006; will be cited as *Nephi's Isaiah.*

Beloved Enos, Denver C. Snuffer, Jr., published by Mill Creek Press, Salt Lake City, 2009; will be cited as *Beloved Enos.*

References to the Bible are to the King James Version.

All other authorities are cited at length.

All spellings in quotes have been left as in the original. To prevent the frequent repetition of "[sic]" we take note of that here, and will not otherwise acknowledge antiquated spellings within the text.

Preface

This book is a collection of thoughts about Jesus Christ. I take responsibility for the content of this book. It is one person's expression of devotion to the Lord. It is written as an act of personal worship. As a result, this is not a typical book about Him. Hopefully its contents draw you closer to Christ.

In the history of the world no one's life has been more important than Jesus Christ. He provided gifts, both before the world began and again in the Meridian of Time, which benefit all the earth's inhabitants. John addressed the futility of any account ever recording all of Christ's acts when he wrote: "And there are also many other things which Jesus did, the which, if they should be written every one, I suppose that even the world itself could not contain the books that should be written." (John 21: 25.) Although much has been written about Christ since John's day, this book should still be a unique addition to the record of Christ's doings because it is my personal testimony about Him.

This book does not attempt to discuss Christ's life in a chronological way, or discuss either His entire mortal life, nor even a preponderance of His life. James E. Talmage, Bruce R. McConkie and Hugh B. Brown are a few Latter-day Apostles whose works are comprehensive in an effort to discuss Christ's life. By comparison, this book takes only a small selection of events and discusses them in an effort to explain neglected doctrine and put it into the context of Christ's life and His teachings not adequately discussed by others. Although the discussion is not chronological, the chronology of Christ's life is mentioned to help the reader put the discussion into context.

Here we assume readers are already familiar with these other, earlier works and already have a foundation concerning Christ. If that is not the case, then this book may not be the right book for you to read first. At a minimum the reader should have previously read *Jesus the Christ* by Elder Talmage and *The Mortal Messiah* series (4 books) by Elder McConkie.

This book contains some new material which you should feel free to disregard, unless the Spirit witnesses to you that the material is worthwhile, true and should be accepted. Teachers are required to follow the Spirit, and you should be able to tell whether or not the content of this book is inspired by the right source. If you believe things in this book to be in error, you are free to give it no further thought. If, however, the Spirit witnesses to you that this testimony adds to your existing understanding of truth about our Lord, then you have something of value in your own search to find Him. The way for you to judge this matter is set out in the Book of Mormon. But the way to judge is accompanied by a warning that you must judge correctly or you will be condemned:

> For behold, **the Spirit of Christ is given to every man, that he may know good from evil**; wherefore, **I show unto you the way to judge**; for **every thing which inviteth to do good, and to persuade to believe in Christ, is sent forth by the power and gift of Christ; wherefore ye may know with a perfect knowledge it is of God**. But whatsoever thing persuadeth men to do evil, and believe not in Christ, and deny him, and serve not God, then ye may know with a perfect knowledge it is of the devil; for after this manner doth the devil work, for he persuadeth no man to do good, no, not one; neither do his angels; neither do they who subject themselves unto him. And now, my brethren, **seeing that ye know the light by which ye may judge, which light is the light of Christ, see that ye do not judge wrongfully; for with that same judgment which ye judge ye shall also be judged**. Wherefore, I beseech of you, brethren, that **ye should search diligently in the light of Christ that ye may know good from evil; and if ye will lay hold upon every good**

> **thing, and condemn it not, ye certainly will be a child of Christ**. (Moroni 7: 16-19, emphasis added.)

Nothing in this test limits who should apply it. If you are given this book to read, you have the means to make the judgment: "every man" has the same tool given to them. Furthermore, the test does not limit where the truth may come from. Even an obscure Latter-day Saint may offer something of value. I hope that is the case with this book.

This book is one person's act of devotion. Writing it has been an act of devotion to the Lord. Any failure in this book is the fault of a flawed author. Any good found in this book, however, is the result of the Lord's mercy in condescending to make these things known to me. So far as I am able to speak the truth, the contents of this book I believe to all be true. However, there are some things which I do not intend to address or clarify in this book.

I want to thank my wife, daughter Kylee, Mill Creek Press and others who have encouraged or supported this book. And I want to thank you, the reader, for taking the time to read this. This is the sixth book I have written. The prior books are: *The Second Comforter: Conversing with the Lord Through the Veil*, published originally in 2006 and in its second edition in 2008; *Nephi's Isaiah*, published in 2007; *Eighteen Verses*, published in 2007; *Ten Parables*, published in 2008; and *Beloved Enos*, published in 2009. All books have been published by Mill Creek Press.

Since this book has been written prayerfully, it will have its greatest meaning to those who read it prayerfully.

Denver C. Snuffer, Jr.
October 6, 2009
Sandy, Utah

COME,
LET US ADORE HIM

Chapter 1, Introduction:
What Think Ye of Christ?

Christ asked a question about Himself that we all must answer: "What think ye of Christ?" (Matt. 22: 42.) There are enough books written about Christ to fill libraries. However, it is still up to each individual to discover for themselves what they think of Christ and what significance He is to have in their lives. Despite all that has been written of Him, we must find Him for ourselves.

Every Fast Sunday members of The Church of Jesus Christ of Latter-day Saints volunteer to testify to their fellow ward members about what Christ means to them. This monthly rite, involving millions of believers, on practically every continent, is still inadequate to describe who the Savior is and what He did for us.

Reading scriptures about Him, hearing testimonies of Him, or studying artists' renderings of Christ may help us get an impression of what He means to others; but each one of us must decide for ourself the depth of the investigation to make of Him. We decide how far to pursue His teachings. The decision should be made in light of Christ's claims: "Jesus saith unto him, I am the way, the truth, and the life: no man cometh unto the Father, but by me." (John 14: 6.) Do you think there may be different levels of coming to the Father through Christ? If so, then why not pursue more deeply into why He is the way, truth and life? I hope this book will help you do that.

He explained that "eternal life" is dependent upon knowing Him: "And this is life eternal, that they might know thee the only true God, and Jesus Christ, whom thou hast sent." (John 17: 3.) He states that each of us must come to **know** Him to obtain eternal life. There is a difference between knowing Him and merely knowing about Him. No one should be content to merely know about Him.

He explained how to meet both Him and His Father: "Jesus saith unto him, Have I been so long time with you, and yet hast thou not known me, Philip? he that hath seen me hath seen the Father; and how sayest thou then, Shew us the Father?" (John 14: 9.) These sayings are as true today as they were when He first uttered them.[1] They mean as much to us as they did to His former disciples.

He occupies the central role in salvation. We are expected to have a testimony of Him. John the Beloved raised the importance of a personal testimony of Christ by directly connecting it with the gift of prophecy: "[T]he testimony of Jesus is the spirit of prophecy." (Rev. 19: 10.) The foundation of the Church established by Christ includes both apostles and prophets.[2] To have

---

[1]I have previously written about Christ's promise in the 14th Chapter of John to come to His followers and, with His Father, to "take up their abode" with His disciples in *The Second Comforter*. Anyone interested in pursuing the subject is referred to that book.

[2]See, e.g., 1 Cor. 12: 28-29; Eph. 2: 20; 3: 5 and 4: 11.

a saving testimony of Him is to become a prophet. It is no wonder, then, Moses wished all men were prophets.[3] We are all invited to get testimonies of Christ and are, therefore, all also invited to become prophets.

What someone else thinks of Christ is not as important as what **you** think of Him. How others relate to Him is not important if **you** do not relate to Him in a deeply personal way.

Paul explained how Christ has improved mankind's potential covenant with God. In this new era described by Paul, it is now possible for each of us to come to Him, know the Father, receive eternal life and possess the spirit of prophecy:

> But now hath he obtained a more excellent ministry, by how much also he is the mediator of a better covenant, which was established upon better promises. For if that first covenant had been faultless, then should no place have been sought for the second. For finding fault with them, he saith, Behold, the days come, saith the Lord, when I will make a new covenant with the house of Israel and with the house of Judah: Not according to the covenant that I made with their fathers in the day when I took them by the hand to lead them out of the land of Egypt; because they continued not in my covenant, and I regarded them not, saith the Lord. For this is the covenant that I will make with the house of Israel after those days, saith the Lord; I will put my laws into their mind, and write them in their hearts: and I will be to them a God, and they shall be to me a people: And they shall not teach every man his neighbour, and every man his brother, saying, Know the Lord: for all shall know me, from the least to the greatest.

---

[3]See Num. 11: 29: "would God that all the Lord's people were prophets, and that the Lord would put his spirit upon them!"

> For I will be merciful to their unrighteousness, and their sins and their iniquities will I remember no more. In that he saith, A new covenant, he hath made the first old. Now that which decayeth and waxeth old is ready to vanish away. (Heb. 8: 6-13.)

In modern revelation we receive the assurance of how intimate a relationship we may all have with Him. We are promised that each of us can obtain our own knowledge of Him. We need not be dependent upon others for that knowledge:

> Until **all shall know me, who remain, even from the least unto the greatest, and shall be filled with the knowledge of the Lord**, and shall see eye to eye, and shall lift up their voice, and with the voice together sing this new song, saying:
> The Lord hath brought again Zion;
> The Lord hath redeemed his people, Israel,
> According to the election of grace,
> Which was brought to pass by the faith
> And covenant of their fathers. (D&C 84: 98-99, emphasis added.)

You should have your own testimony of Him. This book contains a portion of my testimony of Christ. Parts of this book are deeply personal, as any testimony must be. It is offered in the hope that there may be a benefit for you in reading another person's testimony. If there is nothing to be gained by hearing another's testimony then what is the value of having monthly testimony meetings? This book is offered in that same spirit. No one has the right to dictate how or what you should think of Christ. There is also only one person entitled to give commandments to The Church of Jesus Christ of Latter-day Saints. Although all saints may share testimonies, only the President of the High Priesthood, the

President of The Church of Jesus Christ of Latter-day Saints may issue commandments to the Church on behalf of the Lord. Even then, the membership must sustain by common consent the revelations and commandments received by the President before they become binding upon the members. Therefore, it should be clear that if you encounter something new from the testimony contained in this book it is not at all binding upon you, unless the Spirit bears witness that it is true. This book may persuade, but it cannot and does not attempt to command anyone to believe or do anything.

When reading some new things about Christ in this book, remember there are four canonized Gospels written about Christ's life. They differ from each other. Matthew's approach argues that Christ was the living fulfillment of earlier prophecy. Mark's Gospel is Spartan, even primitive when compared with the others. His view of Christ reveals a Savior who was oftentimes exasperated with the foolishness of His disciples. Mark was the youngest of the Gospel writers when he made his observations. Mark's account tells the reader more about him as an observer when contrasted with the other writers. Luke was trusted, even intimate with Christ and His mother. Luke is the only one who recorded the confidential account of how Mary felt in the early history of Christ's birth and youth in his Gospel. Luke was one of the first people Christ visited after the resurrection, meeting with him even before the Twelve Apostles.[4] Luke's account reflects this intimacy

---

[4] I recognize many scholars and even the LDS Bible Dictionary assert that Luke did not become a follower of Christ until after His death. That Dictionary calls the idea of Luke being one of the two disciples who met the Lord on the road to Emmaus "picturesque but historically unsupported." I have a different view, and will explain some

between him, Christ and His mother. John's Gospel is completely different than the other three. For John, Christ was transcendent, His story other-worldly, and His messages steeped in deeper meanings. John used incidents from Christ's life as a setting for transcendent teaching and to reinforce the message. These Gospel writers differed from each other in what they wrote and even in how they viewed Christ. They all believed Him to be the promised Messiah. There is no contradiction between them in that regard. There are only different vantage points from which to view the Lord. We should appreciate these differences because they help us form our own view. But we should also allow these four writers to hold even contradicting memories and express different understandings.

If you compare Michelangelo's sculptures of Christ with Da Vinci's, you will see both similarities and dissimilarities. El Greco's vision of Christ is so otherworldly as to be astonishing; yet it also shares some commonality with other artists. Latter-day artists Minerva Tichert and Jared Barns have different artistic viewpoints and styles, but their artistic interpretations can be seen by an appreciative audience for what insight they may bring. No one would think to criticize these artists' expression of devotion because they were different in style, look, medium, feel and what they communicate to the mind of the observer.

Just like the works of art differ, so also the writings of Elder James E. Talmage, Elder Bruce R. McConkie and Elder Hugh B. Brown differ in view and content. This is true even though all of them are Latter-day Saint Apostles. They wrote as an act of personal devotion, in the hope of inspiring others to have faith in

---

of the reasons for it at the end of this book.

Christ. There is no reason to think the differences between them are inappropriate. They all have something to add.

These diverse expressions of beliefs found in scripture, art and literature illustrate how differently each author or artist testified of Christ. Reading the written testimonies of Christ, or contemplating works of art depicting our Lord should stir within you the realization that Christ lives. He lived a mortal life, died and was resurrected to live again. If you are moved to greater faith by others' testimonies, whether spoken or otherwise, then something wonderful has occurred. These examples confirm to us that we can have our own testimony and understanding of Him even if it is unique from all others. Hope for eternity is achieved only through Him.

This book offers my interpretation of Christ. It is my explanation of faith and my testimony of His message. It shows why I find Christ so compelling. It is offered for your consideration as another way to see the Risen Savior of mankind. If it helps increase your faith in Him, then it has served its purpose. If it does not, then feel at liberty to discard it. As the scripture above tells us: Christ is a revelation of the Father. Coming to Him, knowing Him and learning to understand Him is at the center of life's purpose. When you have reconciled yourself to Christ, you have reconciled yourself to the Father. When you have seen Christ, you have seen the Father, for they are One. Christ's whole ministry was and is to bring others to the Father, that they may also become the "sons and daughters of God."

John explained Christ's purpose in these words: "Behold, what manner of love the Father hath bestowed upon us, that we should be called the sons of God: therefore the world knoweth us not, because it knew him not. Beloved, now are we the sons of God[.]"

(1 John 3: 1-2.) To become such a son you must first know His Firstborn Son.

One of The Book of Mormon's tests for knowing whether something comes from Christ is simple: "And whatsoever thing persuadeth men to do good is of me; for good cometh of none save it be of me. I am the same that leadeth men to all good; he that will not believe my words will not believe me--that I am; and he that will not believe me will not believe the Father who sent me." (Ether 4: 12.) All that brings you to understand Him, seek for Him, believe in and trust Him comes from Him. I hope as you read this book you will find it brings you closer to Him. If it does, then you may know for a certainty that it, like any other true testimony from any disciple of His, comes from Him.

You should be able to recognize truth when you see or hear it. The "Spirit" teaches truth as a gift to everyone.[5] That Spirit allows us to determine whether we are seeing the truth. You should use that gift to learn of Him. He is literally within all of us through that Spirit, to enable us to find Him.

We are told in modern revelation how the process should work. When you use the Spirit of truth within you it allows you to recognize truth:

> Verily I say unto you, he that is ordained of me and sent forth to preach the word of truth by the Comforter, in the Spirit of truth, **doth he preach it by the Spirit of truth or some other way**? And if it be by some other way it is not of God. And

---

[5]See, e.g., D&C 84: 46: "And the Spirit giveth light to every man that cometh into the world; and the Spirit enlighteneth every man through the world, that hearkeneth to the voice of the Spirit." D&C 93: 2: "And that I am the true light that lighteth every man that cometh into the world[.]"

> again, **he that receiveth the word of truth, doth he receive it by the Spirit of truth or some other way**? If it be some other way it is not of God. Therefore, why is it that ye cannot understand and know, that **he that receiveth the word by the Spirit of truth receiveth it as it is preached by the Spirit of truth**? Wherefore, he that preacheth and he that receiveth, understand one another, and both are edified and rejoice together. And **that which doth not edify is not of God, and is darkness. That which is of God is light**; and he that receiveth light, and continueth in God, receiveth more light; and that light groweth brighter and brighter until the perfect day. And again, verily I say unto you, and **I say it that you may know the truth, that you may chase darkness from among you**[.] (D&C 50: 17-25, emphasis added.)

Truth should edify. It should enlighten the mind and heart. It should be filled with light. This is both positive and negative. On the positive side it allows you to find truth. But, on the negative, when you reject truth you are accountable for choosing darkness. If you continually accept light, it will brighten until you near a perfect brightness where you can know truth for yourself. You do not have to rely on others. Be humble and prayerful and you will be able to distinguish that which is of Christ.

As you read this book, consider whether it teaches by the "Spirit of truth" or by some other way. Decide for yourself if it edifies you and contains light, or if, instead, it is filled with darkness.

This book is a personal expression of understanding and testimony. It does not contain any official teaching by or position of any Church or organization. I am a member of The Church of Jesus Christ of Latter-day Saints. However, I do not speak for that Church, nor do the views set out in this book represent views shared by other Latter-day Saints.

There are many books which are comprehensive and cover the entire New Testament account. This book does not. I have chosen to focus on things not well covered by other writers. I may also have a different view point which could help someone understand the Lord differently. This is not even a comprehensive discussion of my personal testimony of Christ. Some of that would be inappropriate to include because of its highly personal meaning. Also, there are many existing Latter-day Saint commentaries which cover the entire life of Christ. I do not intend to merely repeat what has been adequately discussed elsewhere. To the extent that I have something new to add and it does not become overly personal or inappropriate,[6] I have included my personal testimony of Him in this book.

The Christmas hymn from which the title of this book was taken, captures an idea which I like a great deal. The idea of "adoration" for the Lord seems wholly appropriate. I believe the better someone comes to know Christ the more likely they are to find themselves adoring Him.

---

[6]The distinction between what is appropriate and what is not is determined first by the Spirit, which will constrain you to either impart or withhold. (See Alma 12: 9-11.) Secondly, once the discussion passes beyond the initial ordinances of the Gospel, i.e., baptism, laying on of hands for the Holy Ghost, sacrament, ordinations, and Patriarchal Blessings, you then encounter ordinances which are not fully disclosed by the saints beyond mentioning their existence, i.e., washings and anointings, endowment and sealing. There are other ordinances which are not often mentioned. Those distinctions are honored in this book.

There are characteristics of the Lord which are unrelenting, committed and determined. There was never a man who lived with greater resolve than Jesus Christ. He was much tougher, more resolute, more fixed in purpose than I at first imagined. As I have acquired a better understanding of Him, I have grown to greatly appreciate Isaiah's comment: "For the Lord God will help me; therefore shall I not be confounded: therefore have I set my face like a flint, and I know that I shall not be ashamed." (Isa. 50: 7.) Isaiah captured the perfect phrase to describe the Lord's determined will. Surely He "set His face like a flint" as He completed His mortal mission.

Christ came to understand His role early in life. He knew His identity, and accepted His burden. He studied the prophecies about Himself, and then followed the course to its painful end. Although His disciples seemed genuinely surprised by the crucifixion, He was not. He told them He was going up to Jerusalem to be crucified before that final week. As Matthew recorded after the events: "And Jesus going up to Jerusalem took the twelve disciples apart in the way, and said unto them, Behold, we go up to Jerusalem; and the Son of man shall be betrayed unto the chief priests and unto the scribes, and they shall condemn him to death, And shall deliver him to the Gentiles to mock, and to scourge, and to crucify him: and the third day he shall rise again." (Matt. 20: 17-19.) Despite this plain explanation, His closest followers did not understand it. The angels at the tomb had to remind them. To the women who came first to the tomb they declared: "He is not here, but is risen: remember how he spake unto you when he was yet in Galilee, Saying, The Son of man must be delivered into the hands of sinful men, and be crucified, and the third day rise again. And they remembered his words, And returned from the sepulchre, and told all these things unto the eleven, and to all the rest." (Luke 24: 6-9.)

His followers may not have grasped His literal meaning, but He did. He knew why He had come into the world. He was determined to fulfill the mission given Him. Even though His followers may have all had hope for worldly triumph as He entered Jerusalem the week of that final Passover, He knew it was the time for His death. He knew the details of what He would suffer. He had studied them in the prophecies. To say He went willingly is to understate the matter. He went determinedly. He went with His face fixed like flint to suffer the will of the Father in all things, no matter how bitter, no matter how terrible. Nor could His followers' disappointment deter Him. Although there came a moment when He was astonished by how hard it was to bear, He nevertheless submitted.

I have been struck by the Lord's determination that I have previously tried to capture His grit in a parable. In my book *Ten Parables*, there is a story titled *The Horses of Shiloh*, which attempts, by analogy, to describe this aspect of our Lord. He was more fixed in purpose than any man. I cannot describe it any better than did Isaiah. Therefore, I adopt it. Our Lord's face was "fixed like flint" as He moved toward His painful sacrificial suffering and death.

I recognize the contents of this book will differ in some passages quite dramatically from what others have said or taught about Christ. I make no apologies for those differences, and acknowledge they exist. This is one person's testimony. As a reader you should feel no obligation to agree with my personal view, unless the Spirit also confirms to you it is true. Then you will be trusting the Spirit, not me. I want no one to trust or rely only upon me.

Finally, I share the general Latter-day Saint view that the cross is an inappropriate religious symbol. Christ spoke of His Atonement in modern revelation and did not mention the cross. (See D&C 19: 15-19.) He dwelt upon His experience in Gethsemene, and that is why Latter-day Saints always point to the suffering there as being the most important part of the atonement. However, there was a great work done by Christ on the cross for which this book will show respect. His work was not finished in Gethsemene, nor on the cross, nor on the day of His resurrection, nor is it finished still. He continues to work to bring men to God. He continues to succor all who come to Him still.[7]

We turn then to the beginning of the New Testament events in the next chapter.

---

[7]I have discussed His ongoing role in Chapter 15 in my earlier book *Eighteen Verses* on pp. 263-278, which treats Alma 7: 12.

Chapter 2
The Veil Opens

The heavens had been silent for several hundred years when the New Testament account begins. No new revelation was recognized, no prophet known and no angelic visitors had come to Jerusalem for generations. The Jews were despairing from the recently ended Maccabean revolt. Pompey subdued Jerusalem in 63 BC. He not only ended Jewish rule, but as conqueror he entered the Holy of Holies itself to show the returning Roman dominance over these people. Roman political oppression followed. The Hasmonean Dynasty's rule ended only in 37 BC with the appointment of Herod as Rome's subservient ruler.

Into this spiritually desolate landscape the Angel Gabriel came to answer the longstanding and daily repeated prayer of Israel for the light of His countenance to return. The record of the event says:

> There was in the days of Herod, the king of Judaea, a certain priest named Zacharias, of the course of Abia: and his wife was of the daughters of Aaron, and her name was Elisabeth. And they were both righteous before God, walking in all the commandments and ordinances of the Lord blameless. And they had no child, because that Elisabeth was barren, and they both were now well stricken in years. And it came to pass, that while he

> executed the priest's office before God in the order of his course, According to the custom of the priest's office, his lot was to burn incense when he went into the temple of the Lord. And the whole multitude of the people were praying without at the time of incense. (Luke 1: 5-10.)

Zacharias was chosen by lot to bring the incense[8] into the Holy Place and burn it before the veil, atop the Altar of Incense. The veil hung on the west end of the room and separated the Holy Place from the Holy of Holies. The Holy of Holies symbolized the throne room and presence of God. The ritual Zacharias performed had been repeated daily, morning and evening from the time of Moses, with only a brief interruption during the Babylonian exile.

For the ritual, three priests would enter the room. After cleaning the ash, placing hot coals on the golden Altar of Incense and igniting Temple-prepared incense upon the Altar, two of the

---

[8] The formula for the incense was decreed by the Lord to Moses. It was to be used exclusively for Temple service, and never to be made for outside use. "And the Lord said unto Moses, Take unto thee sweet spices, stacte, and onycha, and galbanum; these sweet spices with pure frankincense: of each shall there be a like weight: And thou shalt make it a perfume, a confection after the art of the apothecary, tempered together, pure and holy: And thou shalt beat some of it very small, and put of it before the testimony in the tabernacle of the congregation, where I will meet with thee: it shall be unto you most holy. And as for the perfume which thou shalt make, ye shall not make to yourselves according to the composition thereof: it shall be unto thee holy for the Lord. Whosoever shall make like unto that, to smell thereto, shall even be cut off from his people." (Ex. 30: 34-38.) The purpose of the smell was to remind those who experienced it of the scent of Eden, that original Garden in which God and man associated. The Temple was designed to create a sacred place where the association could be renewed.

priests would withdraw. Zacharias remained alone to offer the prescribed prayer, as the pungent smoke from the incense rose upward. The rising smoke symbolized Israel's prayers ascending to heaven. As the column reached the ceiling it would billow outward against the top of the room. The column and spreading cloud symbolized the trunk and branches from the tree of life in the Garden of Eden. The setting itself was Holy, filled with symbols testifying of God's presence and Israel's history and destiny.

The Table of Shewbread, Menorah, Altar of Incense and rising column of smoke were all in the room in which Zacharias prayed. The words of the prayer Zacharias offered were prescribed:

> Be graciously pleased, Jehovah our God, with Thy people Israel, and with their prayer. **Restore the service to the oracle of Thy house**; and the burnt-offerings of Israel and their prayer accept graciously and in love; and let the service of Thy people Israel be ever well-pleasing unto Thee.
>
> We praise Thee, who art Jehovah our God, and the God of our fathers, the God of all flesh, our Creator, and the Creator from the beginning! Blessing and praise be to Thy great and holy name, that Thou hast preserved us in life and kept us. So preserve us and keep us, and **gather the scattered ones into Thy holy courts**, to keep Thy statutes, and to do Thy good pleasure, and to serve Thee with our whole heart, as this day we confess unto Thee. Blessed be the Lord, unto whom belongeth praise.
>
> Appoint peace, goodness, and blessing; grace, mercy, and compassion for us, and for all Israel Thy people. **Bless us, O our Father, all of us as one, with the light of Thy countenance. For in the light of Thy countenance hast Thou, Jehovah, our God, given us the law of life, and**

> **loving mercy, and righteousness, and blessing, and compassion, and life, and peace**. And may it please Thee to bless Thy people Israel at all times, and at every hour with Thy peace. [May we and all Thy people Israel be remembered and written before Thee in the book of life, with blessing and peace and support.] Blessed be Thou, Jehovah, who blessest Thy people Israel with peace. (Alfred Edersheim, *The Temple, Its Ministry and Services*; Hendrickson Publishers, Massachusetts, 1994; p. 129, emphasis added, brackets in original.)

This prescribed petition offered on behalf of Israel requested the "oracle," or prophetic presence, of God come again to the Lord's House. Although the Temple was the House of the Lord in one sense, all of Israel was the House of the Lord as well. The prayer's request to "gather the scattered ones" was not only a request to return lost Israelites, but also more correctly an entreaty to bring those who had strayed from the truth back to its knowledge. Finally, the prayer for the "light of Thy countenance" asked God to bring His presence among Israel again. Israel expected Him to bring "the law of life, and loving mercy, and righteousness, and blessing, and compassion, and life, and peace." There could not be a more appropriate petition for the birth of Jesus Christ.

The response that came was a specific answer to this prayer, as the Angel Gabriel said. We read Gabriel's explanation in Luke:

> And there appeared unto him an angel of the Lord standing on the right side of the altar of incense. And when Zacharias saw him, he was troubled, and fear fell upon him. But the angel said unto him, **Fear not, Zacharias: for thy prayer is heard**; and thy wife Elisabeth shall bear thee a son, and thou shalt call his name John. And thou shalt have joy and gladness; and many shall rejoice at his

> birth. For he shall be great in the sight of the Lord, and shall drink neither wine nor strong drink; and he shall be filled with the Holy Ghost, even from his mother's womb. And many of the children of Israel shall he turn to the Lord their God. And **he shall go before him in the spirit and power of Elias, to turn the hearts of the fathers to the children, and the disobedient to the wisdom of the just; to make ready a people prepared for the Lord**. (Luke 1: 11-17, emphasis added.)

The prayer for Israel had been heard. God intended to shine the light of His countenance upon them! He would come to give the law of life, loving mercy, righteousness, blessing, compassion, life and peace, just as Zacharias had prayed. But there was something else. Something which seemed oddly disconnected from the prayer he had offered. Zacharias and his wife, Elisabeth, were going to have a son who would go before the light of His countenance and prepare people to receive the coming Lord.

This son, who would go before the Lord and prepare people for Him, was to be "great in the sight of the Lord." He would be consecrated from his birth. Throughout His life he would live the Nazarite oath, abstaining from wine, and being filled with the Holy Ghost.[9] Therefore God's deliverance of Israel, the countenance of

---

[9]The vow of the Nazarite is set out in Numbers 6: 2-8: "When either man or woman shall separate themselves to vow a vow of a Nazarite, to separate themselves unto the Lord: He shall separate himself from wine and strong drink, and shall drink no vinegar of wine, or vinegar of strong drink, neither shall he drink any liquor of grapes, nor eat moist grapes, or dried. All the days of his separation shall he eat nothing that is made of the vine tree, from the kernels even to the husk. All the days of the vow of his separation there shall no razor come upon

God's presence, and the son to be born to Elisabeth were all linked in the angel's message.

Zacharias was a priest. He had been selected to come offer the prayer in the Holy Place by lot. The whole scene was overwhelming to him. Here stood an angel on the "right side of the altar" exactly as one would emerge from the Holy of Holies through the veil. The location symbolized coming from the throne room and presence of God. Zacharias would have understood this. This is the room, and this was the place in that room at which such a heavenly messenger would be expected to stand if he came from heaven. Further, the Temple, as God's House, was where God's messengers would be expected to come. The prayer sought God's presence and asked Him to come. Everything from the timing, setting, and physical elements of this event, this angelic message, was exactly as it should be - with one exception. Zacharias doubted the prophecy about he and his wife. His wife Elisabeth bearing a son did not seem consistent with the rest of the message. Childbirth for Elisabeth seemed so unlikely, that Zacharias asked the following:

---

his head: until the days be fulfilled, in the which he separateth himself unto the Lord, he shall be holy, and shall let the locks of the hair of his head grow. All the days that he separateth himself unto the Lord he shall come at no dead body. He shall not make himself unclean for his father, or for his mother, for his brother, or for his sister, when they die: because the consecration of his God is upon his head. All the days of his separation he is holy unto the Lord." This vow was why John's diet was "locusts and wild honey." (Matt. 3: 4.)

> And Zacharias said unto the angel, Whereby shall I know this? for I am an old man, and my wife well stricken in years. And the angel answering said unto him, I am Gabriel, that stand in the presence of God; and am sent to speak unto thee, and to shew thee these glad tidings. And, behold, thou shalt be dumb, and not able to speak, until the day that these things shall be performed, because thou believest not my words, which shall be fulfilled in their season. (Luke 1: 18-20.)

Zacharias expressed the problem plainly to this heavenly messenger. Anyone in the presence of a heavenly messenger should be so candid. You can never have an answer if you do not ask. The concern was valid and heartfelt.

Gabriel's response reminded Zacharias the message came from God. "I am Gabriel, that stand in the presence of God," he said. The meaning was clear: This messenger was not merely standing on the right side of the altar, where the veil parted, to allow one to emerge from the symbolic presence of God in the Temple; Gabriel was coming from the actual presence of God.

He continued saying he had been "sent to speak unto thee, and to shew thee these glad tidings." Or, to put it more directly, this message came straight from God. Gabriel had been in God's presence. God was the author of the message he was delivering.

As we will consider more carefully at the end of this book, this was a real incident. It happened at a specific place and time. It was an actual event. It is unambiguous. It involved a distinct message, and required no lengthy theological debate. There were at least two pregnancies coming, one of them was to involve Zacharias' aged wife. The birth would produce a son and the child was to be named John. This is how God speaks to men. He does not speak in ambiguities, requiring councils to debate meanings. Revelation does not need generations to pass and clarity only emerging after long discussions and a consensus being reached by men. Revelation is clear, definite, unmistakable and intrudes with sometimes unwelcome or surprising news. If portions of a revelation are veiled in prophecy, it is deliberate. But even veiled meanings become clear as soon as the prophesied event occurs. Councils of men debating and then reaching a consensus is a political event, subject to shifting majorities. Neither God nor his messengers are present.

In light of Zacharias' question, Gabriel gave the sign: Zacharias would be struck dumb, and most likely deaf as well, until the promised child was born. Given the subsequent events, the "sign" of being unable to speak was particularly fitting. The audience who waited outside the Temple was not likely to welcome the glad news of the coming of Jehovah. Ultimately Zacharias would be killed by Herod for refusing to produce John, and the High Priests would conspire to kill John and Jesus. The sign kept the priestly crowd outside from hearing the message, which they would ultimately reject, earlier than necessary.

Luke's record continues:

> And the people waited for Zacharias, and marvelled that he tarried so long in the temple. And when he came out, he could not speak unto them: and they perceived that he had seen a vision

> in the temple: for he beckoned unto them, and remained speechless. (Luke 1: 21-22.)

Those who waited were fellow priests. They would "marvel that he tarried so long" because they knew how long it should take for the set prayer to be offered. He was taking too long. When he finally emerged, if he had **told** these waiting priests what he experienced they likely would not have believed him. But when he could not speak, "they perceived he had seen a vision in the temple." Left with the sign and their own reasoning, they reached the right conclusion. But in later events when a true testimony is given, they rejected it. The sign given by Gabriel was perhaps more appropriate for God's purpose than we may presume. It was not exclusively punishment of Zacharias for asking for proof, as is often taught.

Zacharias' ministry did not immediately end. He continued to serve at the Temple, mute, until his service ended. During this time, the subject of what took him so long, why he was mute, and how this had come to be, would no doubt be the conversation of those serving alongside him. This was the perfect place for this event to happen, to pique curiosity about the son who would be born to this aged priest. In the years that followed, all of Israel would know the public ministries of both John and Jesus had their beginning in the Temple of Herod.

The account continues:

> And it came to pass, that, as soon as the days of his ministration were accomplished, he departed to his own house. And after those days his wife Elisabeth conceived, and hid herself five months, saying, Thus hath the Lord dealt with me in the days wherein he looked on me, to take away my reproach among men. (Luke 1: 23-25.)

True to the word of Gabriel, and the sign which was given, Elisabeth conceived a son. She "hid herself" for five months. We are left to decide whether she hid because she did not dare, in her advanced age, bring the happy news to the attention of others for fear of losing the child. We do know she viewed the pregnancy as a gift from the Lord which took away the reproach of barrenness and made her a mother in Israel. Her hiding was due to her joy and gratitude and not embarrassment.

The Dispensation of Meridian of Time began in the Holy Place. Inside the Temple, just in front of the veil, among the Menorah, Table of Shewbread and Altar of Incense, the long silence of heaven is overturned by the message from the Angel Gabriel. This first event reminds us of the importance of the Temple. It is where heaven and earth meet both symbolically and, in this case, literally. The Holy Place is where the record of the New Testament begins and ends. The Holy Place forms the "bookends" (the first and last location) inside of which the New Testament account unfolds. The symbolism of that ought not be lost on any of us.

As the record continues, the scene shifts from the forerunner to the One who will actually restore the "oracle" and the "light of [God's] countenance" to Israel; while "gathering the scattered ones" back to God. So we move to Nazareth:

> And in the sixth month the angel Gabriel was sent from God unto a city of Galilee, named Nazareth, To a virgin espoused to a man whose name was Joseph, of the house of David; and the virgin's name was Mary. And the angel came in unto her, and said, Hail, thou that art highly favoured, the Lord is with thee: blessed art thou among women. And when she saw him, she was troubled at his

> saying, and cast in her mind what manner of salutation this should be. And the angel said unto her, Fear not, Mary: for thou hast found favour with God. And, behold, thou shalt conceive in thy womb, and bring forth a son, and shalt call his name JESUS. He shall be great, and shall be called the Son of the Highest: and the Lord God shall give unto him the throne of his father David: And he shall reign over the house of Jacob for ever; and of his kingdom there shall be no end. (Luke 1: 26-33.)

It is significant this visit takes place "in the sixth month" of Elisabeth's pregnancy. [Verse 36 clarifies that this is referring to the sixth month of the pregnancy, and not the sixth month of the year.] Elisabeth has been in seclusion for five months. What happens when she emerged from that isolation suggests she knew something more about the One before whom her son would go than the record informs us directly. We will look at that below.

It is significant that the timing of these two births would fall six months apart. Modern revelation tells us Christ's birth was on April 6th. (See D&C 20: 1.) Christ's birth in the spring would symbolize new life, new dispensation and resurrection. John's birth in the fall, on or near October 6th, would symbolize the end, destruction, closing of a dispensation and death. Birth dates matter. Joseph Smith's birth came on the day after the winter solstice, when daylight begins to grow longer and nighttime recedes to symbolize his role as restorer of light. John's birth date symbolized ending one dispensation. Christ's symbolized opening another.

Both were timed by heaven as a further witness to us of their respective missions.[10]

The messenger who had been sent to answer the prayer in the Holy Place, was sent again. The second visit was to the woman who would carry "the light of the countenance" of the Lord in her womb. His greeting called Mary "highly favored" and told her the Lord was with her. Troubled by this greeting, she wondered silently what this meant. Gabriel knew she was troubled. She was the only one who could have provided this information. Her story was recorded only by Luke. This reveals that Luke was trusted by her with sacred information which she was unlikely to have shared with many others.

Her candor with Luke about the incident and her private reservations speak well of her character, and provide us with insight into her soul. She did not expect the greeting. Likely, she did not think she was "highly favoured" as Gabriel said. For her it was troubling; not reassuring. The reaction reveals a humble soul.

Gabriel's next words: "Fear not," tell us volumes as well. Mary was fearful in the angel's presence. She reacted with the same kind of self-doubt and worry which all good people feel when they first encounter a holy messenger.

The message continued and informed her of her impending pregnancy. The promised child was to be a son, whose name would be Jesus (our Greek form of Joshua, or Yesheva). He was to be called "the Son of the Highest" and would possess the throne of David. She was told, this Son of the Highest would rule over the house of Jacob, and His kingdom would have no end. If the

---

[10] In our own dispensation, the Annual General Conference and Semi-annual General Conference coincide with the births of Jesus and John, symbolizing a little-known tribute to these two.

presence of the angel was troubling, and his countenance caused fear, what thoughts must have entered into the heart of Mary as she considered the child promised to her? She would carry a child who was greater than the heavenly messenger who announced His coming! It is hard to take in and wonderful to contemplate.

The account continues:

> Then said Mary unto the angel, How shall this be, seeing I know not a man? And the angel answered and said unto her, The Holy Ghost shall come upon thee, and the power of the Highest shall overshadow thee: therefore also that holy thing which shall be born of thee shall be called the Son of God. And, behold, thy cousin Elisabeth, she hath also conceived a son in her old age: and this is the sixth month with her, who was called barren. For with God nothing shall be impossible. And Mary said, Behold the handmaid of the Lord; be it unto me according to thy word. And the angel departed from her. (Luke 1: 34-38.)

Like Zacharias, the practical issue of the pregnancy is the first thing Mary spoke to the angel about. For Zacharias the issue was his wife's age, but with Mary the issue was her virginity. Both seemed practical impediments to the news Gabriel announced. Both expressed concern about how this prophecy was to unfold.

Gabriel explains the Holy Ghost will initiate the pregnancy. Indiscreet speculators have imposed all manner of conjecture about how this happened. For us it is enough to know that the same God who can enter a locked room without damage to the building can just as easily cause pregnancy while leaving the mother a virgin. With respect to the Holy Ghost, we all experience its presence without injury to our person: "the Holy Ghost has not a body of flesh and bones, but is a personage of Spirit. Were it not so, the

Holy Ghost could not dwell in us." (D&C 130: 22.) So it is enough for us to know the child was conceived through the workings of the Spirit, and without a mortal father. Mary was a virgin.

Gabriel, who promised the child would come through miraculous means, gave Mary cause to believe the promise by telling her about her elderly cousin, Elisabeth, who was then in her sixth month of pregnancy. The angel then made a statement which Christ would later repeat: "For with God nothing is impossible." It is likely this saying to Mary became a family saying within the household in which Christ grew to adulthood; a family saying that Christ may have heard many times growing up. He, in turn, would later tell His disciples: "with God all things are possible." (Matt. 19: 26, see also Mark 10: 27.) Family sayings tend to last for generations. This one has become eternal.

The final comment from Mary to Gabriel shows her submissiveness: "be it unto me according to thy word." What is not often recognized is that those words are also a blessing. While submitting to the role assigned her, she was also pronouncing a blessing upon herself, confirming the promise of God to her. Inspired by this holy encounter she does what Godly people have done under the influence of the Spirit in every generation. She moves the words from outside herself to claim them inside herself as well. Blessings spoken in the language of angels come into the mind. But when she responds with the mortal voice, the words move here, into our world, where they would be fulfilled. There is power in language. One of the reasons we will be judged by our words is because they count; they have power. (See Alma 12: 14.) We should bless one another more often than we do; and we ought never condemn one another. Mary, hearing this message, confirmed its effect upon herself with her benediction: "be it unto me according to thy word."

At the news of her cousin's pregnancy, Mary went to visit with Elisabeth, also a newly called mother in Israel: "And Mary arose in those days, and went into the hill country with haste, into a city of Juda; And entered into the house of Zacharias, and saluted Elisabeth." (Luke 1: 39-40.) We know from this description that Mary went in haste and therefore had to know where to locate her cousin, Elisabeth. This shows how familiar these two were with each other. The exact Judean location, including the home, were somewhere Mary had to know intimately to be able to go in haste. These extended family members were close with each other.

She "saluted" Elisabeth with an unrecorded greeting. Given the fact we have record of other greetings from Gabriel, Elisabeth, Zacharias and Mary we must conclude either Mary or Luke decided this particular greeting did not belong in the public record. There was likely something so intimate or sacred to justify the omission. Whether the greeting referred to Elisabeth, Mary, John or Jesus we are left to ourselves to find out through personal revelation. The record invites us to use pondering and prayer, if we want to know.

Whatever the words were that were spoken, both Elisabeth and the child John within her reacted to the salutation:

> And it came to pass, that, when Elisabeth heard the salutation of Mary, the babe leaped in her womb; and Elisabeth was filled with the Holy Ghost: And she spake out with a loud voice, and said, Blessed art thou among women, and blessed is the fruit of thy womb. And whence is this to me, that the mother of my Lord should come to me? For, lo, as soon as the voice of thy

salutation sounded in mine ears, the babe leaped in my womb for joy. (Luke 1: 41-44.)

Elisabeth's reaction was immediate, inspired, and spoken in a loud, joyful voice. In response to Mary's salutation, she declared: "blessed are thou among women, and blessed is the fruit of thy womb!" This reaction would, no doubt, continue the thought contained in Mary's unrecorded greeting.

As she continued, Elisabeth confirmed what Gabriel had first announced. John was filled with the Holy Ghost from his mother's womb. He, too, reacted with joy at the arrival of Christ's mother. This private reunion, in a humble Judean home, was more important than anything else in all the world happening at the time. Although Caesar Augustus reigned in Rome, and most of mankind living at that time, regarded him as the earth's central historic figure, it was these two pregnant women who were living truly historic lives.

Elisabeth continued by confirming the blessing of Gabriel, and the self-blessing of Mary, by adding her own blessing: "And blessed is she that believed: for there shall be a performance of those things which were told her from the Lord." (Luke 1: 45.) The only words spoken between them before this was the unrecorded salutation. Therefore, Elisabeth no doubt learned of "the things which were told [Mary] from the Lord" by the initial, unrecorded greeting.

Mary continued to speak words of a spontaneous psalm, so wonderfully composed that the scriptures preserve them for us to ponder:

> And Mary said, My soul doth magnify the Lord,
> And my spirit hath rejoiced in God my Saviour.
> For he hath regarded the low estate of his

> handmaiden: for, behold, from henceforth all generations shall call me blessed. For he that is mighty hath done to me great things; and holy is his name. And his mercy is on them that fear him from generation to generation. He hath shewed strength with his arm; he hath scattered the proud in the imagination of their hearts. He hath put down the mighty from their seats, and exalted them of low degree. He hath filled the hungry with good things; and the rich he hath sent empty away. He hath holpen his servant Israel, in remembrance of his mercy; As he spake to our fathers, to Abraham, and to his seed for ever. (Luke 1: 46-55.)

Mary's understanding of her role had grown by the time she came to Elisabeth. She could now declare that it would affect "all generations." She knew she occupied a significant role in the history of man. She also knew the Lord's mercy was extended in greater measure to those who, although obscure to the rest of mankind, were great in the eyes of God. She occupied a "low estate" but "henceforth all generations" would know how blessed she was. Those who fear God are remembered, visited and blessed by Him. Those who had reason to be "proud" of their status in mortality, the great ones of the day, dignitaries, presiding authorities, kings, rulers and magistrates "he hath scattered" like dust. They will be put down from their mighty seats. In their place those of low degree will be exalted. Those who crave knowledge and are hungry to be filled with truth will not reject His messengers, and will be filled. This is so even if the greatest message of the day comes through an elderly woman, pregnant for the first time, and her lowly, still unmarried, pregnant cousin. Oh how wonderful are the workings of God! How little the praise and recognition of man matters! How foolish to men are the ways in which the Lord works in every generation! How easy it is to mistake social standing for God's favor, and to consider lowliness to mean insignificance! This God, who is the same yesterday, today and tomorrow, surely has given us all sufficient warning to let us all know His ways are not, and never will, be man's ways.

Mary's visit lasted another three months: "And Mary abode with her about three months, and returned to her own house." (Luke 1: 56.) Mary remained through the final term of Elisabeth's pregnancy, and would have been among those who were present at John's birth. The "handmaiden of the Lord" had no doubt come for this very purpose. She was directly involved in the mission to bring the "light of [God's] countenance" back to Israel. She began her service as an aid to her elderly cousin. She would first help bring her Son's forerunner into mortality.

The scene which follows, at the birth of John, makes more sense when you realize Mary was present. With her also was the unborn Christ. Zacharias's words referring to Christ fit perfectly with Christ in attendance. The account refers to Mary's presence only by the mention of "cousins" in attendance: "Now Elisabeth's full time came that she should be delivered; and she brought forth a son. And her neighbours and her cousins heard how the Lord had shewed great mercy upon her; and they rejoiced with her." (Luke 1: 57-58.)

Before getting to Zacharias' psalm, the record tells about the naming of John:

> And it came to pass, that on the eighth day they came to circumcise the child; and they called him Zacharias, after the name of his father. And his mother answered and said, Not so; but he shall be called John. And they

> said unto her, There is none of thy kindred that is called by this name. And they made signs to his father, how he would have him called. And he asked for a writing table, and wrote, saying, His name is John. And they marvelled all. (Luke 1: 59-63.)

Zacharias did not name his son John because he or Elisabeth had any preference. He simply declared what the angel had said before: "His name **is** John." This child came already named. His given name was merely being revealed to those in attendance.

When the "sign" was lifted and Zacharias could speak, there was another inspired psalm spoken about God's visitation to Israel and John, who will go before Him:

> And his mouth was opened immediately, and his tongue loosed, and he spake, and praised God. And fear came on all that dwelt round about them: and all these sayings were noised abroad throughout all the hill country of Judaea. And all they that heard them laid them up in their hearts, saying, What manner of child shall this be! And the hand of the Lord was with him. And his father Zacharias was filled with the Holy Ghost, and prophesied, saying, **Blessed be the Lord God of Israel; for he hath visited and redeemed his people, And hath raised up an horn of salvation for us in the house of his servant David; As he spake by the mouth of his holy prophets, which have been since the world began: That we should be saved from our enemies, and from the hand of all that hate us; To perform the mercy promised to our fathers, and to remember his holy covenant; The oath which he sware to our father Abraham, That he would grant unto us, that we being delivered out of the hand of our enemies might serve him**

> **without fear, In holiness and righteousness before him, all the days of our life**. And thou, child, shalt be called the prophet of the Highest: for thou shalt go **before the face of the Lord to prepare his ways**; To give knowledge of salvation unto his people by the remission of their sins, Through the tender mercy of our God; whereby the dayspring from on high hath visited us, To give light to them that sit in darkness and in the shadow of death, to guide our feet into the way of peace. (Luke 1: 64-79, emphasis added.)

All of the bold language refers to Christ. It is fitting that the greater part of Zacharias' psalm would speak of Christ, and the lesser part would speak of his son, John, who would go before Christ to prepare the way. Zacharias and John both recognized what John's role was and that Christ was the greater of the two.

All who heard of these things spread the news about. The coming ministry of these two, John as forerunner and Christ as the light of God's countenance, would vindicate this widespread speculation about "what manner of child shall this be!" Their messages would not bring worldly change to the political and religious institutions of the day. Neither had any official recognition or success. The hierarchy fought against them both. To their followers they offered eternal life. The light broke from behind the veil, and those few who would accept it found not only the "light of God's countenance," but also the promised "law of life, and loving mercy, and righteousness, and blessing, and compassion, and life, and peace." It was just as Zacharias prayed and Gabriel declared to be answered. For the rest, the "light of God's countenance" came and was rejected, dismissed, persecuted and ultimately killed.

How great and terrible is God's work among every generation. How similar are the methods by which He separates His sheep, who hear His voice, from the goats, who are merely religious. Daily, weekly or annual outward observances of religious forms can never save a soul. To be saved mankind must accept His messengers. Those whom He inspires and then sends point to the path back to Him. They alone will point to Him, and not to themselves. They alone will encourage people to come to Him, and not take honor for themselves. Invariably it is the religious who are responsible for persecuting and killing the ones actually sent by God.

Before discussing Christ's birth, we first will examine what it means for a people to be "chosen" by God in the next two chapters.

Chapter 3
Chosen People

The Lord said to Moses: "For thou art an holy people unto the Lord thy God, and the Lord hath chosen thee to be a peculiar people unto himself, above all the nations that are upon the earth." (Deut. 14: 2.) This was a reiteration of what Abraham, Isaac and Jacob had been promised generations earlier. There is irony about being the Lord's "chosen people" which often escapes us. More often than not, the blessing of being "chosen" turns into a burden which the chosen fail in their attempt to carry. It turns them into an example of what *not* to do, how *not* to live, and how to disappoint God. They become the backdrop against which God shows mercy and longsuffering, as well as justice and condemnation; depending upon how the people behave. Almost without exception, being a "chosen" group is a statement of God's patience, commitment and longsuffering. It has little to do with the worthiness of the group itself. From ancient Israel to the remnant of the Jews returning from Babylon, from the family of Lehi to the remnant of the Nephites, and all the "other sheep" whose identities remain presently unknown, all of them failed to keep the Gospel alive although they were given it by the Lord. Chosen people have invariably failed to preserve what they inherited.

Those who are "chosen" presume this means they are right with God. This presumption of superiority feeds pride, haughtiness and arrogance. The chosen people are blind to their actual condition. They never realize they are on display, exhibiting foolishness, excess, pride and disobedience. From a distance, later in time, or from outside, the glaring weaknesses of the chosen become the great lesson to be learned from chosen people. These weaknesses exhibited by those chosen of the Lord teach a valuable lesson to those who are willing to see.

In each generation of those chosen by God, there are individuals who are shown by revelation the pride and arrogance of those who ignorantly celebrate God's peculiar delight in them. These few individuals are the ones upon whom the Lord lays the obligation to declare repentance. These characters are generally outcasts who are disliked and rejected. Oftentimes these people are killed because of the message of repentance they preach. When these messengers are dead, the proud "chosen" can claim the words spoken against them actually vindicate them and condemn others. This pattern repeats itself over and over again. It was a problem inherited by Christ's contemporaries as evidenced when He taught:

> And he said, Woe unto you also, ye lawyers! for ye lade men with burdens grievous to be borne, and ye yourselves touch not the burdens with one of your fingers. Woe unto you! for **ye build the sepulchres of the prophets, and your fathers killed them**. Truly ye bear witness that ye allow the deeds of your fathers: for **they indeed killed them, and ye build their sepulchres**. Therefore

> also said the wisdom of God, I will send them prophets and apostles, and some of them they shall slay and persecute: That the blood of all the prophets, which was shed from the foundation of the world, may be required of this generation; From the blood of Abel unto the blood of Zacharias, which perished between the altar and the temple: verily I say unto you, It shall be required of this generation. **Woe unto you, lawyers! for ye have taken away the key of knowledge: ye entered not in yourselves, and them that were entering in ye hindered**. (Luke 11: 46-52, emphasis added.)

Christ lived among people who were chosen. They exhibited all the dangers and ironies inherent in that status.

Another historical witness of this phenomenon regarding God's chosen people was Stephen. He was an inspired messenger sent by God, and the chosen people had contempt for him. Moments before the Jewish priests killed him, Stephen recounted the following:

> Ye stiffnecked and uncircumcised in heart and ears, **ye do always resist the Holy Ghost: as your fathers did, so do ye. Which of the prophets have not your fathers persecuted**? and they have slain them which shewed before of the coming of the Just One; of whom ye have been now the betrayers and murderers: Who have received the law by the disposition of angels, and have not kept it. (Acts 7: 51-53, emphasis added.)

Angels delivered the messages to the prophets, but the prophets were rejected, persecuted and killed by the Jews. Then after they were dead they were celebrated, venerated and accepted. Their words were studied in hindsight. This is because once dead, the prophets' words could be manipulated or parsed to mean things which the prophets never intended.

Nephi described the Jews' reaction to his father, Lehi, when he spoke his testimony of Christ. Lehi was an obscure descendant of Joseph, unentitled to the Aaronic or Levitical Priesthood. He was not a member of the priestly Levites at all, much less an ecclesiastical leader (although he had priesthood). Yet his testimony came, just as Stephen mentioned, from angels. According to Nephi, the reaction to Lehi's testimony of Christ followed the same pattern: "And when the Jews heard these things **they were angry with him; yea, even as with the prophets of old, whom they had cast out, and stoned, and slain**; and they also sought his life, that they might take it away." (1 Ne. 1: 20, emphasis added.)

We are going to discuss in this chapter what being chosen means. We will look at the good things men are called to do and be when chosen. We will see how they oftentimes fail, and what follows in the wake of persistent failure. Pride in being one of the chosen people is ill conceived at best and inordinate foolishness which damns at worst. Given the scriptural history of such people, we should be alarmed anytime we believe ourselves to be among the chosen.

The Lord has used "chosen people" since the time of Abraham. The question arises then as to why there have been and are still "chosen people." All mankind are children of the same Father in Heaven. Yet there is a minority of these children called "chosen" and the rest left outside this group. That ought to be a curiosity for us; something we take some pains to understand.

Originally the entire family of Adam were on equal footing. They were all taught by their prophet-father, who passed along to all of them faith in the God who was known by Adam.

Unfortunately, from those first born of Adam and Eve, the message of salvation taught by Adam was rejected and their children rebelled against God. "And Adam and Eve blessed the name of God, and they made all things known unto their sons and their daughters. And Satan came among them, saying: I am also a son of God; and he commanded them, saying: Believe it not; and they believed it not, and they loved Satan more than God. And men began from that time forth to be carnal, sensual, and devilish." (Moses 5: 12-13.) Yet all mankind continued to be invited to accept the Gospel.

Priestly authority was passed from Adam through his descendants to Noah. Details about how that happened has been restored in modern revelation.[11] From the start it was intended that

---

[11] "This order was instituted in the days of Adam, and came down by lineage in the following manner: From Adam to Seth, who was ordained by Adam at the age of sixty-nine years, and was blessed by him three years previous to his (Adam's) death, and received the promise of God by his father, that his posterity should be the chosen of the Lord, and that they should be preserved unto the end of the earth; Because he (Seth) was a perfect man, and his likeness was the express likeness of his father, insomuch that he seemed to be like unto his father in all things, and could be distinguished from him only by his age. Enos was ordained at the age of one hundred and thirty-four years and four months, by the hand of Adam. God called upon Cainan in the wilderness in the fortieth year of his age; and he met Adam in journeying to the place Shedolamak. He was eighty-seven years old when he received his ordination. Mahalaleel was four hundred and ninety-six years and seven days old when he was ordained by the hand of Adam, who also blessed him. Jared was two hundred years old when he was ordained under the hand of Adam, who also blessed him. Enoch was twenty-five years old when he was ordained under the hand of Adam; and he was sixty-five and Adam blessed him. And he saw the Lord, and he walked with him, and was before his face continually; and he walked with God three hundred and sixty-five years, making him four hundred and thirty years old when he was translated. Methuselah was one hundred years old when he was ordained under the hand of Adam. Lamech was thirty-two years old

knowledge of God, and authority to minister in the rites of the priesthood, would be available to all mankind.[12] However, mankind was not interested in this opportunity. When mankind was reorganized and a new family root established through Noah, there was a new opportunity. Just as at the time of Adam, with Noah there was a single set of parents who presided over all who lived. Despite this, men began again to fall away. Several generations later the Lord chose Abraham to establish a family line through whom the Gospel would be preserved. From the time of Abraham to the present, the Lord, on occasion, has used a chosen line of people through whom to reveal and then preserve those truths which save.

When a people are "chosen" by the Lord, He generally endows them with specific gifts or blessings. Whether they are ancient or modern, in the Old World or New, they are almost always given a specific set of gifts as part of a covenant. These covenant-based gifts generally include the following, in no particular order:

-A Promised Land.

-Self-government.

-Sacred space with sacred artifacts.

-Angelic visitors.

---

when he was ordained under the hand of Seth. Noah was ten years old when he was ordained under the hand of Methuselah." (D&C 107: 41-52.)

[12]The only exception was a line of murderers descended from Cain. Those alone were not included among the message to repent. Moses 7: 22: "And Enoch also beheld the residue of the people which were the sons of Adam; and they were a mixture of all the seed of Adam save it was the seed of Cain[.]" That line ended with the flood, after which all mankind descended from Noah's line. From Noah all mankind inherited a common bloodline again.

-"Signs" of His presence.

-Sacred records which expand through a growing body of revelation.

-Ordinances.

When chosen people reject the Lord they begin to forfeit some, or all, of these gifts. Even so, the Lord has always persisted in patiently working to reclaim chosen people for generations after they begin to reject Him. He does this for the sake of the fathers, with whom He made covenants. Once the Lord has chosen a people, through all succeeding generations their history will unfold in accordance with a covenant-based plan. This is true even when the chosen are neglectful, rebellious or apostate. Being "chosen" as a people is a reflection on God and His determination, not on the worthiness of man. (Being "chosen" as an individual is different.)

It is through chosen people the Lord performs His "strange act." He put it this way in modern revelation: "That I may proceed to bring to pass my act, my strange act, and perform my work, my strange work, that men may discern between the righteous and the wicked, saith your God." (D&C 101: 95; see also D&C 95: 4.) This description of the Lord's unfolding plan for mankind ("strange act") was used anciently as well. (See Isa. 28: 21.) It **is** strange. The Lord uses people who think they are special and better than others to show in patience over generations how only the humble, the penitent and the poor are His. All others are rejected. He taught a parable about this to His disciples: "And he spake this parable unto certain which trusted in themselves that they were righteous, and despised others: Two men went up into the temple to pray; the one a Pharisee, and the other a publican. The Pharisee stood and prayed thus with himself, God, I thank thee, that I am not as other men are, extortioners, unjust, adulterers, or even as this publican.

I fast twice in the week, I give tithes of all that I possess. And the publican, standing afar off, would not lift up so much as his eyes unto heaven, but smote upon his breast, saying, God be merciful to me a sinner. I tell you, this man went down to his house justified rather than the other: for every one that exalteth himself shall be abased; and he that humbleth himself shall be exalted." (Luke 18: 9-14.) The ironic juxtaposition of the "righteous" and the "sinner" in the parable shows how being chosen is not a reflection of a people's individual standing before God.

By establishing a chosen people, the Lord is able to gather enough people and resources to build Temples. It also allows Him to assemble sufficient numbers to establish a priestly class who can attend to ordinances continually. It allows God to organize a culture which can produce and preserve documents. Chosen people enable God to accomplish with a group what He could never accomplish with individuals. Pooling resources and talents to perpetuate His divine projects is one inevitable result of the Lord choosing a people.

Having a chosen people does not exclude others outside the chosen group from receiving salvation. Anyone can elect to be "chosen" by accepting His faith and receiving His ordinances.[13] Christ invited all, to the ends of the earth, to join with Him:

---

[13]The full history of chosen people and how God has acted in the best interest of all mankind is beyond the scope of this book. Great care has been taken to spread the bloodline of Abraham throughout the world. That is one of the reasons the Lost Ten Tribes were lost, or transplanted into other cultures and intermarried. So, too, was the bloodline of the Southern Kingdom, or the Jews taken captive to Babylon, with only a remnant returning. The remaining stayed behind and intermarried, making much of the current populations of Iraq, Iran and Afghanistan blood descendants of the transplanted Jewish kingdom.

"Therefore, whoso repenteth and cometh unto me as a little child, him will I receive, for of such is the kingdom of God. Behold, for such I have laid down my life, and have taken it up again; therefore repent, and come unto me ye ends of the earth, and be saved." (3 Ne. 9: 22.) The universal nature of Christ's mission and the invitation to come and join His chosen people is set out in modern revelation as well: " For, behold, the Lord your Redeemer suffered death in the flesh; wherefore he suffered the pain of all men, that all men might repent and come unto him." (D&C 18: 11.) But even before the invitation for all to come join, the Lord has always wanted all mankind to be candidates for eternal life.

All nations have been included within God's chosen people at one time or another. As revealed through Nephi: "Know ye not that there are more nations than one? Know ye not that I, the Lord your God, have created all men, and that I remember those who are upon the isles of the sea; and that I rule in the heavens above and in the earth beneath; and **I bring forth my word unto the children of men, yea, even upon all the nations of the earth?** ... For behold, I shall speak unto the Jews and they shall write it; and I shall also speak unto the Nephites and they shall write it; and I shall also speak unto the other tribes of the house of Israel, which I have led away, and they shall write it; and **I shall also speak unto all nations of the earth and they shall write it**." (2 Ne. 29: 7, 12, emphasis added.)

Christ's Gospel was not intended to be exclusive. It is and always has been universal. As Alma put it: "For behold, **the Lord doth grant unto all nations, of their own nation and tongue, to teach his word, yea, in wisdom, all that he seeth fit that they should have**; therefore we see that the Lord doth counsel in wisdom, according to that which is just and true." (Alma 29: 8, emphasis added.) All nations have been chosen to receive some portion of Christ's Gospel. And, after His death, all nations have been invited to receive the fullness of His Gospel, and join in by adoption to the chosen line tracking back to Abraham.

Abraham, his son Isaac and his grandson Jacob/Israel were all promised land. The promise to posses that land was renewed to Abraham, Isaac and Jacob's descendants through Moses. The children of Lehi were also led away and promised a new land. Many groups were led away, promised land, and given an inheritance throughout the world. The parable of the olive tree taught by Zenos, and preserved by Jacob, tells of numerous chosen people put into various lands of promise. (See Jacob, Chapter 5.) When Christ taught His Sermon on the Mount, He promised an eternal inheritance of land to His followers: "Blessed are the meek: for they shall inherit the earth." (Matt. 5: 5.) When Israel rebelled, they lost their promised land. First the Northern Kingdom, or Ten Tribes were carried away by Assyria; then the Southern Kingdom, or Jews were dispossessed by Babylon. Although a remnant returned, ultimately after rejecting Christ, the Jews were scattered again and lost their land until 1948 when it was restored in part to them. Today the remnant of the Jews continue to have a tenuous hold on a piece of their Promised Land.

In addition to a Promised Land, chosen people are given the right to govern themselves. When the Lord's chosen people are in full faith with Him, they are independent of all other civil authorities under heaven. The Lord has always intended His people to be governed by Him alone. Even in this Dispensation He has promised independence for His people: "That through my providence, notwithstanding the tribulation which shall descend upon you, that the church may stand independent above all other creatures beneath the celestial world[.]" (D&C 78: 14.) This is so even though submission to governments is temporarily required.[14] When, however, Christ's plan for His chosen people is in full operation, they are always independent of all other governments, and free to obey only Him. This is true even in our day, for the Lord has said: "That through my providence, notwithstanding the tribulation which shall descend upon you, that the church may stand independent above all other creatures beneath the celestial world[.]" (D&C 78: 14.)

When people are chosen they are given sacred space and equipped with sacred artifacts. They receive Temples, into which are placed sacred symbols of His presence. The Ark of the Covenant, for example, was placed inside the Holy of Holies. The Mercy Seat was the symbol of God's very presence.

Other sacred artifacts which God has entrusted to His people at various times in history include the garment of Adam, the Urim and Thummim, Seer Stones, stone tablets, Aaron's Rod, the Sword of Laban, the Liahona, and gold plates to name a few better known examples. These physical symbols of spiritual power and connection to God were given as a sign of God's favor and presence with His chosen people. When they are lost, the people can know they have lost favor and no longer enjoy His presence.

From Adam to Abraham, from Abraham to Moses, from Moses to Jesus Christ, and from Jesus Christ to Joseph Smith, when the chosen people have been in connection with God they have always received angelic visitors. Indeed angels must come to visit His people or they do not have faith in Him, and no one is

---

[14] See 12th Article of Faith: "We believe in being subject to kings, presidents, rulers, and magistrates, in obeying, honoring, and sustaining the law."

being saved.[15] Therefore, if God has a chosen people, they must have angels visiting with them or they are under condemnation.

In addition to angels, there are always "signs" which accompany the Lord's presence with His chosen people. This is not to create belief in Him, but come as a consequence of people's faith in Him. As He explained in modern revelation: "But, behold, faith cometh not by signs, but **signs follow those that believe. Yea, signs come by faith, not by the will of men, nor as they please, but by the will of God. Yea, signs come by faith, unto mighty works, for without faith no man pleaseth God**; and with whom God is angry he is not well pleased; wherefore, unto such he showeth no signs, only in wrath unto their condemnation." (D&C 63: 9-11, emphasis added.) The connection between God, His people, faith and *signs* of the presence of faith, is indisputable. Signs are one of the great proofs God's chosen are still in favor with Him. When the signs end, their faith has ended as well.

When God chooses people they write sacred records of their association and contact with Him. From the time of Adam to the present, when there is a chosen people there is also a growing body of revelation from Him. In Moses we read about Adam and the beginning of keeping sacred records:

> And Adam knew his wife again, and she bare a son, and he called his name Seth. And Adam glorified the name of God; for he said: God hath

---

[15] Moro 7: 36-37: "Or have angels ceased to appear unto the children of men? Or has he withheld the power of the Holy Ghost from them? Or will he, so long as time shall last, or the earth shall stand, or there shall be one man upon the face thereof to be saved? Behold I say unto you, Nay; for it is by faith that miracles are wrought; and it is by faith that angels appear and minister unto men; wherefore, if these things have ceased wo be unto the children of men, for it is because of unbelief, and all is vain."

> appointed me another seed, instead of Abel, whom Cain slew. And God revealed himself unto Seth, and he rebelled not, but offered an acceptable sacrifice, like unto his brother Abel. And to him also was born a son, and he called his name Enos. And then began these men to call upon the name of the Lord, and the Lord blessed them; **And a book of remembrance was kept, in the which was recorded, in the language of Adam, for it was given unto as many as called upon God to write by the spirit of inspiration**; And by them their children were taught to read and write, having a language which was pure and undefiled. Now this same Priesthood, which was in the beginning, shall be in the end of the world also. Now this prophecy Adam spake, as he was moved upon by the Holy Ghost, and a genealogy was kept of the children of God. (Moses 6: 2-8, emphasis added.)

This pattern has always been followed by God's chosen people. Enoch continued the practice and added to scripture.[16] Abraham received these records, which was one of the reasons he was able to come to know God. Abraham wrote: "But the records of the fathers, even the patriarchs, concerning the right of Priesthood, the Lord my God preserved in mine own hands; therefore a knowledge of the beginning of the creation, and also of

---

[16] Moses 6: 43-46: "And Enoch continued his speech, saying: The Lord which spake with me, the same is the God of heaven, and he is my God, and your God, and ye are my brethren, and why counsel ye yourselves, and deny the God of heaven? The heavens he made; the earth is his footstool; and the foundation thereof is his. Behold, he laid it, an host of men hath he brought in upon the face thereof. And death hath come upon our fathers; nevertheless we know them, and cannot deny, and even the first of all we know, even Adam. For a book of remembrance we have written among us, according to the pattern given by the finger of God; and it is given in our own language."

the planets, and of the stars, as they were made known unto the fathers, have I kept even unto this day, and I shall endeavor to write some of these things upon this record, for the benefit of my posterity that shall come after me." (Abr. 1: 31.)

Although records may be lost by the unfaithful, when God chooses a people He restores the essential missing records to them again. This happened with the Nephites (see 3 Ne. 24: 1 to 25: 6). It has happened again through Joseph Smith in restoring the Book of Mormon, Book of Abraham, Book of Moses and 24th Chapter of Matthew, among other revelations. Through Joseph Smith, in addition to restoring lost and ancient scripture, new, modern revelation has been added in both the D&C and Pearl of Great Price. Oliver Cowdery,[17] John Taylor,[18] Brigham Young,[19] Wilford Woodruff,[20] Joseph F. Smith[21] and Spencer Kimball[22] have all added to the D&C. The Ninth Article of Faith states: "We believe all that God has revealed, all that He does now reveal, and we believe that He will yet reveal many great and important things pertaining to the Kingdom of God." The expectation of ongoing revelation was built into the foundation of The Church of Jesus Christ of Latter-day Saints.

---

[17]Oliver wrote the first draft of Section 20, co-wrote Section 102 and authored Section 134.

[18]He wrote Section 135.

[19]He wrote Section 136.

[20]He added Official Declaration No. 1.

[21]He added Section 138.

[22]He added Official Declaration No. 2.

Finally, God always gives ordinances to His people. When they are His, chosen people are endowed with rites and ordinances that establish their covenantal relationship with Him through sacred ceremonies. His people always come to Him through priestly celebrations designed to teach how to ascend.

Being chosen by God is not an indelible event, separate from the free choices made by the people who are chosen. They are free to neglect or reject what He offers. Rejection has consequences. But a complete loss of chosen status does not come as a result of a single failing, nor as a result of a single generation's failings. Covenants are honored by God long after they have been neglected by men.

When, however, men begin to stray from His rule He reorders their conditions. From among His covenant blessings He first limits access to angels. Angels do not come to the unworthy, except to condemn and judge them.

When men will not accept His rule, they lose their right to govern themselves. Foreign governments displace their home rule, and other nations subject them. Loss of self-rule is one of the certain signs the chosen people are losing favor with the Lord.

When men pollute His sacred ground with unhallowed practices, they lose possession of their promised land. They are displaced by others who hold the ground in opposition to those to whom it was promised. The land does not get returned until the covenant people repent.

When faith in God has been replaced by superstition in relics, men forfeit possession of the sacred artifacts given to them. For example, the Ark of the Covenant was taken from ancient Israel because they started to view it as a talisman which would give them victory in battle.[23] The Urim and Thummim became an historical oddity, both anciently and again in modern times. Its actual use is no longer understood.

After chosen people lose their connection with God, they no longer receive regular or consistent revelation to increase their knowledge and add to their sacred records. The body of scripture first becomes static. Then, because of wickedness, men deliberately suppress, alter and discard past revelations which they are no longer willing to accept. Their canon of scriptures actually diminishes with time.

Despite all this, God's patience with His chosen people persists until finally they alter and reject His ordinances. As Isaiah

---

[23]See, e.g., 1 Sam. 4: 3-11: "Wherefore hath the Lord smitten us to day before the Philistines? Let us fetch the ark of the covenant of the Lord out of Shiloh unto us, that, when it cometh among us, it may save us out of the hand of our enemies. So the people sent to Shiloh, that they might bring from thence the ark of the covenant of the Lord of hosts, which dwelleth between the cherubims: and the two sons of Eli, Hophni and Phinehas, were there with the ark of the covenant of God. And when the ark of the covenant of the Lord came into the camp, all Israel shouted with a great shout, so that the earth rang again. And when the Philistines heard the noise of the shout, they said, What meaneth the noise of this great shout in the camp of the Hebrews? And they understood that the ark of the Lord was come into the camp. And the Philistines were afraid, for they said, God is come into the camp. And they said, Woe unto us! for there hath not been such a thing heretofore. Woe unto us! who shall deliver us out of the hand of these mighty Gods? these are the Gods that smote the Egyptians with all the plagues in the wilderness. Be strong, and quit yourselves like men, O ye Philistines, that ye be not servants unto the Hebrews, as they have been to you: quit yourselves like men, and fight. And the Philistines fought, and Israel was smitten, and they fled every man into his tent: and there was a very great slaughter; for there fell of Israel thirty thousand footmen. And the ark of God was taken; and the two sons of Eli, Hophni and Phinehas, were slain." Although it was regained after this loss, ultimately it was lost forever because of this same kind of superstitious treatment of the Ark.

described the pattern: "**The earth mourneth and fadeth away, the world languisheth and fadeth away, the haughty people of the earth do languish**. The earth also is defiled under the inhabitants thereof; **because they have transgressed the laws, changed the ordinance, broken the everlasting covenant. Therefore hath the curse devoured the earth, and they that dwell therein are desolate**: therefore the inhabitants of the earth are burned, and few men left." (Isa. 24: 4-6, emphasis added.) The break does not come as a result of a lack of understanding the ordinances. He bears with people who foolishly think ordinances are an end in themselves, who never attempt to understand the underlying meaning of the rites they perform. They can go stupidly and endlessly repeating ordinances they no longer understand. However, when they begin to break the covenant and change His ordinances, they bring about a curse in place of the former blessings. So altering ordinances bears grave risks, even if changes are made in a good faith attempt to improve upon them. In all scripture, there is simply no precedent for altering ordinances other than as a New Dispensation is opened.

God's patience with His chosen people also extends to sending messengers from time to time to try and reclaim His people. These messengers attempt to remind His people of the original covenant God made with them. They teach the underlying meaning of the Lord's intent in choosing them. They cry repentance. Although the main body of believers may have lost all contact with God, and no longer receive angelic messengers, His chosen teachers receive all that was once promised to all God's chosen people. They work to try and rekindle the connection between God and man. They make intercession for the wayward covenant people. When Moses reestablished the direct connection between the chosen people and God, the Lord explained to Moses: " And he said, Hear now my words: If there be a prophet among you, I the Lord will make myself known unto him in a vision, and will speak unto him in a dream." (Num. 12: 6.) This foreshadowed the many chosen prophets sent between the time of Moses and the coming of Jesus Christ. During that time very few of the prophets came as presiding authorities, and were often not from the priestly tribe of Levi.

The New Testament account begins with a lone, obscure priest, cycling through his duties at the Temple, and to his surprise, encountering a vision of the Lord's angel, Gabriel. It wasn't Annas, nor Caiaphus, nor any of the Chief Priests or notable scribes or lawyers. Rather it was an obscure, elderly priest chosen from outside the hierarchy to whom the Lord "made Himself known."

A New Dispensation never begins by using leaders from within an existing religious hierarchy. New Dispensations are almost invariably founded by outsiders who are often critical of the chosen. They rarely use encouraging or reassuring words to comfort the chosen. Christ was just such an outside messenger. In the next chapter we will consider the time in which Christ came to minister. We will see how the dynamic described in this chapter unfolded in specific events in the life of our Lord.

Mortal man is here to be tested. The test is not whether they can conform to the expectations of a broad, mainstream, self-congratulating "chosen" people. The test is far more individual than that. It is a lonely quest to find the Chosen One of Israel. Those who really find Him, not an imaginary version of the Living God, but actually meet the Risen Lord, the Savior of mankind, generally do not rely at all upon their chosen status. Rather they are usually somewhat at odds with the chosen mainstream. As Paul described those who, in Israelite history had broken through to see the greater light:

> And what shall I more say? for the time would fail me to tell of ... the prophets: Who **through faith subdued kingdoms, wrought righteousness, obtained promises**, stopped the mouths of lions, Quenched the violence of fire, escaped the edge of the sword, out of weakness were made strong, waxed valiant in fight, turned to flight the armies of the aliens. Women received their dead raised to life again: and **others were tortured, not accepting deliverance; that they might obtain a better resurrection: And others had trial of cruel mockings and scourgings, yea, moreover of bonds and imprisonment: They were stoned, they were sawn asunder, were tempted, were slain with the sword: they wandered about in sheepskins and goatskins; being destitute, afflicted, tormented; (Of whom the world was not worthy:) they wandered in deserts, and in mountains, and in dens and caves of the earth**." (Heb. 11: 32-38, emphasis added.)

Being an individual chosen by God means He will be with you, even when the others claiming to be "chosen" are inclined to attack or reject you. He will provide you with His truth.

For the rest of the "chosen" people, He will send them witnesses. When His people are in the right way, those messengers are inside an established, recognized hierarchy. When His people have left the right way, His messengers may not come from expected bloodlines, nor occupy the chief seats. They may be obscure, outsiders whose only claim to acceptance arises from the words they teach, and not any position they occupy. It is of no consequence, however. For God will remember His chosen people and will always send them true messengers bearing a message from Him. Their credential is the message itself. They speak as if they had authority, even when the "chosen" think they do not. Whether He speaks through His established hierarchy or through apparent outsiders, His voice never changes. Therefore, His sheep should always be able to hear Him no matter who it is that is sent. We should all hope to live worthily, to keep His covenants, and to retain the capacity to always hear Him.

Christ came from the wrong city, with the wrong name, having no recognized authority. He fits the Divine pattern of His predecessors who testified of Him. So we turn to Christ inside the population of the chosen people of God.

Chapter 4

The Time In Which He Came

Christ came at the low point of human misconduct. He came and lived among the most wicked men, on the worst behaved planet created by God. To understand the Lord you must first understand the circumstances in which He chose to come to live His mortality. Everything about it was deliberate. He intended to condescend below all things.

This earth is the most depraved of all God's creations. Enoch left a record (restored through Joseph Smith) in which this planet's fallen state is described:

> And it came to pass that the God of heaven looked upon the residue of the people, and he wept; and Enoch bore record of it, saying: How is it that the heavens weep, and shed forth their tears as the rain upon the mountains? And Enoch said unto the Lord: How is it that thou canst weep, seeing thou art holy, and from all eternity to all eternity? And **were it possible that man could number the particles of the earth, yea, millions of earths like this, it would not be a beginning to the**

> **number of thy creations**; and thy curtains are stretched out still; and yet thou art there, and thy bosom is there; and also thou art just; thou art merciful and kind forever; And thou hast taken Zion to thine own bosom, from all thy creations, from all eternity to all eternity; and naught but peace, justice, and truth is the habitation of thy throne; and mercy shall go before thy face and have no end; how is it thou canst weep? The Lord said unto Enoch: Behold these thy brethren; they are the workmanship of mine own hands, and I gave unto them their knowledge, in the day I created them; and in the Garden of Eden, gave I unto man his agency; And unto thy brethren have I said, and also given commandment, that they should love one another, and that they should choose me, their Father; but behold, they are without affection, and they hate their own blood; And the fire of mine indignation is kindled against them; and in my hot displeasure will I send in the floods upon them, for my fierce anger is kindled against them. Behold, I am God; Man of Holiness is my name; Man of Counsel is my name; and Endless and Eternal is my name, also. Wherefore, I can stretch forth mine hands and hold all the creations which I have made; and mine eye can pierce them also, **and among all the workmanship of mine hands there has not been so great wickedness as among thy brethren**. (Moses 7: 28-36, emphasis added.)

Although God's creations are numberless to us, they are numbered to Him. Sadly, among all those numberless creations, this earth is distinguished by the degree of "great wickedness" found among its people.

Christ came to the worst of the worst. In the history of this wicked world, there was only one group of people who sank into such darkness that they were willing to kill the Son of God. We read:

> Wherefore, as I said unto you, it must needs be expedient that Christ--for in the last night the angel spake unto me that this should be his name--should come among the Jews, among those **who are the more wicked part of the world**; and they shall crucify him--for thus it behooveth our God, and **there is none other nation on earth that would crucify their God**. For should the mighty miracles be wrought among other nations they would repent, and know that he be their God. But because of priestcrafts and iniquities, they at Jerusalem will stiffen their necks against him, that he be crucified. (2 Ne. 10: 3-5, emphasis added.)

It was **not** because these people were Jews. Christ was a Jew, as were Peter, James, John, the other members of the Twelve Apostles, the Seventy, John the Baptist, Mary, Martha, Lazarus, Stephen, Paul, Barnabas, and hundreds of others. Jews made up the foundation of the New Testament Church. Except for Luke, the New Testament was written entirely by Jews. The wickedness that killed Christ was not due to Jewishness. It was because of their "priestcrafts and iniquities" they killed their Messiah. Christ was challenged at every turn by a religious people, whose religious goals consisted of maintaining their "priestcraft," rather than seeking for and receiving the Gift of the Holy Ghost.

The Jews were not the only example of "priestcrafts and iniquities" that resulted in wickedness, abominations, murder and violence. When Historic Christianity gained political control over Europe, the Dark Ages ensued. Those were the days when a benighted and superstitious population followed a religion dominated by clerics speaking Latin in a deliberate attempt to conceal the truth. These Historic Christians were just as committed to priestcrafts as the Jews of Jesus' day had been. This is a universal problem. No population or group is immune to this religious failing. The purpose of studying the time is to prevent ourselves from falling into the same trap of pride, false religion and wickedness.

Christ's contemporaries were in large measure devoid of the Holy Spirit. They suppressed the Light of Christ within them. That was not universally true, as there were still those who were "filled with the Holy Spirit" despite living among a "generation of vipers."[24] Even before Christ taught them, there were those who kept the light of truth alive. For example, John the Baptist's mother, Elisabeth, was a holy vessel among an unholy people: "And it came to pass, that, when Elisabeth heard the salutation of Mary, the babe leaped in her womb; and Elisabeth was filled with the Holy Ghost[.]" (Luke 1: 41.) Zacharias was also familiar with the Holy Spirit: "And his father Zacharias was filled with the Holy Ghost, and prophesied[.]" (Luke 1: 67.) We read of both Simeon and "Anna, a prophetess," (Luke 2: 36) who met Joseph, Mary and the Christ child in the Temple when the days of Mary's purification ended. "[T]he Holy Ghost was upon" Simeon (Id. v. 25). "And it was revealed unto him by the Holy Ghost, that he should not see death, before he had seen the Lord's Christ." (Id. v 26.) We also have a description of John the Baptist which confirms: "For he

[24]This was the phrase used to describe the people of that day by both John the Baptist (Matt. 3: 7: "But when he saw many of the Pharisees and Sadducees come to his baptism, he said unto them, O generation of vipers, who hath warned you to flee from the wrath to come?") and Christ (Matt 12: 34: "O generation of vipers, how can ye, being evil, speak good things? for out of the abundance of the heart the mouth speaketh.")

shall be great in the sight of the Lord, and shall drink neither wine nor strong drink; and he shall be filled with the Holy Ghost, even from his mother's womb." (Luke 1: 15.) John was born with a heart inclined to listen to the Holy Ghost.

It is possible that among people so depraved by false religion that they would kill their God, there also lived men and women who enjoyed the companionship of the Holy Ghost. A "generation of vipers" has never had the power to altogether eliminate righteousness. You can choose to follow God even if the overwhelming majority of those around you walk in darkness.

The wickedness of these people was not a result of a lack of religion. As Nephi recorded, the problem was their "priestcrafts and iniquities." That does not mean a lack of religion, but instead the presence of a false religion. It can also include a true religion practiced abusively.

The Jews were a diminished and subjugated quasi-nationhood, inside the world's dominant superpower, the Roman Empire. Their past glory under Kings David and Solomon had long since faded. The lack of real power rendered this proud people all the more resentful of their humiliating circumstances. How can they claim to be "God's chosen people" when they owe their existence to the tolerance of a greater Roman power? How were they to compensate for this social inferiority?

They learned to practice fanaticism. They resented any challenge to their rights and authority. They learned to defend their claims of righteousness. They became something quite different from what the foundation of their faith tried to make them. Their zeal was based upon defensiveness. Too many historic indignities had made them resent any trespass onto their remaining turf. So they resorted to claiming they had "authority" and that was enough. God "told them" to do what they did. Their "traditions" were handed down from holy sources and were beyond being subject to any questioning. However, when a religious leader is one of God's true messengers, his message will never rely upon a claim of authority as reason to follow him. Indeed, true messengers always understand that no power or influence can or ought to be asserted because of their authority. The words of truth alone are sufficient.[25] Their testimony has authority which transcends any institutional trappings. When there is no Spirit which animates the messenger, then he knows his voice is weak. Because of an internal recognition of this weakness, these religious leaders always buttress their words with claims to priestly authority. This claim of priestly authority empowers them to impose their will upon others. This is one of the reasons it is so abhorrent to "take the name of the Lord, thy God, in vain," which was included as one of the Ten Commandments.[26]

The religious leaders of Christ's day lacked any spiritual authority. Therefore, they jealously guarded their right to claim leadership by asserting authority handed down from Moses' day to their own. Their appointment to leadership offices, the presence of priestly trappings, and possession of the Temple were all used to buttress their claimed rights to preside and exercise control and

---

[25]See, e.g., D&C 121: 41-42: "No power or influence can or ought to be maintained by virtue of the priesthood, only by persuasion, by long-suffering, by gentleness and meekness, and by love unfeigned; By kindness, and pure knowledge[.]"

[26]"Whenever someone proclaims their own agenda in the name of the Lord they take His name in vain. It is not swearing, but rather when one claims to speak for the Lord when they do not, that violates the command against vainly using the Lord's name." *Beloved Enos*, p. 166-167.

dominion over the Jews. Jesus, as a Jew, never challenged this legal right. Indeed, He defended it, as we will see later in this book. He had no place in their hierarchy. You needed to have a recognized place or you were not credible in their culture. These rule-bound but blind guides were strictly hierarchical. When they confronted Christ about the woman taken in adultery, His answer defeated their trap. Then they withdrew. But **how** they withdrew tells a great deal about them. John records: "And they which heard it, being convicted by their own conscience, went out one by one, **beginning at the eldest, even unto the last**: and Jesus was left alone[.]" (John 8: 9, emphasis added.) Deference to the hierarchy was everything. It even controlled the order they entered or left a room! Imagine what kind of rigid social order this was and how little room there was for inspiration, innovation or creativity. It killed the human and Divine spirit. It stifled. Submission to the existing order alone controlled everything. Christ failed to fit in.

When John and Jesus began their ministries they were both confronted with challenges to their right to teach. When John first taught we read of this confrontation:

> And this is the record of John, when the Jews sent priests and Levites from Jerusalem to ask him, **Who art thou**? And he confessed, and denied not; but confessed, I am not the Christ. And they asked him, **What then? Art thou Elias? And he saith, I am not. Art thou that prophet? And he answered, No. Then said they unto him, Who art thou**? that we may give an answer to them that sent us. What sayest thou of thyself? He said, I am the voice of one crying in the wilderness, Make straight the way of the Lord, as said the prophet Esaias. And they which were sent were of the Pharisees. And they asked him, and said unto him, **Why baptizest thou then, if thou be not that**

> **Christ, nor Elias, neither that prophet**? John answered them, saying, I baptize with water: but there standeth one among you, whom ye know not; He it is, who coming after me is preferred before me, whose shoe's latchet I am not worthy to unloose. These things were done in Bethabara beyond Jordan, where John was baptizing. (John 1: 19-28, emphasis added.)

These people knew and respected Annas and Caiaphas, because they presided with recognized institutional authority. But John, a son of a lowly Levite, was too obscure to be authorized to teach and baptize in such a public way.

Luke begins his Gospel by referencing the great and notable government and religious leaders of the time. It is written: "Now in the fifteenth year of the reign of Tiberius Caesar, Pontius Pilate being governor of Judaea, and Herod being tetrarch of Galilee, and his brother Philip tetrarch of Ituraea and of the region of Trachonitis, and Lysanias the tetrarch of Abilene, **Annas and Caiaphas being the high priests**, the word of God came unto John the son of Zacharias in the wilderness." (Luke 3: 1-2, emphasis added.) John held no such recognized authority. He may have been called of heaven, but the presiding authorities were so distant from heaven they were neither told of John's calling, nor were they able to recognize heaven's imprint on his ministry.

When Christ began His ministry, the same presiding authorities were quick to confront Him with questions about His right to teach. In reply, Christ was unwilling to reveal the real answer to them. We read:

> And when he was come into the temple, the chief priests and the elders of the people came unto him as he was teaching, and said, **By what authority doest thou these things**?

> and who gave thee this authority? And Jesus answered and said unto them, I also will ask you one thing, which if ye tell me, I in like wise will tell you by what authority I do these things. The baptism of John, whence was it? from heaven, or of men? And they reasoned with themselves, saying, If we shall say, From heaven; he will say unto us, Why did ye not then believe him? But if we shall say, Of men; we fear the people; for all hold John as a prophet. And they answered Jesus, and said, We cannot tell. And he said unto them, Neither tell I you by what authority I do these things. (Matt. 21: 23-27, emphasis added.)

For those who have no connection with heaven, authority is always everything. Once they establish they have "authority" the debate is over, so far as such people are concerned. They never learn that the rights of their priestly authority are inseparably connected with the powers of heaven; and when they have no connection to heaven they have no authority.

Most of those present were likewise baffled at Christ's ability to perform acts which showed He had authority from heaven. It was puzzling to them. All the doctrine they understood assured them that the presiding High Priest, the Priests and Levites and recognized Rabbis were the ones who held God's authority. It seemed doctrinally unsound to them for Christ to have authority from heaven itself:

> And there was in their synagogue a man with an unclean spirit; and he cried out, Saying, Let us alone; what have we to do with thee, thou Jesus of Nazareth? art thou come to destroy us? I know thee who thou art, the Holy One of God. And Jesus rebuked him, saying, Hold thy peace, and come out of him. And when the unclean spirit had

> torn him, and cried with a loud voice, he came out of him. And they were all amazed, insomuch that they questioned among themselves, saying, What thing is this? **what new doctrine is this? for with authority commandeth he even the unclean spirits, and they do obey him**. (Mark 1: 23-27, emphasis added.)

It did not occur to them Christ could possess independent authority received directly from heaven itself. For them, the institutional trappings of those who controlled the Temple site, presided at the official functions, wore the priestly garb, and collected the tithes, offerings and sacrifices were all that mattered. That alone defined power and authority. Christ paid tithing to them. Christ acted subordinate to them. Christ never challenged their right to preside. To the faithful members of that religious tradition Christ was unauthorized to teach, lead or initiate anyone into a higher order. Indeed, Christ was a threat to the established order of things.

It is important to understand this context in order to understand our Lord. He ministered among the most wicked of men, in the most wicked generation, on the most wicked creation. These people were wicked **because** of their religion. They were blind to what Jesus really taught. They had an order in their society they thought Christ threatened. He was not a bona fide source of anything. He was an outsider, an interloper. Leaders worried He was a threat and that he would cause a schism among their people. They did not want a deceiver to lead them away.

Even the wise men who came from the east inquired of the established authorities to find the newborn King of the Jews:

> Now when Jesus was born in Bethlehem of Judaea in the days of Herod the king, behold, there came

> wise men from the east to Jerusalem, Saying, Where is he that is born King of the Jews? for we have seen his star in the east, and are come to worship him. When Herod the king had heard these things, he was troubled, and all Jerusalem with him. And when he had gathered all the chief priests and scribes of the people together, he demanded of them where Christ should be born. And they said unto him, In Bethlehem of Judaea: for thus it is written by the prophet, And thou Bethlehem, in the land of Juda, art not the least among the princes of Juda: for out of thee shall come a Governor, that shall rule my people Israel. Then Herod, when he had privily called the wise men, enquired of them diligently what time the star appeared. And he sent them to Bethlehem, and said, Go and search diligently for the young child; and when ye have found him, bring me word again, that I may come and worship him also. (Matt. 2: 1-8.)

Expectations driven by cultural traditions and social standing led everyone, even inspired and true worshipers of Christ, to presume He would come as one having status in the community. To the credit of these wise men, however, they were able to hear inspiration from heaven. They were "**warned of God in a dream that they should not return to Herod**, they departed into their own country another way." (Id. v. 12, emphasis added.) They not only received direction from God, they followed it. Those two go together. When people will not listen to what heaven tells them, heaven stops speaking to them.

So we find our Lord choosing to live in a society filled with religious men, preoccupied with authority and devout in their faith. Even in their devotion these people were so distant from heaven they were unable to receive revelation telling them they were beholding the Christ. Nor were they able to understand any doctrine which would justify the apparent interloper. They simply could not "hear" Him.

As Isaiah put it: "there is no beauty that we should desire him." (Isa. 53: 2.) Or, to paraphrase Isaiah: "He was not bonafide. He did not have credentials deserving respect." He was nobody.

The Lord has always sent His messengers without credentials. From Enoch, who made this self assessment: "Why is it that I have found favor in thy sight, and am but a lad, and all the people hate me; for I am slow of speech; wherefore am I thy servant?" (Moses 6: 31) to Joseph Smith who "frequently fell into errors, and displayed the weakness of youth, and the foibles of human nature;" (JS-H 1: 28), God's servants are almost never found at the head of society. They are often like Abinadi or Samuel the Lamanite - belittled, persecuted and violently opposed. They always pay their tithing, but rarely collect it. It is not likely this pattern will ever change.

The Jews of Jesus' day had plenty of warning. They should have been able to identify Christ. They knew that throughout the dispensation of Moses the prophets raised up by God were frequently outcasts, interlopers and challengers to the established authorities. They had come crying repentance to the whole society. Only in the case of Samuel did the presiding authority (Eli) get displaced by the Lord's chosen prophet (Samuel). In all the other instances true prophets were persecuted, hated and killed.

Prophets receive praise only when they are dead. Once gone, their words can be adapted, interpreted and parsed to mean what the corrupt authorities want them to mean. And so they adorned the tombs of the dead prophets, all the while admitting they were the children of those who killed them. As Christ explained: "Woe unto you, scribes and Pharisees, hypocrites! because ye build the tombs of the prophets, and garnish the sepulchres of the righteous, And say, If we had been in the days of our fathers, we would not have been partakers with them in the blood of the prophets. Wherefore ye be witnesses unto yourselves, that ye are the children of them which killed the prophets. Fill ye up then the measure of your fathers. Ye serpents, ye generation of vipers, how can ye escape the damnation of hell?" (Matt. 23: 29-33.)

Therefore, to understand our Lord, it is necessary to understand how He appeared and how He will appear. He comes "as a thief in the night." (Matt. 24: 43.) This is always the case. We read this unflattering association of the Lord's return to a "thief," and assume this could not be referring to anything about His character. We assume He is referring to the way in which any "thief" practices his craft. However, the Lord is more deliberate in picking analogies than that. Not only will His return be a surprise to many, but it will also be as unwelcome as a "thief" is to a homeowner. He will steal authority from the pretenders. His return will threaten the wicked. Whenever any of us is brought into His presence we are immediately convicted of our sins, which makes us recoil. Only His grace and mercy allow us to be in His presence without recoiling. He threatened the established, authorized, and entrenched powers of His day. His return will be unwelcome by all that is Babylon.

He requires us to cast aside institutional securities and collective thinking. Each of us must find Christ for ourselves. Popular opinion, and the collective view of who are God's "chosen people" cannot be trusted. There has never been a safe, broad mainstream which reliably prepared or can prepare anyone to receive Him. It has never happened that way. We delude ourselves into thinking it will be otherwise for us. It was always designed that the Gospel of Christ requires you to find Him in His solitary way. His way is that of a "thief" who comes without credentials, without trappings and without public acclaim. His only sign of authority may be that your heart will burn within you as He speaks to you while in the way. Often times He will require you to first accept the unlikely truths which save, originating from unlikely sources, before He will permit you to come to the Throne of Grace. As we will see in this book, Christ came before as a "thief" and not as the recognized Master of the house.

The life of Christ illustrates the need to distinguish between a necessary order, organization or "chosen people" among whom He will always work, on the one hand, and actually receiving Him as individuals, on the other. His work with mankind begins when He first establishes a people. They are "chosen" to receive a body of teachings which preserve truths and gather tithes to build a House of the Lord. Then He allows those people who are chosen to live freely, exercising their agency to preserve or neglect the light He has dispensed to them. In every past dispensation, including the one established by the Lord in the Meridian of Time, there was always a foundational prophet or dispensation head. The new dispensation's teachings were then perpetuated, in a less-than-perfect way, by stewards who inherited the presiding offices. The tradition quickly eroded, and what remained was a hollow, spiritless entity which venerated the founder, claimed to follow His (or His messenger's) teachings, but drifted away from contact with heaven. Because of this drifting away in past dispensations, there have always been sub-dispensations. From among those who claimed to perpetuate the true faith, the Lord from time to time choose individuals to cry repentance. These characters given sub-dispensations were almost always unpopular, and never in the seat of power. They were the voices crying in the wilderness, because they came from outside the established structure.

From Moses to Jesus Christ there was a single great dispensation. However, during this Dispensation of Moses there were many other prophets who were called and given sub-dispensations of the Gospel. As to these sub-dispensations Joseph Smith taught: "All Priesthood is Melchizedek, but there are different portions or degrees of it. That portion which brought Moses to speak with God face to face was taken away; but that which brought the ministry of angels remained. **All the prophets had the Melchizedek Priesthood and were ordained by God himself.**" (*TPJS*, p. 180, emphasis added.) This means that the existing hierarchy between Moses and Jesus Christ could not have ordained these prophets of the Old Testament because that hierarchy did not have the authority to do so. The portion of the priesthood authority which let men speak face to face with God was bestowed by God directly upon these prophets, independent of the mainstream of the people and their leadership.

These independently ordained prophets were called in precisely in the same way Moses, the Dispensation Head, had revealed. Moses recorded the Lord commanding: "Hear now my words: If there be a prophet among you, I the Lord will make myself known unto him in a vision, and will speak unto him in a dream." (Num. 12: 6.) Direct contact between God and His prophets was not only set as the rule, but it was also the practice throughout that dispensation. We have seen that Joseph Smith taught "All the prophets had the Melchizedek Priesthood and were ordained by God himself." (*Supra.*)

In contrast to this independent and uncontrollable prophetic tradition, the control, command or presiding authority was institutionalized among the "chosen people." It was given through Moses to be handed down through the generations, and belonged to the people who inherited these offices. Despite the hierarchy's continual failure to measure up, God's prophets did not overturn the hierarchy or supplant them, with one single exception. Only in the case of Samuel supplanting Eli did the Lord remove a Presiding High Priest and replace him with a prophet. When Christ commented on the corrupt and worldly hierarchy of His own day would He say: "All they bid you do, that do ye." (See Matt. 23: 3-4) True prophets may teach, but they do not supplant. Hierarchies established by Dispensation Heads are allowed to go forward without being molested or made afraid by those who receive sub-dispensations of the Gospel. This pattern has been true throughout. When Lehi finished crying repentance, he departed. His sub-dispensation functioned without any attempt to supplant. God Himself then intervened to discipline Jerusalem. His prophets fled; but His presiding priestly class was forcibly removed to Babylon.

The Lord, who is ever the same, establishes a system in which the "chosen people" can continue to perpetuate both their true and false traditions, while also providing the means for truth to be kept alive by the "few, who are the humble followers of Christ." (2 Ne. 28: 14.) The Book of Mormon is quick to add, with respect to these "few" of our day that "nevertheless, they are led, that in many instances they do err because they are taught by the precepts of men." (Id.)

Christ's message **is** His authority. His words are what distinguish His true ministers from false ones He never sent.

Anyone teaching His truth should be recognized as His messenger. He taught this to Moroni. Those who will receive Christ in any generation do so because they hear and recognize His words.[27] Anyone who will not believe in His words, no matter who He sends to speak them, will not believe in Christ or His Father. Those who trust only institutional sources of truth, whether they are Catholic, Baptist, Lutheran, or Latter-day Saint, believe in an institution, and do not believe in Christ. The ability to individually recognize His words distinguishes those who are saved from those who are lost.

Control of the budgets, collection of the tithes, the right to control the Temples, to preside, to conduct, and ceremonial authority is all vested by the Lord in a self-perpetuating hierarchy for His covenant people. However, the Lord never allows a hierarchy to control all teaching. For example, in our own Dispensation of the Fullness of Time, just as in all prior dispensations, the obligation to teach is not confined to a small group. It is instead spread broadly among all His people. Everyone who receives the Spirit is directed - indeed commanded - to teach. The command to "teach one another" the doctrines of the kingdom is repeated five times in the D&C. (See, e.g., D&C 38: 23; 88: 77; 88: 118; 107: 85; and 109: 7.) The obligation to teach, exhort and expound is also imposed upon anyone ordained to an office in The Church of Jesus Christ of Latter-day Saints. In the Doctrine and Covenants we read the command to expound

---

[27] Ether 4: 12: " And whatsoever thing persuadeth men to do good is of me; for good cometh of none save it be of me. I am the same that leadeth men to all good; he that will not believe my words will not believe me--that I am; and he that will not believe me will not believe the Father who sent me. For behold, I am the Father, I am the light, and the life, and the truth of the world."

doctrine given to not only an Apostle (D&C 20: 42), but also to all those who are Priests (v. 46), Teachers (v. 59) and Deacons (v. 59). Moses not only refused to rebuke those who showed prophetic gifts, he went further and wished all men were prophets.[28] The New Testament church included prophets and prophetesses who were not presiding general church officers.[29] Spiritual gifts, prophecy and inspired teaching has always been expected to come from all ranks of believers, without regard to office, among the Lord's chosen people.

The Book of Mormon teaches that angels minister to men, women and even children; not just to a hierarchy. The hierarchy is not mentioned at all in Alma's teachings to the humble outcasts, who had been rejected by the presiding authorities. Given the audience, the message of his description of the ministering of angels becomes all the more clear:

> I say unto you, it is well that ye are cast out of your synagogues, that ye may be humble, and that ye

---

[28] See, e.g., Num. 11: 27-29: "And there ran a young man, and told Moses, and said, Eldad and Medad do prophesy in the camp. And Joshua the son of Nun, the servant of Moses, one of his young men, answered and said, My lord Moses, forbid them. And Moses said unto him, Enviest thou for my sake? would God that all the Lord's people were prophets, and that the Lord would put his spirit upon them!"

[29] See, e.g., Acts 21: 8-11: "And the next day we that were of Paul's company departed, and came unto Caesarea: and we entered into the house of Philip the evangelist, which was one of the seven; and abode with him. And the same man had four daughters, virgins, which did prophesy. And as we tarried there many days, there came down from Judaea a certain prophet, named Agabus. And when he was come unto us, he took Paul's girdle, and bound his own hands and feet, and said, Thus saith the Holy Ghost, So shall the Jews at Jerusalem bind the man that owneth this girdle, and shall deliver him into the hands of the Gentiles."

may learn wisdom; for it is necessary that ye should learn wisdom; **for it is because that ye are cast out, that ye are despised of your brethren because of your exceeding poverty, that ye are brought to a lowliness of heart; for ye are necessarily brought to be humble**. And now, because ye are compelled to be humble blessed are ye; for a man sometimes, if he is compelled to be humble, seeketh repentance; and now surely, whosoever repenteth shall find mercy; and he that findeth mercy and endureth to the end the same shall be saved. And now, as I said unto you, that because ye were compelled to be humble ye were blessed, do ye not suppose that they are more blessed who truly humble themselves because of the word? Yea, **he that truly humbleth himself, and repenteth of his sins, and endureth to the end, the same shall be blessed**--yea, much more blessed than they who are compelled to be humble because of their exceeding poverty. Therefore, blessed are they who humble themselves without being compelled to be humble; or rather, in other words, blessed is he that believeth in the word of God, and is baptized without stubbornness of heart, yea, without being brought to know the word, or even compelled to know, before they will believe. ... And now, behold, I say unto you, and I would that ye should remember, that **God is merciful unto all who believe on his name**; therefore he desireth, in the first place, that ye should believe, yea, even on his word. And now, **he imparteth his word by angels unto men, yea, not only men but women also. Now this is not all; little children do have words given unto them many times, which confound the wise and the learned**. (Alma 32: 12-16, 22-23; emphasis added.)

It is not because of position, rank or office that angels come to minister. Rather it is the humility of the person which attracts notice from heaven. The reason the "wise and learned" are confounded is because they are neither wise nor learned, but are arrogant. They trust their wisdom, they trust their learning, and they deny the Spirit which gives utterance. This has always been toxic. It is this problem which created the spiritually sterile environment of the Jewish hierarchy when Christ lived.

None of this information does us any good if we fail to apply it to us. Unless we realize we can lose the light restored to us, these teachings do nothing except make us falsely believe that we are better than these earlier generations. We are just as vulnerable. We need to take heed of these grave risks which destroy faith and cost entire generations their salvation. We are required to be vigilant. Nephi lectured on this problem in his closing remarks in 2 Nephi. In addressing these remarks directly to us, he reminds us that the pattern which showed up in all prior Dispensations would again return in the Dispensation of the Fullness of time.

Christ also lamented the future failure of the Gentile Latter-day Church. His prophecy and caution tells us what we are to expect will happen among us. Christ warned us:

> And thus commandeth the Father that I should say unto you: **At that day when the Gentiles shall sin against my gospel, and shall reject the fulness of my gospel, and shall be lifted up in the pride of their hearts above all nations, and above all the people of the whole earth, and shall be filled with all manner of lyings, and of deceits, and of mischiefs, and all manner of hypocrisy, and murders, and priestcrafts, and whoredoms, and of secret abominations**; and if they shall do all those things, and shall reject the fulness of my gospel, behold, saith the Father, **I**

> **will bring the fulness of my gospel from among them. And then will I remember my covenant which I have made unto my people, O house of Israel, and I will bring my gospel unto them.** And I will show unto thee, O house of Israel, that the Gentiles shall not have power over you; but I will remember my covenant unto you, O house of Israel, and ye shall come unto the knowledge of the fulness of my gospel. But if the Gentiles will repent and return unto me, saith the Father, behold they shall be numbered among my people, O house of Israel. And I will not suffer my people, who are of the house of Israel, to go through among them, and tread them down, saith the Father. But **if they will not turn unto me, and hearken unto my voice, I will suffer them, yea, I will suffer my people, O house of Israel, that they shall go through among them, and shall tread them down, and they shall be as salt that hath lost its savor, which is thenceforth good for nothing but to be cast out, and to be trodden under foot of my people, O house of Israel.** Verily, verily, I say unto you, **thus hath the Father commanded me--that I should give unto this people this land for their inheritance.** (3 Ne. 16: 10-16.)

Note the Lord does not say "if" but "when" the Gentiles will be filled with this kind of corruption. Notice, too, the Lord does not say when this happens there will be a second restoration of the Gospel. Rather, He will sweep away the unworthy and replace them with the worthy. The Gospel will be taken from among the proud but wicked Gentiles, and given to the remnant of the earlier inheritors of the land. Of course those who have followed the teachings of the Gospel, who are penitent, and therefore not full of lyings, deceits, mischiefs, hypocrisy, priestcrafts, whoredoms and secret abominations, even though they are Gentiles, will remain among the chosen. They will not be swept away, but instead will be numbered among God's people because such persons are always His. They have nothing to fear. They are in no danger of being tread down, cast out and trodden under foot.

So while there is no safe "broad mainstream" to protect any of us, God will always care for those who are His. Personal righteousness is always a singular thing. This is the way it was in the days of Christ. This is the way it is it today.

The Lord has given us revelations to let us approach Him. But the test now, as when the Lord was in His mortal ministry, is the same. To understand His day is to understand our own. To correctly weigh and understand the forces of truth and light, against error and darkness which compete for our souls is to see the same tension in which Christ lived. There is no difference. There has never been and never will be a different test.

He told us how to find our way back:

> And I give unto you, who are the first laborers in this last kingdom, a commandment that you assemble yourselves together, and organize yourselves, and prepare yourselves, and **sanctify yourselves; yea, purify your hearts, and cleanse your hands and your feet before me**, that I may make you clean; That I may testify unto your Father, and your God, and my God, that you are clean from the blood of this wicked generation; that I may fulfil this promise, this great and last promise, which I have made unto you, when I will. Also, I give unto you a commandment that **ye shall continue in prayer and fasting from this time forth**. And **I give unto you a commandment that you shall teach one another the doctrine of the kingdom. Teach ye diligently and my grace shall attend you, that you may be instructed more perfectly in theory,**

> **in principle, in doctrine, in the law of the gospel**, in all things that pertain unto the kingdom of God, that are expedient for you to understand; Of things both in heaven and in the earth, and under the earth; things which have been, things which are, things which must shortly come to pass; things which are at home, things which are abroad; the wars and the perplexities of the nations, and the judgments which are on the land; and a knowledge also of countries and of kingdoms--That ye may be prepared in all things when I shall send you again to magnify the calling whereunto I have called you, and the mission with which I have commissioned you. Behold, I sent you out to testify and warn the people, and **it becometh every man who hath been warned to warn his neighbor**. Therefore, they are left without excuse, and their sins are upon their own heads. **He that seeketh me early shall find me, and shall not be forsaken**. (D&C 88: 74-83.)

We need to be taught the truth. As we have seen, there is no single person who holds the obligation to teach His truth. Every person who has been warned should warn his neighbor. All those who have been ordained as a Deacon, Teacher, Priest, Elder, High Priest or Apostle are obligated to exhort, expound and teach the truth. Those who fail to do so jeopardize their salvation.

Those who declare vain, idle or selfish words and claim them to be from the Lord are taking the Lord's name in vain, and will be condemned. Those who listen to and are persuaded by them will suffer a similar fate. They have been warned about using His name to teach foolishness: "And the Spirit shall be given unto you by the prayer of faith; and **if ye receive not the Spirit ye shall not teach**." (D&C 42: 14.)

It is the obligation of all of us to obtain the Spirit and then to speak. As the Lord explained in revelation to those gathered when The Church of Jesus Christ of Latter-day Saints was founded: "And also gave commandments to others, that they should proclaim these things unto the world; and all this that it might be fulfilled, which was written by the prophets-- The weak things of the world shall come forth and break down the mighty and strong ones, that man should not counsel his fellow man, neither trust in the arm of flesh-- But **that every man might speak in the name of God the Lord, even the Savior of the world**; That faith also might increase in the earth; That mine everlasting covenant might be established; That the fulness of my gospel might be proclaimed by the weak and the simple unto the ends of the world, and before kings and rulers." (D&C 1: 18-23; emphasis added.)

In Christ's day the test for His generation was whether they would choose truth and light from a teacher who came bearing nothing *but* the truth. He controlled no synagogue, was not authorized to minister in the Temple because He was not a Levite. He did not hold any official position among the well established hierarchy, did not have wealth, political position, nor traditional learning. But He came with the power of the Spirit. When He spoke words of truth those who heard could feel within them the validity of His message. These faithful followers were not intimidated by the opposition which gathered against them. They were not deterred by threats from men. They relied upon the Spirit.

To some few it is given to know. To a larger group it is given to believe on their words. (See, e.g., D&C 42: 12-13.) These gifts belong to the Lord's Church. (Id., v. 10.) Only a fool will oppose those gifts when they are manifested. And fools opposed the Lord. Well intentioned and devout followers of a false tradition rejected

Him solely because they trusted in the traditions handed down to them. They wrongly believed God would never send someone to tell them anything important unless he were to occupy a position of authority among them. And so they rejected our Lord because He was not in the hierarchy. With that rejection they also forfeited their own salvation.

We may be in a unique position to better understand Christ than any past generation. We get to relive some of the very same dynamics. We also get to enjoy the risk of living with the eternal consequences of the choice we make.

So we turn to examples from the life of Christ in these pages to discover for ourselves how to obtain that "pearl of great price" which is worth all that we possess. As we shall see, Christ's final great public sermon addressed these very issues. He challenged those who killed Him to leave their false beliefs behind. They did not. Instead, they killed Him to silence His criticism and to put an end to His example. They failed. He triumphed.

Chapter 5

Christ's Birth and Early Childhood

Luke established the time of Christ's birth by referencing Caesar Augustus and Cyrenius, the Roman political leaders of the day. These two Roman leaders were notable. Christ was obscure. It was necessary to associate Christ with these political leaders for Luke to establish for readers the time in which He was born. In the centuries after Christ's life, we now refer to Caesar in relationship to Christ's birth. Although not well known during his short life, He has since gained significance and historic recognition. This is often the case. The Lord and His true messengers acquire greater importance only after they die.

He came, as He promised to return, as a thief in the night. (See Matt. 24: 37-51.) He was not expected. There was no fanfare. Only a few recognized Him. He was not popular among his peers. Only after his death has he occupied a singular place in history. We presume we would have recognized Him. The likelihood is that we would not have been any more open to His claims than those whose history and tradition made them skeptical. He was different than they expected. If you strip away the two millennia of tradition affirming He **was** the Lord, and go back to the setting in which He was born, we would be far less likely to have accepted Him than we think. At the time, it required those who elected to follow Him to ignore tradition. It required them to reject the authority structure of the religion they believed and the leaders who presided over them. It required them to accept a vastly different set of meanings than they had ever been taught before. The Messiah would come as a lamb, rather than as a lion. He would suffer, die and be resurrected. He would show perfection by the meekness of His example. Those who 'heard His voice' and knew Him as their shepherd were required to become revolutionaries who stepped out of existing social orders and controls to accept a radically different world view. This is true of all his followers in every generation in every culture and subculture. His ways are not man's ways.[30] Therefore, whenever the Lord is nearby, we are required to drop our vain traditions and foolish thoughts and follow Him.

Luke's account reads:

---

[30]"Seek ye the Lord while he may be found, call ye upon him while he is near: **Let the wicked forsake his way, and the unrighteous man his thoughts: and let him return unto the Lord**, and he will have mercy upon him; and to our God, for he will abundantly pardon. **For my thoughts are not your thoughts, neither are your ways my ways, saith the Lord. For as the heavens are higher than the earth, so are my ways higher than your ways, and my thoughts than your thoughts**. For as the rain cometh down, and the snow from heaven, and returneth not thither, but watereth the earth, and maketh it bring forth and bud, that it may give seed to the sower, and bread to the eater: So shall my word be that goeth forth out of my mouth: it shall not return unto me void, but it shall accomplish that which I please, and it shall prosper in the thing whereto I sent it." (Isa. 55: 6-11, emphasis added.)

> And it came to pass in those days, that there went out a decree from Caesar Augustus, that all the world should be taxed. (And this taxing was first made when Cyrenius was governor of Syria.) And all went to be taxed, every one into his own city. And Joseph also went up from Galilee, out of the city of Nazareth, into Judaea, unto the city of David, which is called Bethlehem; (because he was of the house and lineage of David:) To be taxed with Mary his espoused wife, being great with child. And so it was, that, while they were there, the days were accomplished that she should be delivered. And she brought forth her firstborn son, and wrapped him in swaddling clothes, and laid him in a manger; because there was no room for them in the inn. (Luke 2: 1-7.)

Christ, the God of Heaven, entered mortality away from the gaze of the Bethlehem crowd. The population of Judea was unaware of this momentous event. There was no room for Him or His family because no one outside his family attached any significant to His birth. This King of kings spent His first night in mortality in a manger.

The isolated and rough circumstances of Christ's birth preclude all excuses by those who claim they are justifiably resentful that they were born to difficult conditions. He had as much cause to complain about His life's beginning as anyone. He never did so.

He "descended below all things" willingly, gracefully, and without complaint. (See, e.g., D&C 88: 6; 122: 8.) Although He came through the house and lineage of David, the hereditary throne had long been forfeited. In place of David's descendants, a Roman vassal political appointment belonging to the house of Herod ruled. This was a corrupt and only quasi-Jewish ruler whose allegiance was to Rome, not to the Jews. To the extent the Davidic lineage mattered at all at the time, it was a detriment. Because of His lineage, He inherited no throne. Instead he inherited an obligation to travel to Bethlehem to be part of the Roman-decreed census.

Mankind may have taken little notice of His coming, but heaven knew Him. His arrival was not without testimony from the heavenly host:

> And there were in the same country shepherds abiding in the field, keeping watch over their flock by night. And, lo, the angel of the Lord came upon them, and the glory of the Lord shone round about them: and they were sore afraid. And the angel said unto them, Fear not: for, behold, I bring you good tidings of great joy, which shall be to all people. For unto you is born this day in the city of David a Saviour, which is Christ the Lord. And this shall be a sign unto you; Ye shall find the babe wrapped in swaddling clothes, lying in a manger. And suddenly there was with the angel a multitude of the heavenly host praising God, and saying, Glory to God in the highest, and on earth peace, good will toward men. (Luke 2: 8-14.)

Consider this scene from Luke for a moment: Shepherds were on watch in the spring fields, protecting their flock by night. This was in the spring,[31] when lambs were being born. The shepherds' nightly duty to "keep watch" required them to minister to and protect the newborn lambs. Many of these animals would be destined for ritual sacrifice. These men were attending to the symbols of the Lamb of God when the glory of God shone about

---

[31]Modern revelation in D&C 20: 1 fixes the date of Christ's "coming ... in the flesh" as April 6th.

them and interrupted the quiet. When the light appeared, as is always the case, they were caught unprepared to see such holiness, glory and power. They recoiled. They were afraid. They were troubled by the gulf between their humble lives and the messenger of glory standing before them. They likely doubted their senses. This was all so unexpected.

We do not know the shepherds' names. We do not know their ages, home towns or backgrounds. We do not know their spiritual preparation, or even their reason for being the ones on watch this particular night. Their story about the events of this night had to be told to others, by them, who in turn reported it to Luke. How this happened is lost to history. It is likely that Christ's mother Mary, repeated it to Luke. This is alluded to later in the account.

The message they received was an introduction of Christ by heaven to mankind: Good tidings! Great joy! Born **to you** a Savior! The personal nature of this announcement was emphatic. This wasn't just a baby who would matter to heaven, but one who mattered **to them**. He was **their** Savior. Heaven is always interested in each of us. We matter, however unlikely it may seem.

Thankfully this heavenly message has been preserved. The witnesses' account is certain and unmistakable in meaning. But they were content to remain unknown shepherds, who kept watch by night. Their story and testimony have remained, but their identities are lost to history. For them it was enough to be known by heaven. They felt no need to claim any earthly notice. Their story keeps the focus where it belongs: upon the Child who was born as Savior.

The account continues:

> And it came to pass, as the angels were gone away from them into heaven, the shepherds said one to another, Let us now go even unto Bethlehem, and see this thing which is come to pass, which the

> Lord hath made known unto us. And they came with haste, and found Mary, and Joseph, and the babe lying in a manger. (Luke 2: 15-16.)

They said to each other: "Let us now go." The emphasis being on "now." Let us go and "see this thing which is come to pass." Heaven proclaimed the arrival. They needed to act quickly to see it for themselves. There was no hesitation. They went "with haste" and were able to find Mary, Joseph and Christ "lying in a manger." It appears that in their haste they were able to arrive on the night of His birth.

Mary and Joseph received an immediate reminder of who it was who had been entrusted to their care. This child was perhaps only a few hours old when these excited messengers arrive to worship Him and proclaim their story about heavenly choirs singing praises of this newborn. If either Mary or Joseph entertained any doubt about how their child's life was to unfold, this event gave unmistakable forewarning.

While still in the manger, the shepherds told any who would listen about this newborn Savior. They continued to announce throughout the Judean countryside the news of Him who was born "Christ, the Lord." We read:

> And when they had seen it, they made known abroad the saying which was told them concerning this child. And all they that heard it wondered at those things which were told them by the shepherds. But Mary kept all these things, and pondered them in her heart. And the shepherds returned, glorifying and praising God for all the things that they had heard and seen, as it was told unto them. (Luke 2: 17-20.)

Luke has just revealed where he received his information regarding this momentous event. Only Mary would have known what she "pondered in her heart." Given her personal introspection, it seems Mary would necessarily have been the source for Luke's account. Although the shepherds were busily announcing His birth, His mother was quietly considering what all this meant. She had the responsibility of raising Him. She had to consider what this widespread announcement was going to do to complicate her responsibilities. She also had to consider the daunting task of mothering "Christ, the Lord."

Those who initially heard this story "wondered at those things which" the shepherds said. No doubt they would wonder about the incongruence of this Heavenly King lying in the manger. Everything about the circumstance was humble, even homely. On the one hand they hear about angels, choirs, songs of praise and a newborn Lord. On the other hand they hear the excited but lowly shepherds and their message, the manger, and the humble family. The likelihood of anyone royal coming into the world this way seems improbable. It would only be normal for those who heard these things to "wonder at those things" the shepherds were saying.

How often the work of God is done in unlikely ways! Men want Him to fit their pattern. The Lord's pattern is unexpected and inconvenient. It is heralded by unlikely messengers. It is the message alone by which His comings are marked. It is not the circumstances. He doesn't use expected fanfare. He comes or sends the unexpected. You must listen to hear Him. His sheep **hear** His voice. They recognize Him in the message. He is not found in the trappings, orders, institutions, genealogical lines, chief seats, traditions or expectations. We should carefully consider that pattern as we decide what and who we believe and trust. The test for us cannot be any different than the test all others have been required to pass in mortality. Hear His voice and be gathered, don't and be lost. It is always the same.

Following the first announcement by the shepherds, Mary and Joseph received additional witnesses after Christ was circumcised and the days of purification ended. When they brought Him to the Temple, the following took place:

> And when eight days were accomplished for the circumcising of the child, his name was called JESUS, which was so named of the angel before he was conceived in the womb. And when the days of her purification according to the law of Moses were accomplished, they brought him to Jerusalem, to present him to the Lord; (As it is written in the law of the Lord, Every male that openeth the womb shall be called holy to the Lord;) And to offer a sacrifice according to that which is said in the law of the Lord, A pair of turtledoves, or two young pigeons. And, behold, there was a man in Jerusalem, whose name was Simeon; and the same man was just and devout, waiting for the consolation of Israel: and the Holy Ghost was upon him. And it was revealed unto him by the Holy Ghost, that he should not see death, before he had seen the Lord's Christ. And he came by the Spirit into the temple: and when the parents brought in the child Jesus, to do for him after the custom of the law, Then took he him up in his arms, and blessed God, and said, Lord, now lettest thou thy servant depart in peace, according to thy word: For mine eyes have seen thy salvation, Which thou hast prepared before the face of all people; A light to lighten the Gentiles, and the glory of thy people Israel. And Joseph and his mother marvelled at those things which were spoken of him. And Simeon blessed them, and said

> unto Mary his mother, Behold, this child is set for the fall and rising again of many in Israel; and for a sign which shall be spoken against; (Yea, a sword shall pierce through thy own soul also,) that the thoughts of many hearts may be revealed. (Luke 2: 21-35.)

When Christ was brought to the Temple for the purification offering, His parents met Simeon. We know only that Simeon is "just and devout," which is to say that he was unlike others. He knew through revelation that Christ would come before he died. We presume Simeon was elderly, because he says he can now "depart in peace." We do not know how many years passed after the witness of the Holy Ghost told him he would not die before seeing the Father's Christ. But we can be sure the Lord tried his patience just as He tries ours. Blessings are given after the trial of our faith. It was likely many years between when Simeon first knew he would see the Christ child and the day this event occurred.

This was the day, however, when Simeon finally "came by the Spirit into the Temple" knowing he would finally see Him who had been promised. As soon as he saw Christ, he knew. It is not hard to envision the scene. This gentle, elderly soul approached with his arms extended. Just as he came **by** the Spirit to the Temple, he also came **with** the Spirit. Mary could not resist his outstretched entreaty, and she gave him the child to hold. "Then took he him up in his arms, and blessed God, and said, Lord ... mine eyes have seen thy salvation." From Gabriel His birth was promised by Heaven. To the shepherds His birth was certified by choirs of angels. To Simeon the testimony of His arrival came by the inspiration of the Holy Spirit. For great missions there are great witnesses given to the humble. Joseph and Mary, as the parents of this little child, were given multiple witnesses in rapid succession to assure them of the significance of their calling to be His earthly parents.

Simeon went on to prophesy Christ would be a light to the Gentiles. Although it makes sense to us because of the centuries which followed, that prophecy would foretell an unexpected role for Israel's King and Savior. He would be expected to be "the glory of ... Israel," as Simeon promised, but His role to the Gentiles would be surprising, even though Isaiah mentions it three times.[32] Joseph and Mary "marveled" at all which Simeon said about their Son. Presumably there was more said than what the record preserves.

Simeon went on to bless Christ's parents as well. His prophecy to Mary was ominous. He foretold that many will fall, but many will rise, as a result of this Child's mission. Some would fall from grace because they reject Him. Others would rise to glory and exaltation because of Him. The mighty, content, prosperous and secure have almost universally rejected Him. But the weak, the infirm, the outcast, the bedraggled have accepted Him and what He offers. This prophecy remains in effect. His mission still causes many to fall and some to rise.

Simeon predicted Mary's heartbreak at her son's sacrificial death. He told her that a "sword shall pierce through they own soul also" as she sees His life end before her own. Glory and sacrifice go hand in hand. Suffering and exaltation are inseparable. Christ will always expose the thoughts of our hearts by what we say and do regarding His message. Righteousness is always purchased with a price.

---

[32]See, e.g., Isa. Isa 42: 6; 49: 6 and 60: 3.

If these messengers and witnesses had not been enough, the scriptures tell of yet another. A woman, prophetess, also of great age was at the Temple as well, and Luke preserves her witness for us in these words:

> And there was one Anna, a prophetess, the daughter of Phanuel, of the tribe of Aser: she was of a great age, and had lived with an husband seven years from her virginity; And she was a widow of about fourscore and four years, which departed not from the temple, but served God with fastings and prayers night and day. And she coming in that instant gave thanks likewise unto the Lord, and spake of him to all them that looked for redemption in Jerusalem. (Luke 2: 36-38.)

Anna's testimony as a prophetess confirmed the Lord is no respecter of persons. All are alike unto Him; whether male or female, young or old, bond or free, everyone is entitled to the ministering of angels and gift of prophecy. (See Alma 32: 23.) If we seriously believe our claim to be a restoration of the ancient faith, we would be well advised to encourage the gifted, including the "prophetesses" among us, to speak up when moved upon by the Holy Spirit. Whenever there are people of faith there are always spiritual gifts and gifted believers, including prophetesses. In the New Testament era, both before Christ established a Church and after, prophetesses were expected and accepted.[33] Latter-day Saints are uncomfortable with the idea of women declaring prophecy. Unlike us, the New Testament includes reference to Anna's inspired testimony of the Christ child with no jealousy or hint of disfavor toward gifted women offering inspired testimony.

---

[33] See also, e.g., Acts 21: 9.

Spiritually weak, insecure men feel threatened by women's spiritual gifts. A discussion of that subject is beyond the scope of this book, however, so we can make only passing reference to it.

Anna thanked the Lord for Christ's arrival. She testified of Him to "all them that looked for redemption in Jerusalem." This would have involved more than the few standing nearby, and would have continued for the rest of her life. To the extent that anyone hoped for redemption in Jerusalem, this woman of "great age" spent her remaining days testifying that the Day of Redemption had come and Christ was then among them.

The stir which the pregnancies and births of John and Christ caused was nevertheless confined to few enough people that it escaped King Herod's attention. He moved in different circles. Visitors from the east brought it directly to his notice. Matthew records:

> Now when Jesus was born in Bethlehem of Judaea in the days of Herod the king, behold, there came wise men from the east to Jerusalem, Saying, Where is he that is born King of the Jews? for we have seen his star in the east, and are come to worship him. When Herod the king had heard these things, he was troubled, and all Jerusalem with him. (Matt. 2: 1-3.)

Little is known about these "wise men" from the east. They understood enough about the true faith to know a Savior was one day coming, and He would be known as the King of the Jews. They knew He would come to the land of Jerusalem. And they trusted in the promise of this King enough to bring Him gifts worthy of royalty.

How they maintained the knowledge of these things while living in an undisclosed eastern location, is not known. We do not know how many of them came. Because there were three categories of gifts, some assume that meant there were three wise men. That conclusion is likely wrong.

It made sense that they would seek the newborn king in Herod's palace. The King of the Jews was not found there, nor were the palace occupants aware of His birth. As soon as Herod heard of this new citizen of his kingdom, he was "troubled." The news of Christ's arrival was no longer limited to the lower classes of society who had heard these tidings two years earlier, but "all Jerusalem" was now troubled. News would have traveled quickly from the throne into the outlying cities.

The account continues:

> And when he had gathered all the chief priests and scribes of the people together, he demanded of them where Christ should be born. And they said unto him, In Bethlehem of Judaea: for thus it is written by the prophet, And thou Bethlehem, in the land of Juda, art not the least among the princes of Juda: for out of thee shall come a Governor, that shall rule my people Israel. (Matt. 2: 4-6.)

Herod knew nothing of the prophecy identifying where to look for the King of the Jews. But his courtesans read and understood the scriptures. It is good to have a command of the scriptures. Such knowledge is useful, even in the employ of an evil king.[34] It would be better, of course, for a scriptorian instead to study the scriptures

---

[34]See, e.g., Luke 16: 8-9: "And the lord commended the unjust steward, because he had done wisely: for the children of this world are in their generation wiser than the children of light. And I say unto you, Make to yourselves friends of the mammon of unrighteousness; that, when ye fail, they may receive you into everlasting habitations."

for his salvation. Christ would later be confronted about the scriptural propriety of healing on the Sabbath. In response to scripture-based criticism He rebuked the scripture-quoting critics with: "Search the scriptures; for in them ye think ye have eternal life: and they are they which testify of me." (John 5: 39.) It is not the words of scripture which matter. It is the Spirit which inspired the words which gives life. Without that Spirit, you may be able to find an answer to a question, but it will not be for your salvation.

The chief priests and scribes found the answer in the scriptures. If they had the right Spirit about them, they would have already known that Christ their rightful king was among them. It took inspired men from the east to bring it to their attention. This incident shows, yet again, how knowledge of the scriptures alone does not have the power to save anyone. Knowledge may be power, but such power is not necessarily the same thing as salvation.

Knowing "where" (i.e., Bethlehem) does not mean you know "when" (i.e., how old the new King should be). So Herod had to ask:

> Then Herod, when he had privily called the wise men, enquired of them diligently what time the star appeared. And he sent them to Bethlehem, and said, Go and search diligently for the young child; and when ye have found him, bring me word again, that I may come and worship him also. When they had heard the king, they departed; and, lo, the star, which they saw in the east, went before them, till it came and stood over where the young child was. When they saw the star, they rejoiced with exceeding great joy. (Matt. 2: 7-10.)

Herod inquired, but it isn't until verse 16 that we learn the answer to his inquiry. The child had been born two years earlier: "Then

Herod, when he saw that he was mocked of the wise men, was exceeding wroth, and sent forth, and slew all the children that were in Bethlehem, and in all the coasts thereof, from two years old and under, according to the time which he had diligently enquired of the wise men." (Id. v. 16.) This lets us know Christ's age at the time and that the wise men had been traveling for approximately two years. This gives some indication of the significant distance they must have traveled to get there. It also gives a clue about the distance one body of His "other sheep" was from Jerusalem. As the Risen Christ, He would visit various places where there were believing bodies of "other sheep" who kept alive faith in the Lord. But those matters are beyond the scope of this book and can only be mentioned in passing.

Matthew lets us know the wise men learned of Christ's birth because they were studying the heavens and saw a new star. The Nephites saw a heavenly sign testifying of Christ's birth, also. Their sign of Christ's birth was a day, a night and a day without darkness. These wise men came from a place where they saw an unmistakable heavenly message.

Herod's request to the wise men to 'bring him word,' so he could 'come and worship' Christ was a lie. The wise men did not know at the time that Herod was lying. It would require a heavenly message to intervene and tell them of the threat Herod posed. Here again we see an example of the fallibility of good and inspired men. We always have critics who think it is right to belittle inspired men because they make mistakes. But these accusers of good men should consider the example of the wise men. They were not unworthy merely because they failed to detect Herod's lies. They were not rejected by God because Herod intended to kill Christ and use the wise me to accomplish it. They were still wise, despite being misled. They were still worthy of revelation and direction from God, as we shall presently see.

The account continues:

> And when they were come into the house, they saw the young child with Mary his mother, and fell down, and worshipped him: and when they had opened their treasures, they presented unto him gifts; gold, and frankincense, and myrrh. And being warned of God in a dream that they should not return to Herod, they departed into their own country another way. (Matt. 2: 11-12.)

It had been two years since the birth, and at that point Joseph, Mary and Christ lived in a "house." When the wise men first arrived they found "the young child with Mary his mother," but no mention is made of Joseph being there. The men worshiped Christ, and presented gifts to Him.

It is not known how long they stayed, but presumably overnight because they received revelation in a dream. To protect His Son, the wise men were warned "in a dream that they should not return to Herod." This was the means by which Heavenly Father saved the life of His young Son. Messages sent to us in dreams are very important. Our own lives may be spared if we take such messages seriously.

We also see how the wise men were forewarned by God, making their error with Herod no longer mattered. Because they were open to revelation they got revelation. They were inspired, even if they were poor judges of Herod's character and intent. We worship a perfect God who sent a perfect Son, but there has never been a perfect servant of God. God's work continues by and through mortal men who, in spite of their flaws, receive revelation, are willing to listen and act on that revelation and inspire others to do the same. Therefore in the true gospel of Christ there is no room for worshiping His imperfect servants. We do not rise or kneel as worship of mere mortals. God does not want us to surrender our agency to another man. Good men, inspired men, wise men make mistakes. We all do. All true worship is properly limited to God the Father in the name of His Son, by the power of the Holy Ghost.

Matthew next adds:

> And when they were departed, behold, the angel of the Lord appeareth to Joseph in a dream, saying, Arise, and take the young child and his mother, and flee into Egypt, and be thou there until I bring thee word: for Herod will seek the young child to destroy him. When he arose, he took the young child and his mother by night, and departed into Egypt: And was there until the death of Herod: that it might be fulfilled which was spoken of the Lord by the prophet, saying, Out of Egypt have I called my son. (Matt. 2: 13-15.)

The dream sent to the wise men and the dream sent to Joseph could not have been on the same night. Joseph's dream came after the departure of the wise men on different nights.

In Joseph's dream it was "the angel of the Lord" who appeared. This added detail is not included in the dream warning the wise men.

Joseph was told by the angel of the Lord that Herod will attempt to kill Christ. To prevent this, Joseph was directed to take his family to Egypt for refuge. (Matthew's comment that this fulfilled the prophecy that God's Son would be called out of Egypt was an explanation by Matthew, and not part of what the angel said to Joseph. Throughout his Gospel, Matthew makes personal commentary about the events in Christ's life which fulfill prophecy.)

Joseph's departure was the same night as his dream. He arose and fled "by night" toward Egypt. This immediate action by Joseph testified of his faithfulness to God and devotion to Christ. He was eager to obey.

We read of Herod's reaction when he learned the wise men were not going to return with news of where to locate Christ:

> Then Herod, when he saw that he was mocked of the wise men, was exceeding wroth, and sent forth, and slew all the children that were in Bethlehem, and in all the coasts thereof, from two years old and under, according to the time which he had diligently enquired of the wise men. Then was fulfilled that which was spoken by Jeremiah the prophet, saying, In Rama was there a voice heard, lamentation, and weeping, and great mourning, Rachel weeping for her children, and would not be comforted, because they are not. (Matt. 2: 16-18.)

There are scholars who doubt this happened. They cannot find any independent record of this slaughter and argue that there would have been evidence to support such an event. Matthew was a faithful recorder of the events of Christ's life, and we have no reason to doubt him on this account. Matthew's record of the Sermon on the Mount, when compared with the Nephite account, shows just how reliable a historian he was. I accept that Herod did kill the children who were two years old and younger. Matthew knew there had been this lamentation by mothers throughout Judea. He knew of the slaughter of their children. It was because of this he made this reference to Jeremiah's prophecy.

This killing was necessary. It will influence later events in Christ's life. When He was twelve, He and John would have been notable Judean survivors of this earlier slaughter of children. This is likely why he was noticed while visiting the Temple. This will be discussed later in this chapter.

Matthew continues:

> But when Herod was dead, behold, an angel of the Lord appeareth in a dream to Joseph in Egypt, Saying, Arise, and take the young child and his mother, and go into the land of Israel: for they are dead which sought the young child's life. And he arose, and took the young child and his mother, and came into the land of Israel. But when he heard that Archelaus did reign in Judaea in the room of his father Herod, he was afraid to go thither: notwithstanding, being warned of God in a dream, he turned aside into the parts of Galilee: And he came and dwelt in a city called Nazareth: that it might be fulfilled which was spoken by the prophets, He shall be called a Nazarene. (Matt. 2: 19-23.)

Here again we get insight into Joseph. He independently worried about Christ's safety because of Herod's son. His concern was confirmed to him "being warned of God in a dream," again. He took the family to Nazareth, outside the kingdom which Herod's son ruled, to protect the Son of God.

We do not know how long the family stayed in Egypt. If Christ was two when they went, and twelve when they go to the Temple from Nazareth, the time could be no more than approximately nine to ten years. It could have been several years shorter. Christ would have lived in Egypt acquiring education for some time during His formative years. Given the Latter-day Saint interest in the things of Egypt because of the Book of Abraham, we should at least consider how the Osirian traditions of a slain, resurrected son of Horus may have influenced Christ's thinking about His own mission. Latter-day Saints, unlike Historic Christians, are rightly interested in this subject. Joseph Smith forced the issue upon us when The Book of Abraham was translated. Hugh Nibley has done a wonderful service for the Church in addressing this subject in multiple volumes of his collected works.[35] It is beyond this book to discuss these things, but the reader should contemplate the potential significance of Christ's early life in Egypt and what He may have learned there. Just as Abraham, Joseph, Moses and early Israel spent time in Egypt as part of their experience, Christ was also sent by the "angel of the Lord" to Egypt for a season. Egypt held an important role for Christ as well as for Israel.

Between the return from Egypt and His adult ministry there are two significant events in Christ's life. The first involves the visit to the Temple when Christ was twelve. It comes from Luke and reads as follows:

> Now his parents went to Jerusalem every year at the feast of the passover. And when he was twelve years old, they went up to Jerusalem after the custom of the feast. And when they had fulfilled the days, as they returned, the child Jesus tarried behind in Jerusalem; and Joseph and his mother knew not of it. But they, supposing him to have been in the company, went a day's journey; and they sought him among their kinsfolk and

[35]See, e.g., *Abraham in Egypt*, Salt Lake City: Deseret Book, 1981; *The Joseph Smith Papyri: An Egyptian Endowment*, Deseret Book, Salt Lake City, 1975; *An Approach to the Book of Abraham*, Deseret Book, Salt Lake City, 2009. His final book on Abraham, *One Eternal Round*, is expected to be published early in 2010.

> acquaintance. And when they found him not, they turned back again to Jerusalem, seeking him. And it came to pass, that after three days they found him in the temple, sitting in the midst of the doctors, both hearing them, and asking them questions. And all that heard him were astonished at his understanding and answers. And when they saw him, they were amazed: and his mother said unto him, Son, why hast thou thus dealt with us? behold, thy father and I have sought thee sorrowing. And he said unto them, How is it that ye sought me? wist ye not that I must be about my Father's business? And they understood not the saying which he spake unto them. And he went down with them, and came to Nazareth, and was subject unto them: but his mother kept all these sayings in her heart. And Jesus increased in wisdom and stature, and in favour with God and man. (Luke 2: 41-52.)

We know a great deal from this single incident. First, Christ's parents went to the Temple every Passover, perhaps even during the years in Egypt. The statement leaves out Christ or His younger siblings. But when twelve, He was taken along. Under Jewish law, this was the year of His manhood, and He would have been expected to assume the responsibility of coming. His cousin John would be twelve this year also. He too, would have been expected at the Temple for Passover. I believe both cousins were there on that occasion.

There would have been fewer twelve year-olds that year because there were many who were slain by Herod a decade earlier. Both John and Jesus survived the purge of Judean children. John survived at the expense of his father, Zacharias.[36] Christ survived at the inconvenience of spending His youth in Egypt; John at the inconvenience of spending his youth hidden in the Judean wilderness. Both were at the Temple for Passover on this occasion.

These two former Judean infants were now twelve. The fact they survived the slaughter, and one of them was the son of a former Temple priest, would have brought some attention to them. We know Christ wound up in a discussion with the doctors. The record does not tell us how the discussion began, but, the conversation could have lasted up to five days. It is likely John and Jesus were conspicuous to any who remembered King Herod's slaughter of the children. It is likely John and Jesus would have been together and conversing with one another during much of this time. More likely it was the conversation between these two cousins which attracted the Temple doctor's notice. Whatever the initial cause, by the fifth day, when Mary and Joseph returned, Christ was making no secret of His greater light. The doctors were "astonished at his understanding and answers."

Christ's mother rebuked Him, as mothers feel free to do. Joseph does not. This seems consistent with what we know of Joseph elsewhere. He was always trusted with the child's life. Finding Christ alive and well in the Temple was apparently enough

---

[36]"Let us come into New Testament times-so many are ever praising the Lord and His apostles. We will commence with John the Baptist. When Herod's edict went forth to destroy the young children, John was about six months older than Jesus, and came under this hellish edict, and Zacharias caused his mother to take him into the mountains, where he was raised on locusts and wild honey. When his father refused to disclose his hiding place, and being the officiating high priest at the Temple that year, was slain by Herod's order, between the porch and the altar, as Jesus said." *TPJS*, p. 261.

for Joseph. He was content and relieved to be able to take Him back home. For Mary, however, she could not stop herself from being impatient with her Son. In reply to her rebuke, Christ reminded her of His real Father and His real mission. He did, after all, come from heaven on "His Father's business." According to Luke His parents did not understand the comment.

It would be about eighteen years before we have any record of Christ and His cousin reuniting. But the visit of these two to the Temple when twelve served all Jerusalem notice that these were no ordinary men. They were sent. They would be heard from again, exactly as the Angel Gabriel had foretold. Whether they met again during that interim is unrecorded. But John recognized Jesus on the day of His baptism. They were familiar enough with one another for John to recognize his cousin instantly.

The final incident in His childhood comes from Joseph Smith's Translation of the New Testament, and records the following:

> And it came to pass that Jesus grew up with his brethren, and waxed strong, and waited upon the Lord for the time of his ministry to come. And he served under his father, and he spake not as other men, neither could he be taught; for he needed not that any man should teach him. And after many years, the hour of his ministry drew nigh. (JST-Matt. 3: 24-26.)

This is a wonderful description filled with insight into Christ. He "waited upon the Lord for the time of his ministry to come." This standing-by and waiting was not short. It was "many years" before the time of His ministry finally came. Consider for a moment that the Lord, Redeemer, Savior of mankind was required to wait for many years after He was ready. He was fully prepared, able to undertake His assignment, yet required to wait. During this time He couldn't be taught, because no one could offer Him any insight He had not already obtained. He didn't need any man to teach Him because He was taught by the Spirit, gaining light in the only proper way: directly from heaven.

If the Father felt it no great wrong to require Christ to stand down for years, despite his preparation, then we ought to be patient with the things which the Lord sees fit to impose upon us. Should we presume our own patient development is less important that Christ's? It is an interesting thing to contemplate. The one who is "more intelligent than them all"[37] was required to labor as a carpenter under the stewardship of his father for "many years."

This daily regimen of manual labor was important for Christ to experience. He understands us by the things which He experienced. In turn, we should understand Him by realizing He also experienced the mundane waiting we all experience in life. There is no indication He did anything to be noticed during this time. He "served under [H]is father" and "waited."[38]

His public ministry lasted 3 years. He waited 18 years. It is a profound example for all of us. We should expect to wait. We should stand by serving modestly for "many years" in our own lives. If we do not, we have been cheated of the opportunity to gain what can only be understood by such direct experience through eager, prepared and anxious enduring in patience for "the hour ... to draw nigh."

---

[37]See Abraham 3: 19: " I am the Lord thy God, I am more intelligent than they all."

[38]I have tried to capture this concept about Christ in the parable of *The Rich Young Man* in my earlier book *Ten Parables.*

Chapter 6
Bookends

Life, for each of us, tends to have "bookends" in which a similar sequence of events begins and ends a process. We encounter a difficulty in life, overcome it, then are required to face it again later. This is not just deja vu. It is a repeating cycle which proves us, and proves us again. It is distinctly recognizable in life when it happens. It happens to all of us. Christ's life was no exception. His ministry began and ended by facing three similar temptations, in conflict with the devil and his mortal surrogates. In this chapter we will look at these two bookend events.

Christ's public ministry began when He came to John, who was baptizing in the Jordan River. As soon as Christ was baptized He departed into the wilderness to fast and pray for forty days before beginning to preach. When His fasting and the time apart was drawing to an end, we read this account from Luke:

> And the devil said unto him, **If thou be the Son of God**, command this stone that it be made bread. And Jesus answered him, saying, It is written, That man shall not live by bread alone, but by every word of God. And the devil, taking him up into an high mountain, shewed unto him all the kingdoms of the world in a moment of time. And the devil said unto him, All this power will I give thee, and the glory of them: for that is delivered unto me; and to whomsoever I will I give it. **If thou therefore wilt worship me, all shall be thine**. And Jesus answered and said unto him, Get thee behind me, Satan: for it is written, Thou shalt worship the Lord thy God, and him only shalt thou serve. And he brought him to Jerusalem, and set him on a pinnacle of the temple, and said unto him, **If thou be the Son of God**, cast thyself down from hence: For it is written, He shall give his angels charge over thee, to keep thee: And in their hands they shall bear thee up, lest at any time thou dash thy foot against a stone. And Jesus answering said unto him, It is said, Thou shalt not tempt the Lord thy God. And when the devil had ended all the temptation, he departed from him for a season. (Luke 4: 3-13, emphasis added.)

The three challenges tempted Christ to demonstrate or prove He is the Son of God. What Satan is really asking is for Christ to question His status as the Son of God. He is suggesting Christ doubt His divine nature, His status as the One sent to deliver Israel. The challenge draws into question His parentage, what His mother taught Him, and things He learned over His lifetime.

When He was twelve and came to the Temple, He had tarried behind for several days teaching the Temple priests. When finally found by His parents, His mother scolded Him with a reminder He ought to have been more courteous to His parents. The record says: " And when they saw him, they were amazed: and his mother said unto him, Son, why hast thou thus dealt with us? behold, thy father and I have sought thee sorrowing." (Luke 2: 48.) In response Christ both explained His absence and reminded His mother that His real Father was God: "And he said unto them, How is it that ye sought me? wist ye not that I must be about my Father's business?" (Id. v. 49.) This incident shows that Christ was certain about who His Father was at the early age of twelve.

So as Satan questioned Christ's status as the Son of God, he was challenging a long held conviction that governed Christ's conduct from early in life. Satan was throwing into question what He had been taught by His mother, and what He no doubt had confirmed by revelation. Satan wanted Christ to prove His status and claim that He was mankind's Redeemer by performing a demonstration of physical power over the elements.

The challenge to transform stone into bread came after a forty day fast. Satan knew Christ had the pressing physical need for sustenance. Like any of us, Christ needed to eat to live. Christ was suffering from lack of food. Asking Him to "prove" His divine Sonship by satisfying a physical need was asking Him to seek normal, physical relief for a mortal necessity. It was a modest request which another, earlier righteous man had made and it had been given to him. We read this of the Lord feeding Elijah by miraculous means:

> And the word of the Lord came unto him, saying, Get thee hence, and turn thee eastward, and hide thyself by the brook Cherith, that is before Jordan. And it shall be, that thou shalt drink of the brook; and I have commanded the ravens to feed thee there. So he went and did according unto the word of the Lord: for he went and dwelt by the brook Cherith, that is before Jordan. And the ravens

> brought him bread and flesh in the morning, and bread and flesh in the evening; and he drank of the brook." (1 Kgs. 17: 2-6.)

Elijah, along with a widow and her son, would be fed by miraculous means for "many days." (See 1 Kings 17: 8-16.) If He could feed Elijah by miraculous means, why not change stone to bread and relieve His own hunger? The request would not only relieve His physical discomfort, it was scripturally consistent with Elijah's experience.

In Exodus we have the account of how the Lord provided manna from heaven to feed Israel when they were hungry in the wilderness:

> And the Lord spake unto Moses, saying, I have heard the murmurings of the children of Israel: speak unto them, saying, At even ye shall eat flesh, and in the morning ye shall be filled with bread; and ye shall know that I am the Lord your God. And it came to pass, that at even the quails came up, and covered the camp: and in the morning the dew lay round about the host. And when the dew that lay was gone up, behold, upon the face of the wilderness there lay a small round thing, as small as the hoar frost on the ground. And when the children of Israel saw it, they said one to another, It is manna: for they wist not what it was. And Moses said unto them, This is the bread which the Lord hath given you to eat. This is the thing which the Lord hath commanded, Gather of it every man according to his eating, an omer for every man, according to the number of your persons; take ye every man for them which are in his tents. And the children of Israel did so, and gathered, some more, some less. And when they did mete it with an omer, he that gathered much had nothing over, and he that gathered little had no lack; they

> gathered every man according to his eating. (Exo. 16: 11-18.)

So if the Lord fed Elijah by the ravens, and fed Israel with manna, surely Christ has no reason to refuse to feed Himself by miraculous means. There is a difference between God, in His mercy, miraculously providing food for men in times of famine, and an act which was to serve as a sign to Satan that Christ was the Son of God. Christ was purposefully fasting. His hunger was deliberate, and could have been relieved without a miracle. Indeed one of the reasons for the temptation was to end the fast on Satan's terms, rather than on the Lord's. This temptation was designed to appeal to selfishness, vanity and insecurity. For Christ to do as He was asked would have been an act of doubt. No matter what past precedents may have existed for feeding the hungry by miraculous means, this request by Satan was not comparable to anything before. It was subtle, it preyed on doubt, and it asked Christ to spare Himself from personal inconvenience using divine power. So He who would turn water into wine for His mother,[39] and would feed the five-thousand when asked,[40] and the four-thousand who were faint from fasting,[41] would do nothing to spare Himself from the pangs of near starvation. For others He had mercy. For Himself there was only strict observance and careful obedience.

In the second temptation, Satan offered Christ power in this world in exchange for surrendering worship to the devil. Christ could establish Himself as a king, as a lord, over the whole earth.

---

[39]See John 2: 1-11.

[40]See, e.g., Matt. 14: 14-21.

[41]See, e.g., Matt. 15: 32-38.

Since this was His promised destiny anyway, Satan was suggesting He could achieve this more quickly by worshiping him. Every knee will bow, every tongue will confess that Christ is Lord over all mankind. (See Isa. 45: 23.) So the devil was not asking Christ to do anything other than what His destiny already held. But the price of worshiping the devil made it altogether a different proposition. Even if Christ knew at the time He would be a future King of kings and Lord of lords, He was not to assume that role in this Telestial world. He would eventually explain to Pilate: "My kingdom is not of this world: if my kingdom were of this world, then would my servants fight, that I should not be delivered to the Jews: but now is my kingdom not from hence." (John 18: 36.) There was no reason for Him to assert kingship while here a mortal. It would be vain and unnecessary. So the offer from Satan was impossible to consider. It was not time. It was an offer to speed things up, take them out of season, and appealed to impatience and ambition. Although this was Christ's inevitable status, and He would only be claiming what would eventually be His anyway, the offer was clothed in evil. Impatience may have made a twelve year-old Jesus seek to do His Father's will the first time He stepped foot on the Temple grounds, but He later submitted to His role as Son, and returned to Nazareth to labor under Joseph. In the years since then, Christ overcame all impatience. As the JST records, after returning from the Temple visit as a twelve year old: "Jesus grew up with his brethren, and waxed strong, and waited upon the Lord for the time of his ministry to come. And he served under his father, and he spake not as other men, neither could he be taught; for he needed not that any man should teach him. And after many years, the hour of his ministry drew nigh." (JST Matt. 3: 24-26.) After waiting "many years" for "the hour of his ministry [to] draw nigh," Christ was not going to be hurried by Satan's trick. He would not consider an offer to become a worldly king, when His kingdom was not of this world. Nor would He consider kingship before completing His stewardship as a servant.

The final request asked Christ to make a public display of His divine power. Satan tempted Him to put on a show, so the people would know He came with power and authority.

Signs follow those who believe, after all. (See D&C 63: 9.) The problem with the request is that faith does NOT come by signs. (Id.) Signs follow faith, they do not precede it. It is after all, "A wicked and adulterous generation seeketh after a sign; and there shall no sign be given unto it, but the sign of the prophet Jonas." (Matt. 16: 4.) Giving people of that generation a sign may have resulted in followers, but the followers would have been wicked and adulterous. They would not have been willing to receive the message of repentance Christ was sent to deliver. The sign of His Divine power would have defeated the very thing He was sent to accomplish.

Here the request was to try and accomplish the impossible. He was being asked to show off, impress onlookers in order to gain worldly acclaim. Had Christ fallen to the temptation, He would have impressed and attracted wicked and unrepentant sign-seekers who wanted to follow a celebrity-Lord who could perform miracles as a sign of his power. This would have frustrated the Lord's ability to attract followers from among the penitent, the humble and the submissive. In effect Satan wanted Christ to attract "goats" and repel "sheep." Satan wanted to undermine the whole of His ministry with this one flamboyant act.

These three temptations were directed at Christ as He began His public ministry. He refused all three. He did not alter His plan to go forward in humility, a man of sorrows who would be acquainted with grief. He intended to be stricken, smitten and afflicted. He was to be the suffering servant before He returns as the King.

This was the first of the bookends. It came at the start of His ministry. The other bookend came at the end of His ministry and during the last hours of His mortal life.

At the end of His public ministry, when He hung in agony on a cross offering Himself as sacrifice to finish His work, He was again tempted three times while in physical distress. The record states:

> And the people stood beholding. And the rulers also with them derided him, saying, He saved others; let him save himself, **if he be Christ**, the chosen of God. And the soldiers also mocked him, coming to him, and offering him vinegar, And saying, **If thou be the king of the Jews**, save thyself. And a superscription also was written over him in letters of Greek, and Latin, and Hebrew, THIS IS THE KING OF THE JEWS. And one of the malefactors which were hanged railed on him, saying, **If thou be Christ**, save thyself and us. (Luke 23: 35-39, emphasis added.)

Once again there are three challenges. They are all asking Him to prove publicly what He has said, taught, believed and testified to for three years. These three, just as the first three, challenge Him to prove His claim of being the Son of God.

The demand was designed to have Him show publicly that He was the Son of God. But had He not been doing this for three years already? Were not His miracles well known? In particular, did not the return of Lazarus to life bring crowds to get a glimpse of them together?[42] At this point, there was nothing being asked of Him which was any different from what He had been doing during His ministry. After all, He said to the Sanhedrin that they would see Him coming in the clouds of heaven.[43] If He made that declaration, what could be different in making a public display of the truthfulness of the assertion?

Once again the temptation would have disrupted His appointed course. He could only comply by failing to complete His sacrificial offering as part of the required Atonement for sin. Everything hinged on this final agony and death. If He were to succumb to the temptation it would have destroyed mankind's hope.

In the first request He was again asked to attend to His physical needs and end His torment. Just as He was asked to provide proof of His divine Sonship by relieving the pangs of hunger, at the end He was asked to end His suffering using divine power selfishly. All He need do was come down from the cross, and in the process convert the collected on-lookers. He had saved others from disease, illness, even death, had He not? If He spared them, why not spare Himself? The demand was designed to equate Christ's relieving the suffering of the lepers, restoring sight to the blind, raising the dead, and the many other miraculous acts of

---

[42]See, e.g., John 12: 9: "Much people of the Jews therefore knew that he was there: and they came not for Jesus' sake only, but that they might see Lazarus also, whom he had raised from the dead."

[43]Christ told them, during His trial: "Jesus saith unto him, Thou hast said: nevertheless I say unto you, Hereafter shall ye see the Son of man sitting on the right hand of power, and coming in the clouds of heaven." (Matt. 26: 64.)

mercy He performed with showing that same mercy to Himself by ending His suffering. There was, of course, no such equivalency. Indeed, this final act of suffering and death was consistent with all His prior acts healing mankind. It was His final act of healing others. Through it, He would at last conquer death for all who ever lived. To come down from the cross would not have been proof of His Divine Sonship. It would have contradicted, violated and ultimately frustrated all He had done before. He could not comply. The request seemed to rely on what He had been doing for three years, but was a twisted perversion of His ministry's true meaning.

Christ was offered vinegar to drink. This would heighten his thirst and be a further temptation for Him to relieve his physical distress. Just as Satan tempted Him by preying on his physical need for food, the guards want Him to satiate His thirst by offering Him vinegar. The thirst could be relieved if He were to just come down from the cross. He was being asked to end His torment, relieve His physical distress, come down and put this agony behind Him. He could no more satisfy His thirst while on the cross than He could satisfy His hunger in the wilderness.

The third request came from a fellow-sufferer. This man was condemned for theft. Surely the death penalty was disproportionate to his wrongdoing. Certainly the same Lord who forgave the adulterer, the unjust tax collector, and other sinners who came to Him could and would forgive this petitioner. This request for salvation from sin and death was no different from the many other requests He had granted to those who had come to Him throughout His ministry. Surely this request was the most invidious of all: for it pitted His merciful, forgiving and redeeming nature against Himself. If He would not come down from the cross for

His own relief, He would undoubtedly come down to relieve the suffering of another.

Once again He was being asked to do something wrong for a good reason. He was being asked to bless another, and in the process He was being tempted to fail in His mission. The whole circumstance is laced with irony. This merciful God could not show mercy to His petitioner without destroying mercy for all mankind. How like Adam's dilemma. Which commandment was Adam to obey: To not partake of the fruit of the forbidden tree? Or, instead, to multiply and replenish the earth? He could not obey both. Nor could Christ. He could not show mercy to the petitioning thief without condemning all mankind.

Once again in His final temptations He is offered public acclaim, public influence, and a crowd of followers if He will just prove His power. He is being put through the same ordeal by Satan's minions as Satan had put Him through earlier. The previous temptations from a disembodied spirit tempter were no more successful than the later temptation coming from His fellow man.

Here before Him, in this last temptation, was a representative constituency of mankind. These were those He came to save by dying for them. Even as His final sacrifice was being made, they added to His humiliation, to His suffering, and to His struggle to complete the course.

It ends as it began. He was called upon to measure the matter correctly. He had to weigh the consequences in the proper scale and to press forward to the final end. He must pour out His offering. He studied the law and prophets. He was acquainted with the Psalms. He knew what they said of His mission. For this cause He came to Golgotha. As He suffered He expected to confront this awful scene, foretold by David's Psalm: "They gaped upon me with their mouths, as a ravening and a roaring lion. I am poured out like water, and all my bones are out of joint: my heart is like wax; it is melted in the midst of my bowels. My strength is dried up like a potsherd; and my tongue cleaveth to my jaws; and thou hast brought me into the dust of death." (Ps. 22: 13-15.)

It is one thing to know these prophecies foretold this final agony, and it is another to confront them. How appealing these final three requests seemed as He suffered. How easy the rationalizations were to believe. Christ was deprived of blood, weak from torment, struggling in semi-consciousness as the temptations were shouted to Him. This burden could all be ended by giving the rulers what they asked; showing the same proof now as He had shown so often in the preceding years. The torment could stop if He but came down and showed His kingship. The wrenching struggle could be over if He but showed mercy to a petitioner who, like Him, suffered this public humiliation. Yes, it was one thing to know the scriptures, to read the prophecies and to understand what the Messiah must do. It was another thing to endure this torment and not succumb. Yet He did.

He gave full meaning to the Psalmist's words, and lived the events described in the brutal poetry. It is important enough to repeat:

They gaped upon me with their mouths, as a ravening and a roaring lion.
I am poured out like water, and all my bones are out of joint: my heart is like wax;
it is melted in the midst of my bowels.
My strength is dried up like a potsherd; and my tongue cleaveth to my jaws;
and thou hast brought me into the dust of death.

For dogs have compassed me:
the assembly of the wicked have inclosed me:
they pierced my hands and my feet.
I may tell all my bones: they look and stare upon me.
(Ps. 22: 13-17.)

How can any of us fail to be moved by this final, terrible suffering of a God who laid His majesty by, and came to redeem us? How can we fail to adore this God of love who, to the very end, spared not Himself for our salvation?

Those who saw it, both before it happened through vision, or who stood there on that dread day, or who have since had the vision opened to their view; all understand the meaning of Isaiah's proclamation:

The Lord God hath opened mine ear, and I was not rebellious, neither turned away back.
I gave my back to the smiters, and my cheeks to them that plucked off the hair:
I hid not my face from shame and spitting.
For the Lord God will help me; therefore shall I not be confounded:
therefore have I set my face like a flint, and I know that I shall not be ashamed.
He is near that justifieth me; who will contend with me? let us stand together:
who is mine adversary? let him come near to me.
(Isa. 50: 5-8.)

The Lord's ministry carried a heavier burden than any man is able to bear for himself. But that burden, once carried, brought with it salvation from death and hell for all mankind. The sentence of death passed upon mankind as a result of our first parent's transgression could not claim this Man. Death was, for Christ, completely unjust. Therefore under the eternal law of justice Christ could demand His life back again. Death could not claim Him.

Because for Christ death was unjust, justice folded over on itself, and irony once again works, this time for the redemption of mankind. By allowing Himself to die unjustly, Christ made the justice of death for all descendants of Adam unjust. He was a descendant of Adam and also the exception. Death had no proper claim on Him. Dying was, for innocent blood, morally wrong. "Therefore, according to justice, the plan of redemption could not be brought about, only on conditions of repentance of men in this probationary state, yea, this preparatory state; for except it were for these conditions, mercy could not take effect except it should destroy the work of justice. Now the work of justice could not be destroyed; if so, God would cease to be God. And thus we see that all mankind were fallen, and they were in the grasp of justice; yea, the justice of God, which consigned them forever to be cut off from his presence. And now, the plan of mercy could not be brought about except an atonement should be made; therefore God himself atoneth for the sins of the world, to bring about the plan of mercy, to appease the demands of justice, that God might be a perfect, just God, and a merciful God also." (Alma 42: 13-15.) It was as wrong for Christ to die as it would have been for Adam to live forever in his sins. Adam needed to die. Christ, on the other hand, needed to be resurrected. What began with Adam was reversed in Christ.

Christ passed the test at the commencement of His ministry. Christ faced the same temptations at the end. Illustrated by bookends, these three temptations to have Him succumb to the request to prove Himself, "if He be the Son of God" by failing to bear patiently all God saw fit to inflict upon Him, did not work. As

He slipped into death, and the earth shook beneath the cross, the Roman guard exclaimed what His death proclaimed: "Truly this man was the Son of God." (Mark 15: 39; see also Matt. 27: 54.)

We will consider His crucifixion more fully later. Here we have considered only the three temptations which He faced at the beginning, and again at the end, of His ministry. The bookends of the mortal trial which He met and overcame perfectly both times.

Chapter 7

The Ten Lepers

There is an interesting account of an incident late in Christ's ministry recorded in the 17th Chapter of Luke. The account states the following:

> And it came to pass, as he went to Jerusalem, that he passed through the midst of Samaria and Galilee. And as he entered into a certain village, there met him ten men that were lepers, which stood afar off: And they lifted up their voices, and said, Jesus, Master, have mercy on us. And when he saw them, he said unto them, Go shew yourselves unto the priests. And it came to pass, that, as they went, they were cleansed. And one of them, when he saw that he was healed, turned back, and with a loud voice glorified God, And fell down on his face at his feet, giving him thanks: and he was a Samaritan. And Jesus answering said, Were there not ten cleansed? but where are the nine? There are not found that returned to give glory to God, save this

> stranger. And he said unto him, Arise, go thy way: thy faith hath made thee whole. (Luke 17: 11-19.)

This chapter discusses the profound doctrinal implications of this event. The incident tells us a great deal about our Lord.

The account comes from Luke. He was born to Gentile parents, and was probably a convert to Judaism. Although a writer of one of the Synoptic Gospel's, he was not one of the Apostles and it is questionable whether he was present at the time of this event. It is probable that a great deal of what Luke writes of Christ comes second-hand from someone who was there. This was true of earlier events in Christ's life that Luke heard from Mary and possibly others. Therefore, just like those earlier events which he learned from Mary, he may also have learned about the ten lepers second-hand from someone who had been present.

We do not know if these lepers were Jewish or Samaritan. Once they were lepers such distinctions became less important. Whether one or the other, they clearly recognized Christ. When He told them to "Go shew yourselves unto the priests," they all understood what He was instructing them to do. They immediately began the trek to find priests and follow the rites of the Law of Moses. It is noteworthy that Luke did not identify the city they were in. He chose to call it a "certain village." This leaves the corridor from central Galilee to central Samaria open for the location of possible villages.

Christ was entering an unidentified village. The lepers were outside the village, standing afar off as would be expected under the Law of Moses. The law imposed these restrictions for lepers living among the children of Israel: "the Lord spake unto Moses, saying, Command the children of Israel, that they put out of the camp every leper, and every one that hath an issue, and whosoever is defiled by the dead: Both male and female shall ye put out, without the camp shall ye put them; that they defile not their camps, in the midst whereof I dwell. And the children of Israel did so, and put them out without the camp: as the Lord spake unto Moses, so did the children of Israel." (Num. 5: 1-4.) Since they were excluded from society, required to live "outside the camp" or city, these ten lepers were required to "stand afar off," as the account in Luke states.

Lepers could not engage in commerce. Any food they might grow would be ceremonially unclean and potentially diseased. It could not be sold to provide them money for their support. Any other product they might make would also be unclean and pose the same risk. Therefore, lepers were completely dependent upon the charity of others for their survival. Living close, but outside a village was the practical way for them to receive charitable support from the larger society.

For those who had adult onset leprosy, the sudden exclusion from the society they had grown up in would be terrible to bear. No doubt they would long to return to their former friends and associations. These ten individuals lived a painful, wrenching existence.

The account reports that while "afar off" these lepers called to Christ. They must have been expecting him and watching for his arrival. Perhaps there were ten of them because they came together as a delegation to petition for help. We do not know how many were local, or if they all came from other towns. The fact that all of them cried out to Christ shows this was likely a planned meeting for them.

The fact they could recognize Christ from "afar off" also tells us something about how easily Christ could be recognized. His physical appearance was distinct enough that He could be seen and recognized from a distance. In all likelihood it was His height, since He was taller than the average height of His day.[44]

The cry from the ten began with the shout: "Jesus, Master." The name and title were important. These men were calling Him by name and acknowledging His authority by using the title "Master." The term had varying applications but almost invariably it meant "teacher" or ruler (which in the Book of Mormon is the same thing.)[45] John defined this term in these words: "Then Jesus turned, and saw them following, and saith unto them, What seek ye? They said unto him, Rabbi, (which is to say, being interpreted, Master,) where dwellest thou?" (John 1: 38.) The term is frequently applied to Christ by believers using the term respectfully (see, e.g., Mark 4: 28; Mark 9: 5; Luke 5: 5; Luke 8: 45), and doubters or challengers, using the term in an attempt to mislead Christ into thinking they were showing respect. (See, e.g., Matt. 12: 38; Matt. 22: 24; Luke 10: 25; Luke 20: 21.) The term was also used by Judas, when betraying Him. "And forthwith he came to Jesus, and said, Hail, master; and kissed him." (Matt. 26: 49.)

Christ cautioned against using the term for anyone other than Himself: "But be not ye called Rabbi: for one is your Master, even Christ; and all ye are brethren. And call no man your father upon the earth: for one is your Father, which is in heaven. Neither be ye

---

[44]I have discussed Christ's physical appearance in *Nephi's Isaiah*, pp. 207-214.

[45]The context of Abraham 3: 23 also compels the conclusion that the "rulers" foreordained from the "noble and great" are those who in this life teach saving truth.

called masters: for one is your Master, even Christ." (Matt. 23: 8-10.) Truth has a single source. That source is the One True Teacher.

Members of the Sanhedrin were to the Jews what General Authorities are to Latter-day Saints, or Cardinals are to Catholics. They were society's highest ecclesiastical authorities. In an incident involving a member of the Sanhedrin, Christ used the term "master" to describe the pretended understanding of that body of men. Christ and Nicodemas had this exchange: "Nicodemus answered and said unto him, How can these things be? Jesus answered and said unto him, Art thou a master of Israel, and knowest not these things?" (John 3: 9-10.) That is, Nicodemas pretended to teach, yet did not understand what Christ was teaching. The ordained, established, authorized authority was questioning to understand what the Teacher of Truth was saying. Christ had no credentials, belonged to no presiding body, and did not lay claim to any right to preside over the Jews. Yet it was Christ, and not Nicodemas, who had the answers.

It is in the most respectful sense that the lepers used the title "Master" when calling out to Christ. Therefore, when Christ heard the prayer "Jesus, Master" coming from them He knew they had faith in Him. He knew they were showing genuine regard. He accepted the title when they used it.

Immediately following this address came the petition: "have mercy on us." They show respect and faith and ask for a blessing. Christ healed the lepers because they asked. If they had not come and asked Him, He may never have even noticed them. Or, even if He had noticed, if they hadn't petitioned Him with such respect, He would likely have done nothing.

The account continues: "And when he saw them..." It suggests the only reason He saw them was because they called out and came to Him. It is just like that today. Only those who seek Him will find Him. Only those who recognize their need to be freed from the disease of uncleanliness will cry out to Him and ask Him to take notice of them. We are all equal before Him. Some of us recognize how much we lack, cry out, and come to Him seeking to be healed. But **we** must start the process.

After seeing them, He had no physical contact with them. Instead, He spoke the words: "Go shew yourselves unto the priests." His word was and is law. His word is power. He did not need to minister other than to speak. He did not need to touch, to anoint, to pour oil, wash, or sprinkle. He needed only to speak. (See, e.g., D&C 1: 38.)

The lepers understood what it meant to show themselves to the priests. There was a ceremony for cleansed lepers. However, they were not yet healed when they departed for the ceremony. It was only "as they went" that "they were cleansed." The lepers had to have faith to leave Christ and travel to the priests to participate in a ceremony pronouncing them clean. These lepers had already announced their faith with the words: "Jesus, Master" when calling to Him in the beginning. So they turned from Him and went to do as He told them. They were obeying Him, but their obedience began before they knew He had healed them. It took faith for them to begin the journey.

Faith to be healed, however, is not the same as the faith to be taught. Christ could heal the sick Nephites because they had faith enough for that (see 3 Ne. 17: 6-10). But He could not teach them, because they lacked the faith necessary to understand what He had been commanded to tell them (see 3 Ne. 17: 2-3). I discuss this in

The Second Comforter on pp. 96-100, including the footnotes found there. As this account unfolds we see the same thing happens in the incident of the ten lepers.

First, however, the ceremony involving the priests needs to be understood. We have only a few accounts of someone being cleansed from leprosy in the Bible. There is the account of Naaman, captain of the host of the king of Syria, whose leprosy was cleansed by Elisha. (See 2 Kings 5.) Moses' sister Miriam was stricken with leprosy, then healed. (See Num. 12: 10-15.) For those few accounts we have of a person being healed from leprosy, we never have an account of an offering performed by the priests for the one who had been healed.

Despite its unusual and limited occurrence, the Law of Moses included a ceremony to commemorate cleansing of a leper. Here is a description of the full ceremony found in Leviticus:

> And the Lord spake unto Moses, saying, This shall be the law of the leper in the day of his cleansing: He shall be brought unto the priest: And the priest shall go forth out of the camp; and the priest shall look, and, behold, if the plague of leprosy be healed in the leper; **Then shall the priest command to take for him that is to be cleansed two birds alive and clean**, and cedar wood, and scarlet, and hyssop: And the priest shall command that **one of the birds be killed** in an earthen vessel over running water: As for the living bird, he shall take it, and the cedar wood, and the scarlet, and the hyssop, and shall dip them and the living bird in the blood of the bird that was killed over the running water: And **he shall sprinkle upon him that is to be cleansed from the leprosy seven times, and shall pronounce him clean**, and shall **let the living bird loose into the open field**. And he that is to be cleansed shall wash his clothes, and shave off all his hair, and **wash**

himself in water, that he may be clean: and after that he shall come into the camp, and shall tarry abroad out of his tent seven days. But it shall be on the seventh day, that he shall shave all his hair off his head and his beard and his eyebrows, even all his hair he shall shave off: and **he shall wash his clothes, also he shall wash his flesh in water, and he shall be clean.** And **on the eighth day he shall take two he lambs without blemish**, and one ewe lamb of the first year without blemish, and three tenth deals of fine flour for a meat offering, mingled with oil, and one log of oil. And the priest that maketh him clean shall present the man that is to be made clean, and those things, before the Lord, at the door of the tabernacle of the congregation: And **the priest shall take one he lamb, and offer him for a trespass offering**, and the log of oil, and wave them for a wave offering before the Lord: And **he shall slay the lamb in the place where he shall kill the sin offering and the burnt offering, in the holy place**: for as the sin offering is the priest's, so is the trespass offering: it is most holy: And **the priest shall take some of the blood of the trespass offering, and the priest shall put it upon the tip of the right ear of him that is to be cleansed, and upon the thumb of his right hand, and upon the great toe of his right foot**: And the priest shall take some of the log of oil, and pour it into the palm of his own left hand: And **the priest shall dip his right finger in the oil that is in his left hand, and shall sprinkle of the oil with his finger seven times before the Lord**: And of **the rest of the oil that is in his hand shall the priest put upon the tip of the right ear of him that is to be cleansed, and upon the thumb of his right hand, and upon the great toe of his right foot,** upon the blood of the trespass offering: And **the remnant of the oil that is in the priest's hand**

he shall pour upon the head of him that is to be cleansed: and the priest shall make an atonement for him before the Lord. And the priest shall offer the sin offering, and make an atonement for him that is to be cleansed from his uncleanness; and afterward he shall kill the burnt offering: And the priest shall offer the burnt offering and the meat offering upon the altar: and the priest shall make an atonement for him, and he shall be clean. And if he be poor, and cannot get so much; then he shall take one lamb for a trespass offering to be waved, to make an atonement for him, and one tenth deal of fine flour mingled with oil for a meat offering, and a log of oil; And two turtledoves, or two young pigeons, such as he is able to get; and the one shall be a sin offering, and the other a burnt offering. And he shall bring them on the eighth day for his cleansing unto the priest, unto the door of the tabernacle of the congregation, before the Lord. And the priest shall take the lamb of the trespass offering, and the log of oil, and the priest shall wave them for a wave offering before the Lord: And he shall kill the lamb of the trespass offering, and the priest shall take some of the blood of the trespass offering, and put it upon the tip of the right ear of him that is to be cleansed, and upon the thumb of his right hand, and upon the great toe of his right foot: And the priest shall pour of the oil into the palm of his own left hand: And the priest shall sprinkle with his right finger some of the oil that is in his left hand seven times before the Lord: And the priest shall put of the oil that is in his hand upon the tip of the right ear of him that is to be cleansed, and upon the thumb of his right hand, and upon the great toe of his right foot, upon the place of the blood of the trespass offering: And the rest of the oil that is in the priest's hand he shall put upon the head of him that is to be cleansed, to make an atonement for

> him before the Lord. And he shall offer the one of the turtledoves, or of the young pigeons, such as he can get; Even such as he is able to get, the one for a sin offering, and the other for a burnt offering, with the meat offering: and the priest shall make an atonement for him that is to be cleansed before the Lord. This is the law of him in whom is the plague of leprosy, whose hand is not able to get that which pertaineth to his cleansing. (Lev. 14: 1-32.)

These acts are steeped in symbolism and tie directly to the Lord and His atoning sacrifice. Briefly, these symbols suggest the following: The two doves, one to be killed and one to be set free, point to ceremony on the Day of Atonement. A discussion of this can be found in the Appendix to *Eighteen Verses*, which I will not repeat here. Letting the one bird free after it has been wet by the blood of the other symbolizes Christ's gift of freedom to all who live under the curse of mortal frailty and sin, but come to receive His sacrificial blood. What better symbolism of freedom than the bird in flight? This must be how the leper feels when freed from the stigma of his unclean disease.

Washing of the leper's body is another symbol of cleanliness, renewal, rebirth and baptism. All these point to Christ and the cleansing He can bring for us all.

Putting blood, then oil on the right ear, right thumb and right big toe are all important symbols. The right side is the symbol of being blessed. Christ used the right side to symbolize blessedness, and the left to symbolize cursing. He taught: " When the Son of man shall come in his glory, and all the holy angels with him, then shall he sit upon the throne of his glory: And before him shall be gathered all nations: and he shall separate them one from another, as a shepherd divideth his sheep from the goats: And he shall set the sheep on his right hand, but the goats on the left. Then shall the King say unto them on his right hand, Come, ye blessed of my Father, inherit the kingdom prepared for you from the foundation of the world." (Matt. 25: 31-34.) The blood and oil on the right thumb symbolizes putting the cleansing power of Christ's sacrifice and the Holy Spirit into the works of the man's hands. Putting these on the right ear is to symbolize listening to the words of God, hearkening to the right way, and keeping the mind focused on the words of God. Anointing the right big toe symbolizes to walk in the right path. Once a person begins to walk the right path in the right way, their big toe goes first. The right foot, the right way, the right words and the right works are all symbolized by this anointing.

The seven days of the ceremony, the seven sprinkles of the oil, are tied to the symbolic meaning of the number seven. It symbolizes a new creation, perfection or completion. It means "the whole" or all. With this ceremony all the past burdens of leprosy are gone, and the man becomes a new creation.

The ceremony is powerful and brings the recipient into full fellowship with the Camp of Israel. For any leper wanting to return to his friends, family and society this ceremony would be a moment filled with profound meaning. One can imagine how tears would flow from the healed lepers who got the opportunity to celebrate this rite.

However, the incident of the ten lepers records something even more profound. There was one of the healed who, upon seeing he was freed from his disease "turned back, and with a loud voice glorified God, and fell down on his face at his feet, giving him thanks." One returned to Christ. The other nine were still on their way to the priests to receive their washings and anointings.

The deeper meaning of the incident can only be understood by what Christ then said: "Were there not ten cleansed? But where are the nine?"

The obvious answer to Christ's question is: they were doing as He told them to do. That is, they were on their way to the priests.

But the true answer to Christ's question is: these other nine failed to understand Who the Priest really was. Nine went to the priests who performed ceremonies. They went to see the symbol of Christ. But they went without understanding the priests officiated merely as a substitute symbol which pointed to Christ. One, however, came to the True Priest. Only one understood and did exactly as Christ had directed. He alone came to the True Priest.

Nine would go through a public ceremony, be anointed, washed, reunited with society and enjoy public recognition and reunification. One would hear the words from the Great High Priest Himself declaring: "Arise, go thy way: thy faith hath made thee whole."

For this leper who returned, no further ceremony was needed. While nine were seeking comfort from the symbols and ceremonies, the one who returned received relief from the Master, Himself. While nine were to be ceremonially clean, one was becoming clean indeed. For this one there was no need to comply with the Law of Moses, because the One who gave the Law of Moses declared him to be "whole." Christ's personal declaration **to** a man is more important than any ceremony or rite performed **by** men. Men may endlessly repeat the ceremonial return to Christ's presence, but it means nothing unless the man actually returns to Him.

For anyone who does return to the Lord's presence, the rites are not what are important. It is when they hear the voice of God declaring to them: "Arise, go thy way: thy faith hath made thee whole" which makes them confident in the Day of Judgment. If Christ declares a man to be "whole" then the man is whole indeed.

From this incident we see how Christ was respectful, even deferential, to the religious authorities of His day. Though they lacked any real authority over Him, He did not openly challenge their right to preside and administer the priestly ordinances. When He healed these lepers, He sent all ten of them to the authorities to have the rights performed. The "priests" He sent them to constantly challenged His right to cure, His right to teach, and His authority to attract a following. They condemned Him. He, in turn, sent those He healed to them to receive ordinances at their hands.

In our day the Lord commands His followers: "Wherefore, be subject to the powers that be, until he reigns whose right it is to reign, and subdues all enemies under his feet." (D&C 58: 22.) Christ obeyed this same commandment. Therefore, no matter what level a person's understanding is, there is never any reason to be jealous of, nor any reason to show disrespect to the authorities who preside over you. God is over all. His purposes will not fail. Men must be given the opportunity to succeed or fail. Often, leadership is as much a test of the heart for the one assigned to lead as it is for those asked to follow. Respect for authority is as important for you as it was for Christ. His example leaves us no room to rebel against even unworthy authorities.

Christ did not compel any of the lepers to recognize Him as the True High Priest. In fact, He seemed almost resigned to how few would recognize Him when He commented: "There are not found that returned to give glory to God, save this stranger." It is always the same. Only the rare person realizes where light and truth, which is the glory of God, can be found. For the rest there is an abundance of rites, ordinances, observances, rituals, and symbols. While all of these point to the real thing, they are not the real thing itself. Therefore we find still that "there are not found that return to give glory to God, save [a few]."

This incident encapsulates the whole dilemma of the second estate. The test we are taking is exactly the same now as it was from the beginning. The people we read about in the Gospel of Luke are exactly as the people of our own day. We are being tested to determine whether or not we can be blinded by traditions, presumptions, trappings and priestcrafts; or if we can see through those things to find the Son of God. What a marvelously consistent, perfectly equal chance all of us are given here. This plan and its author are perfect. "Wherefore, take heed, my beloved brethren, that ye do not judge that which is evil to be of God, or that which is good and of God to be of the devil." (Moro. 7: 14.)

Chapter 8

Significant Ordinances

Historic Christianity is only familiar with incomplete ordinances which have been passed down in the Catholic and Protestant traditions. As a result of the restoration of the fullness of the Gospel of Jesus Christ, it is apparent there are ordinances which have been lost. Those who are familiar with the complete Gospel can still see remnants of the original rites in the New Testament. In this chapter we will look at some of the forgotten ordinances Christ received while He was mortal. We will not discuss the ordinances which the New Testament makes clear, and which Historic Christianity still imitates, including baptism and the sacrament of the Lord's Supper. This chapter will only deal with what may be properly termed: higher ordinances.

Any discussion of higher ordinances must be careful and discreet. It is never appropriate to "cast pearls before swine." This is one of the reasons the ordinances were lost to Historic Christianity. We are not forbidden to know about them, but are denied the right to teach them openly. For some things the Lord will either personally instruct someone, send a messenger with authority to reveal things, or they cannot be known.

Christ was the perfect example. He is the prototype of the "saved man." If anyone hopes to be saved they must do as He did. He was the example we are expected to follow. As the Lectures on Faith explain:

> Where shall we find a prototype into whose likeness we may be assimilated, in order that we may be made partakers of life and salvation? or, in other words, **where shall we find a saved being**? for if we can find a saved being, we may ascertain without much difficulty what all others must be in order to be saved. We think that it will not be a matter of dispute, that two beings who are unlike each other cannot both be saved; for whatever constitutes the salvation of one will constitute the salvation of every creature which will be saved; and if we find one saved being in all existence, we may see what all others must be, or else not be saved. We ask, then, **where is the prototype? or where is the saved being? We conclude, as to the answer of this question, there will be no dispute among those who believe the bible, that it is Christ: all will agree in this, that he is the prototype or standard of salvation; or, in other words, that he is a saved being**. And if we should continue our interrogation, and ask how it is that he is saved? the answer would be-because he is a just and holy being; and **if he were anything different from what he is he would not be saved; for his salvation depends on his being precisely what he is and nothing else**; for if it were possible for him to change, in the least degree, so sure he would fail of salvation and lose all his dominion, power, authority and glory, which constitute salvation; for salvation consists in the glory, authority, majesty, power and dominion

> which Jehovah possesses and in nothing else; and no being can possess it but himself or one like him. Thus says John, in his first epistle, third chapter, second and third verses: "Beloved, now are we the sons of God, and it doth not yet appear what we shall be; but we know that, when he shall appear, we shall be like him, for we shall see him as he is. And every man that hath this hope in him purifieth himself, even as he is pure." Why purify themselves as he is pure? Because if they do not they cannot be like him. (*Lectures* 7: ¶ 16, emphasis added.)

Since we are expected to be like Christ and nothing less, we should understand as much as possible about what Christ's mortal example included. We should strive to examine His life very closely. Even though we should never "cast pearls before swine," which means we cannot state fully or directly what is forbidden to be revealed, we are certainly allowed to refer to what is contained in scripture. The scriptures give us direction so that we know what we need to do in order to be like Him.

The scriptures often record events which contain such sensitive subjects that the discussion is limited. It is often quite obvious the account is deliberately veiling something. We can learn a great deal by looking at what is happening in the account as the veil is drawn. The prophets who write the scriptures tell us things which are intended to help us find what is not written. We will consider only a few examples to illustrate the point. You should press this subject in your personal scripture studying, pondering and prayer. God does not stop any of us from learning. But we must be willing to "knock, seek, and ask." Otherwise we are left without knowing.

The first of the events is the Mount of Transfiguration. Later in this chapter we will take a closer look at that event. Now, however, we only consider what happened on that day beginning with what Matthew recorded:

> [He] was transfigured before them: and his face did shine as the sun, and his raiment was white as the light. And, behold, there appeared unto them Moses and Elias talking with him. Then answered Peter, and said unto Jesus, Lord, it is good for us to be here: if thou wilt, let us make here three tabernacles; one for thee, and one for Moses, and one for Elias. While he yet spake, behold, a bright cloud overshadowed them: and behold a voice out of the cloud, which said, This is my beloved Son, in whom I am well pleased; hear ye him. And when the disciples heard it, they fell on their face, and were sore afraid. And Jesus came and touched them, and said, Arise, and be not afraid. And when they had lifted up their eyes, they saw no man, save Jesus only. And as they came down from the mountain, Jesus charged them, saying, Tell the vision to no man, until the Son of man be risen again from the dead. (Matt. 17: 2-9.)

In this example the witnesses were told not speak of the incident until after Christ's resurrection. When they were finally able to talk about what happened they limited what they said to three things: The transfiguration, Elias' and Moses' appearance, the Father's voice declaring Christ was His beloved Son. They never said what else happened in the encounter. Modern revelation expands on the event and adds this:

> Nevertheless, he that endureth in faith and doeth my will, the same shall overcome, and shall receive an inheritance upon the earth when the day of transfiguration shall come; **When the earth shall be transfigured, even according to the pattern which was shown unto mine apostles upon the**

> **mount**; of which account the fulness ye have not yet received. (D&C 63: 20-21, emphasis added.)

Unlike Historic Christians, Latter-day Saints know from a revelation given to Joseph Smith that the three Apostles saw the pattern of the earth's future transfiguration as part of this event. Yet the Apostles involved in the Transfiguration held this information back from the saints in the New Testament era. Only in modern revelation do we get a brief, passing reference to it.

President Spencer W. Kimball (while a member of the Twelve) made another reference to what happened on the Mount. Elder Kimball was speaking about what Christ taught to the Nephites during His visit with them. He explained:

> As they looked into his kindly eyes and wondered about his wounds, he told them of his birth and ministry. He repeated to them the vital and priceless sermons on the mount, on the Sea of Galilee, in Samaria, in Jerusalem. He taught them the power of faith, of the battle between truth and evil. He told them of the voice of God, his Father, at the time of his baptism, and **of the special endowments to Peter, James, and John on the Holy Mount of Transfiguration**, when they also heard the voice of God, the Father. (*CR*, October 1959, pp. 58-59, emphasis added.)

President Joseph Fielding Smith also elaborated on the Temple ordinances involved on the Mount of Transfiguration:

> These keys were given to Peter, James, and John on the mount when they received this power from Elias and Moses, the latter conferring the keys of the gathering of Israel. Christ told these three men, **who I believe received their endowments on the mount**, that they were not to mention this vision and what had taken place until after he was

> resurrected. Therefore, the exercise of this authority had to wait until Christ had prepared the way." (*Doctrines of Salvation*, Vol. 2, p. 165, emphasis added.)

Latter-day Saints understand the limited nature of what can be properly discussed when it comes to the Temple endowment ceremony, but they also understand they are able to access this information by personally attending the Temple. Similarly, the further revelation about the earth's future transfiguration is not beyond the reach of a faithful Saint who seeks and asks. Just as the conditions for entering the Temple must be met before receiving that sacred information, so also the conditions for receiving this further revelation must be met: We must ask of God, who giveth to all men liberally: "If any of you lack wisdom, let him ask of God, that giveth to all men liberally, and upbraideth not; and it shall be given him. But let him ask in faith, nothing wavering. For he that wavereth is like a wave of the sea driven with the wind and tossed." (James 1: 5-6.) This is the gate through which all truth is accessible.[46]

In a second example from the New Testament, the Apostle Paul wrote about sacred knowledge which could not be shared: "And I knew such a man, (whether in the body, or out of the body,

---

[46]As it is explained in Moroni 10: 4-5: "And when ye shall receive these things, I would exhort you that ye would ask God, the Eternal Father, in the name of Christ, if these things are not true; and if ye shall ask with a sincere heart, with real intent, having faith in Christ, he will manifest the truth of it unto you, by the power of the Holy Ghost. And by the power of the Holy Ghost ye may know the truth of all things." For a discussion of this, see Chapter 14, *Knowing All Truth*, in my earlier book, *Eighteen Verses*, pp. 241-262; see also *The Second Comforter*, where the doctrine, scripture and teachings about the entire process of being taught mysteries by Christ is explained.

I cannot tell: God knoweth;) How that **he was caught up into paradise, and heard unspeakable words, which it is not lawful for a man to utter**." (2 Cor. 12: 3-4, emphasis added.) In this example, the witness saw paradise where God was present. What he saw was not for public consumption. That information must be obtained directly from God.

In his earlier letter to the Corinthian saints, Paul wrote, probably contemplating the same vision of paradise he refers to in his later letter:

> But as it is written, Eye hath not seen, nor ear heard, neither have entered into the heart of man, **the things which God hath prepared for them that love him**. But **God hath revealed them unto us by his Spirit: for the Spirit searcheth all things, yea, the deep things of God**. (1 Cor. 2: 9-10.)

In this earlier letter to the Corinthian saints, Paul writes about the final, post-mortal plan for those who love God. Knowledge of this is also limited and can only be obtained by direct revelation to the person who seeks it. Again however, modern revelation has informed Latter-day Saints a great deal more about post-resurrection life. A whole flood of light came to us in Section 76 of the Doctrine and Covenants.

There are many examples in the Book of Mormon. One of them involved a moment in Christ's visit with a group of Nephites at the Bountiful Temple after His resurrection. All the group who were present on that day witnessed the incident. But the record we have of it is limited because the content was unlawful to fully record:

> And it came to pass that after he had ascended into heaven--the second time that he showed himself

> unto them, and had gone unto the Father, after having healed all their sick, and their lame, and opened the eyes of their blind and unstopped the ears of the deaf, and even had done all manner of cures among them, and raised a man from the dead, and had shown forth his power unto them, and had ascended unto the Father--Behold, it came to pass on the morrow that the multitude gathered themselves together, and they both saw and heard these children; yea, even **babes did open their mouths and utter marvelous things; and the things which they did utter were forbidden that there should not any man write them**. (3 Ne. 26: 15-16, emphasis added.)

Although these things are not written for us, everyone in the audience that day heard and witnessed them. The point is not that some information cannot be learned. Rather the point is that it cannot be taught. Or, more correctly, it can only be taught by the Lord or someone sent by Him with authority to teach such things.

The Lord's willingness to teach these things, including the forbidden afterlife scene shown to the Apostle Paul, is clear from the closing verses of the revelation about the three degrees of glory given to Joseph Smith and Sidney Rigdon. These verses contain the following promise:

> But great and marvelous are the works of the Lord, and the mysteries of his kingdom which he showed unto us, which surpass all understanding in glory, and in might, and in dominion; Which he commanded us we should not write while we were yet in the Spirit, and are not lawful for man to utter; Neither is man capable to make them known, for **they are only to be seen and understood by the power of the Holy Spirit, which God bestows on those who love him, and purify themselves before him; To whom he grants**

> **this privilege of seeing and knowing for themselves**; That through the power and manifestation of the Spirit, **while in the flesh**, they may be able to bear his presence in the world of glory. (D&C 76: 114-118, emphasis added.)

The promise that all who "love [H]im, and purify themselves before [H]im," can see these same things shows us how very open and approachable our Lord is. The fact that these things ought to be viewed "while in the flesh" so as to enable us to "bear [H]is presence in the world of glory" serves us notice that we will be disappointed if we fail to seek after this knowledge in mortality. We may find ourselves unable to bear His presence in the next life unless we obtain the keys to do so by enduring it here first. This scripture implies as much.

Many more examples could be given and much more could be said. There is enough, however, to make the point without belaboring it. Lines are drawn about things which are sacred which make it inappropriate to discuss details openly. Sacred things are kept for disclosure in sacred settings to prevent us from misunderstanding the truth, or rejecting it because we have not been properly prepared to receive it. But if we prepare, and seek for it, we can have it while mortal.

There is every reason to believe Jesus Christ did more than just obey the Law of Moses, which He came to fulfill. He no doubt lived the same higher Gospel He taught. We should expect to see evidence in the New Testament of ordinances which belong to the complete Gospel of Jesus Christ. This chapter will consider some of the glimpses of those rites which Latter-day Saints should be able to recognize.

He asked to be baptized by John, telling John that He intended to "fulfill all righteousness" by submitting to the ordinance. As the account explains, the discussion was as follows:

> Then cometh Jesus from Galilee to Jordan unto John, to be baptized of him. But John forbade him, saying, I have need to be baptized of thee, and comest thou to me? And Jesus answering said unto him, Suffer it to be so now: for thus it becometh us to fulfil all righteousness. Then he suffered him. (Matt. 3: 13-15.)

The Book of Mormon gives a more detailed explanation:

> And now, if the Lamb of God, he being holy, should have need to be baptized by water, to fulfil all righteousness, O then, how much more need have we, being unholy, to be baptized, yea, even by water! And now, I would ask of you, my beloved brethren, wherein the Lamb of God did fulfil all righteousness in being baptized by water? Know ye not that he was holy? But notwithstanding he being holy, he showeth unto the children of men that, according to the flesh he humbleth himself before the Father, and witnesseth unto the Father that he would be obedient unto him in keeping his commandments. (2 Ne. 31: 5-7.)

If Christ intended to obey all the commandments, then the first commandment given to Adam and Eve, to multiply and replenish the earth, would be a commandment Christ would keep as well. That command has never been revoked. (Gen. 1: 28.)

Modern best-selling books which claim there has been a vast historical conspiracy to cover up the marriage and progeny of Christ have become international best sellers. Dan Brown's fiction book, *The Da Vinci Code*, based upon the earlier non-fiction *Holy*

Blood, Holy Grail, attracted worldwide notice. The idea of a married Christ who fathered children may be news to Historic Christianity, but it was this subject which caused a good deal of the persecution of Latter-day Saints in the 1800's. This may be a new, titillating subject to the general public, but it is old news to Latter-day Saints.

First, remember the New Testament account of the marriage in Cana described in John's Gospel, is part of the basis for comments made by early Latter-day Saint leaders:

> And the third day there was a marriage in Cana of Galilee; and the mother of Jesus was there: And both Jesus was called, and his disciples, to the marriage. And when they wanted wine, the mother of Jesus saith unto him, They have no wine. Jesus saith unto her, Woman, what have I to do with thee? mine hour is not yet come. His mother saith unto the servants, Whatsoever he saith unto you, do it. And there were set there six waterpots of stone, after the manner of the purifying of the Jews, containing two or three firkins apiece. Jesus saith unto them, Fill the waterpots with water. And they filled them up to the brim. And he saith unto them, Draw out now, and bear unto the governor of the feast. And they bare it. When the ruler of the feast had tasted the water that was made wine, and knew not whence it was: (but the servants which drew the water knew;) the governor of the feast called the bridegroom, And saith unto him, Every man at the beginning doth set forth good wine; and when men have well drunk, then that which is worse: but thou hast kept the good wine until now. This beginning of miracles did Jesus in Cana of Galilee, and manifested forth his glory; and his disciples believed on him. (John 2: 1-11.)

Why was Mary hosting this event? Why were she and Jesus so directly involved? Was this a marriage involving her immediate household? Was this Christ's marriage? Was Christ under the obligation to marry? Was marriage also part of "fulfilling all righteousness?" If He were required to obey every commandment, did He have to obey the first commandment given to Adam and Eve to multiply and replenish the earth?

Modern revelation describes what is required of anyone who would receive the kind of celestial glory God has in eternity. The following has been revealed plainly to us:

> In the celestial glory there are three heavens or degrees; And **in order to obtain the highest, a man must enter into this order of the priesthood [meaning the new and everlasting covenant of marriage]**; And **if he does not, he cannot obtain it. He may enter into the other, but that is the end of his kingdom; he cannot have an increase**. (D&C 131: 1-4, emphasis added, brackets in original.)

We should have no doubt that Christ entered into the highest glory available to man. Therefore we should have no doubt that He married.

Early in The Church of Jesus Christ of Latter-day Saints there was an open discussion about this subject. Orson Hyde, one of the Twelve Apostles, spoke openly in General Conference on the subject.[47] Five months later, after criticism from the press, he

---

[47]Referring to the marriage in Cana he taught: "Now there was actually a marriage; and if Jesus was not the bridegroom on that occasion, please tell who was. If any man can show this, and prove that it was not the Savior of the world, then I will acknowledge I am in error. We say it was Jesus Christ who was married, to be brought into the relation whereby he could see his seed, before he was crucified. 'Has he indeed passed by the nature of angels, and taken upon himself the seed of Abraham, to die without leaving a seed to bear his name on the earth?' No. But when the secret is fully out, the seed of the blessed shall be

reiterated the teaching.[48] We avoid talking about Christ's marriage because of the connection made to the practice of plural marriage in Orson Hyde's sermons. But eternal marriage and plural marriage are two different things. Eternal marriage is a constant obligation, and plural marriage is instituted and rescinded, depending upon the conditions prevailing among the Lord's people. The Book of Mormon has made it clear that plural marriage is the forbidden exception, only to be practiced when specifically commanded.[49] I have discussed the folly of splinter groups continuing the practice of plural marriage in my earlier book *Beloved Enos*, and would refer

---

gathered in, in the last days; and he who has not the blood of Abraham flowing in his veins, who has not one particle of the Savior's in him, I am afraid is a stereotyped Gentile, who will be left out and not be gathered in the last days; for I tell you it is the chosen of God, the seed of the blessed, that shall be gathered. I do not despise to be called a son of Abraham, if he had a dozen wives; or to be called a brother, a son, a child of the Savior, if he had Mary, and Martha, and several others, as wives; and though he did cast seven devils out of one of them, it is all the same to me." (Orson Hyde, October 6, 1854, *JD* Vol. 2, p. 82-83.)

[48]"I discover that some of the Eastern papers represent me as a great blasphemer, because I said, in my lecture on Marriage, at our last Conference, that Jesus Christ was married at Cana of Galilee, that Mary, Martha, and others were his wives, and that he begat children." (Orson Hyde, March 18, 1855, *JD* Vol. 2, p. 210.)

[49]"Wherefore, my brethren, hear me, and hearken to the word of the Lord: For **there shall not any man among you have save it be one wife**; and concubines he shall have none; For I, the Lord God, delight in the chastity of women. And whoredoms are an abomination before me; thus saith the Lord of Hosts. Wherefore, this people shall keep my commandments, saith the Lord of Hosts, or cursed be the land for their sakes. For if I will, saith the Lord of Hosts, raise up seed unto me, I will command my people; otherwise they shall hearken unto these things." (Jacob 2: 27-30, emphasis added.)

the reader to the discussion there on pp. 130-133, should you care to consider the subject further.

Two years later, in 1857, Orson Hyde made another statement about Christ's wedding.[50] He reaffirmed that the incident in Cana was Christ's marriage. These teachings, however acceptable they may be today, with the popularity of *The Da Vinci Code* and *Holy Blood, Holy Grail*, were, at the time, used by critics to accuse Latter-day Saints of blasphemy. From the Edmunds-Tucker Act, through the march of Johnson's Army, and the Reed Smoot Senate Confirmation Hearings, Latter-day Saints learned from rough treatment that speaking openly about such a subject can only excite persecution. Latter-day Saints have certainly learned from history that public opinion matters. We have suffered a great deal from ignoring public opinion. Since openly discussing Christ's marriage causes resentment and anger, it is among the distinct teachings which Latter-day Saints have let lapse into obscurity. However, since I am writing this as a lay member, and cannot speak for the Church, I am free to describe my own beliefs concerning Christ. In turn, you are likewise free to decide whether you believe the Lord married and fathered children. The Church does not have an official position.

In the official biography of Christ published by The Church of Jesus Christ of Latter-day Saints, the following states the Church's present position:

---

[50]"It will be borne in mind that once on a time, there was a marriage in Cana of Galilee; and on a careful reading of that transaction, it will be discovered that no less a person than Jesus Christ was married on that occasion. If he was never married, his intimacy with Mary and Martha, and the other Mary also whom Jesus loved, must have been highly unbecoming and improper to say the best of it." (Orson Hyde, March 1857, *JD*, Vol. 4: p. 259-260.)

> Soon after the arrival of Jesus in Galilee we find Him and His little company of disciples at a marriage party in Cana, a neighboring town to Nazareth. The mother of Jesus was at the feast, and for some reason not explained in John's narrative, she manifested concern and personal responsibility in the matter of providing for the guests. Evidently her position was different from that of one present by ordinary invitation. **Whether this circumstance indicates the marriage to have been that of one of her own immediate family, or some more distant relative, we are not informed**. (Talmage, James E., *Jesus the Christ*, p. 135, emphasis added.)

This does not force anyone to accept that it was Christ's marriage. Nor does it rule it out. The Church has decided to avoid any direct teaching that Christ was married. However, the scriptures state plainly that marriage is a condition for exaltation. Christ is the prototype of the saved man, and He said He came to "fulfill all righteousness" by obedience. It is left to us to reason out in our own minds if we believe He was married or not.

Scriptures which speak of the necessity of the marriage covenant for exaltation include the following:

> For behold, **I reveal unto you a new and an everlasting covenant; and if ye abide not that covenant, then are ye damned; for no one can reject this covenant and be permitted to enter into my glory**. For all who will have a blessing at my hands shall abide the law which was appointed for that blessing, and the conditions thereof, as were instituted from before the foundation of the world. And as pertaining to the new and everlasting covenant, it was instituted for the fulness of my glory; and he that receiveth a fulness thereof must and shall abide the law, or he shall be

> damned, saith the Lord God. And verily I say unto you, that the conditions of this law are these: All covenants, contracts, bonds, obligations, oaths, vows, performances, connections, associations, or expectations, that are not made and entered into and sealed by the Holy Spirit of promise ... are of no efficacy, virtue, or force in and after the resurrection from the dead; for all contracts that are not made unto this end have an end when men are dead. (D&C 132: 4-7, emphasis added.)

Therefore we know the new covenant (requiring marriage) requires obedience for any person to enter into God's glory. The revelation continues:

> Therefore, **if a man marry him a wife in the world, and he marry her not by me nor by my word**, and he covenant with her so long as he is in the world and she with him, their covenant and marriage are not of force when they are dead, and when they are out of the world; therefore, they are not bound by any law when they are out of the world. Therefore, **when they are out of the world they neither marry nor are given in marriage; but are appointed angels in heaven, which angels are ministering servants, to minister for those who are worthy of a far more, and an exceeding, and an eternal weight of glory. For these angels did not abide my law; therefore, they cannot be enlarged, but remain separately and singly, without exaltation, in their saved condition, to all eternity**; and **from henceforth are not gods, but are angels of God forever and ever**. And again, verily I say unto you, if a man marry a wife, and make a covenant with her for time and for all eternity, if that covenant is not by me or by my word, which is my law, and is not sealed by the Holy Spirit of promise, through him whom I have anointed and appointed unto this

> power, then it is not valid neither of force when they are out of the world, because they are not joined by me, saith the Lord, neither by my word; when they are out of the world it cannot be received there, because **the angels and the gods are appointed there, by whom they cannot pass; they cannot, therefore, inherit my glory**; for my house is a house of order, saith the Lord God. (Id., v. 15-18, emphasis added.)

I conclude Christ, the prototype of saved man, must necessarily have followed this law. Therefore, He was certainly married. The New Testament account omits direct reference to it, as does Latter-day revelation. This is one of those doctrines best left without elaboration because foolish men struggle with the propriety of it. The best approach in contemplating the subject of sacred, eternal marriage is to note that it is necessary for exaltation and remember that Christ was exalted. Among the ordinances Christ would have received, eternal marriage would certainly have been one.

Another rite or blessing He would have received would have been the sealing power or authority. We looked earlier at the incident Matthew described on the Mount of Transfiguration as an example of how not all information is disclosed by scripture. We are going to look at the event again, this time to specifically discuss the sealing authority. For your convenience Matthew's account is set out again below:

> And after six days Jesus taketh Peter, James, and John his brother, and bringeth them up into an high mountain apart, And was transfigured before them: and his face did shine as the sun, and his raiment was white as the light. And, behold, there appeared unto them Moses and Elias talking with him. Then answered Peter, and said unto Jesus, Lord, it is good for us to be here: if thou wilt, let us

> make here three tabernacles; one for thee, and one for Moses, and one for Elias. While he yet spake, behold, a bright cloud overshadowed them: and behold a voice out of the cloud, which said, This is my beloved Son, in whom I am well pleased; hear ye him. And when the disciples heard it, they fell on their face, and were sore afraid. And Jesus came and touched them, and said, Arise, and be not afraid. And when they had lifted up their eyes, they saw no man, save Jesus only. (Matt. 17: 1-8.)

This incident has significant meaning to Latter-day Saints who associate the power to seal on earth and in heaven with Elijah's ministry. Joseph Smith described this authority:

> Now for Elijah, the spirit power & calling of Elijah is that ye have power to hold the keys of the revelations ordinances, oricles powers & endowments of the fulness of the Melchezedek Priesthood & of the Kingdom of God on the Earth & to receive, obtain & perform all the ordinances belonging to the Kingdom of God even unto the sealing of the hearts of the hearts fathers unto the children & the hearts of the children unto the fathers even those who are in heaven. (*Words of Joseph Smith.* Salt Lake City: Bookcraft, 1981; at p. 329, spellings and punctuation as in original.)

The authority which came from Elijah on the Mount of Transfiguration has been repeatedly discussed by various General Authorities in General Conference.[51] Elder Jeffrey R. Holland

---

[51]See, e.g., Elder Russell M. Nelson, *The Spirit of Elijah*, Ensign (CR), November 1994, p. 84: "Joseph compared Moroni's teaching to a similar prophecy by Malachi-that Elijah would come again. We know that Elijah did return-at least twice-after Malachi's promise. At Christ's transfiguration, Elijah appeared on the mount to Peter, James, and John. At the Kirtland Temple, April 3, 1836, Elijah appeared to the Prophet

referred to this subject in the April General Conference in 2005, when he taught:

> The essential function of the priesthood in linking time and eternity was made explicit by the Savior when He formed His Church during His mortal ministry. To His senior Apostle Peter He said, "I will give unto thee the keys of the kingdom of heaven: and whatsoever thou shalt bind on earth shall be bound in heaven: and whatsoever thou shalt loose on earth shall be loosed in heaven." Six days later He took Peter, James, and John to a mountaintop where He was transfigured in glory before them. Then prophets from earlier dispensations, including at least Moses and Elijah, appeared in glory also and conferred the various keys and powers that each held. (*Our Most Distinguishing Feature*, Ensign, May 2005, p. 43.)

These speakers link the arrival of the sealing keys on the Mount of Transfiguration to Christ possessing and transferring them to His Apostles. It is clear, however, from what has been said that the full significance of what this entailed is not disclosed in scripture. However, since Christ is the prototype of a saved man, we will

---

and Oliver Cowdery and said, 'The keys of this dispensation are committed into your hands.'" Also, Elder Theodore M. Burton, *Neither Cryptic Nor Hidden*, Ensign (CR), May 1977, p. 28: "Now the sealing power mentioned by Paul was given to Peter, James, and John on the Mount of Transfiguration. This same sealing power restored by Elijah the prophet was later given by Jesus to all his apostles as recorded in Matthew." Also Elder Theodore M. Burton, *The Power of Elijah*, Ensign (CR), May 1974, p. 61: "So important was this scripture, that it is the only one I know of which is quoted almost word for word in all four standard works. The prophet Elijah, with the keys of this sealing power, did come just as predicted. Those keys of the priesthood were restored in perfect order and harmony, as was done on the Mount of Transfiguration. Each prophet holding special keys of the priesthood appeared and restored them to prophets on the earth. Moses appeared. Elias came."

have to experience this same sealing authority if we expect to inherit the same kingdom as Christ. A further discussion of this is probably best left to the individual to pray, ponder and seek to understand. Chapters 10 through 12 of *Beloved Enos* have a discussion which the reader may find helpful.

The final ordinance, which may escape notice from the casual reader, involves an incident occurring shortly before His death. The scriptural account has become quite muddled, and I am not going to make any effort to sort it out. It is important to bear in mind that for nearly a thousand years the sole custodian of official scripture texts was a single institution which taught celibacy for its priesthood. They altered the text. Things which were once plain have become vague. As the prophet Nephi saw in vision and explained in his testimony:

> And the angel of the Lord said unto me: Thou hast beheld that **the book proceeded forth from the mouth of a Jew; and when it proceeded forth from the mouth of a Jew it contained the fulness of the gospel of the Lord**, of whom the twelve apostles bear record; and they bear record according to the truth which is in the Lamb of God. Wherefore, these things go forth from the Jews in purity unto the Gentiles, according to the truth which is in God. And after they go forth by the hand of the twelve apostles of the Lamb, from the Jews unto the Gentiles, **thou seest the formation of that great and abominable church, which is most abominable above all other churches; for behold, they have taken away from the gospel of the Lamb many parts which are plain and most precious; and also many covenants of the Lord have they taken away.** And all this have they done **that they might pervert the right ways of the Lord, that they might blind the eyes and harden the hearts of**

> **the children of men.** Wherefore, thou seest that after the book hath gone forth through the hands of the great and abominable church, that **there are many plain and precious things taken away from the book, which is the book of the Lamb of God**. And after these plain and precious things were taken away it goeth forth unto all the nations of the Gentiles; and after it goeth forth unto all the nations of the Gentiles, yea, even across the many waters which thou hast seen with the Gentiles which have gone forth out of captivity, thou seest – **because of the many plain and precious things which have been taken out of the book, which were plain unto the understanding of the children of men, according to the plainness which is in the Lamb of God--because of these things which are taken away out of the gospel of the Lamb, an exceedingly great many do stumble**, yea, insomuch that Satan hath great power over them. (1 Ne. 13: 24-29, emphasis added.)

These omissions from the scriptures make much of what was once clear now unclear. Although someone familiar with the fullness of the Restored Gospel of Jesus Christ might be able to plainly recreate the ordinance involved, it is not appropriate to do so in print, in a book available to the public. Therefore in the case of the incident below I do not feel at liberty to elaborate. I will just suggest that this be read as though recording an ordinance, and not merely an obscure event recorded about His final hours:

> Now when Jesus was in Bethany, in the house of Simon the leper, There came unto him a woman having an alabaster box of very precious ointment, and poured it on his head, as he sat at meat. But when his disciples saw it, they had indignation, saying, To what purpose is this waste? For this ointment might have been sold for much, and

> given to the poor. When Jesus understood it, he said unto them, Why trouble ye the woman? for she hath wrought a good work upon me. For ye have the poor always with you; but me ye have not always. For in that she hath poured this ointment on my body, she did it for my burial. Verily I say unto you, Wheresoever this gospel shall be preached in the whole world, there shall also this, that this woman hath done, be told for a memorial of her. (Matt. 26: 6-13.)

If this is an ordinance, then any restoration of the Christ's original Gospel would include this rite. We should expect it to be more clear when restored than it is in this New Testament account. Finally, until we have information which allows us to see what is going on in this sacred event, we have not yet heard the same Gospel Christ referred to as "this gospel" by Him in Matthew. Beyond that it is best not to comment.

These are not all the ordinances received or conducted by Christ during His ministry. But these are ones appearing in scripture often overlooked.

Finally, the life of Christ included several occasions on which He was acknowledged by the Father as His Son. At His baptism, the New Testament records there was a voice from heaven that declared: "This is my beloved Son, in whom I am well pleased." (Matt. 3: 17; see also Mark 1: 11; Luke 3: 22.) On the Mount of Transfiguration a voice out of the cloud declared: "This is my beloved Son, in whom I am well pleased; hear ye him." (Matt. 17: 5.) The text of what the voice actually declared was likely altered because of the theological debates over Christ's status as "Son" during the third and fourth centuries. The words which were originally spoken, and originally in scripture, came from Psalms 2: 7, and state: "Thou art my Son; this day have I begotten thee."

However, this statement gave support to the "adoptionist" theory which claimed Christ was just an ordinary man until His adoption by the Father at baptism. To negate this heretical interpretation, the scriptures were changed to read as they do now. They failed to change Hebrews, however, and it still reads: "For unto which of the angels said he at any time, Thou art my Son, this day have I begotten thee? And again, I will be to him a Father, and he shall be to me a Son?" (Heb. 5: 5.)

For our purposes it is important to understand that Christ received this declaration by the Father because He was obedient to the Father's instructions. Following the example of the prototype for salvation, we should realize we are all expected to hear the voice of God declaring from heaven the words: "thou art my son, this day have I begotten thee." In modern revelation it is explained in these words: "The more sure word of prophecy means a man's knowing that he is sealed up unto eternal life, by revelation and the spirit of prophecy, through the power of the Holy Priesthood." (D&C 130: 5.) Christ set the example in all things. He was sealed up unto eternal life, fulfilled all righteousness, and "receive[ed] all those ordinances in the house of the Lord, which are necessary for [Him], after [He] departed this life, to enable [Him] to walk back to the presence of the Father, passing the angels who stand as sentinels, being enabled to give them the key words, the signs and tokens, pertaining to the holy Priesthood, and gain [His] eternal exaltation in spite of earth and hell." (Brigham Young, *Discourses of Brigham Young,* selected and arranged by John A. Widtsoe, p. 416.) We are expected to follow Him. We are expected to participate in the same ordinances, follow the same path. He is our Great High Priest. To love Him is to follow Him. To follow Him is to receive all He offers. If we can understand what ordinances He received, then we can understand what ordinances we should also be seeking to receive.

My testimony of Christ includes a witness that He followed all the rites, ordinances and endowments which He offers to us as a part of His Gospel. From baptism to being sealed up to eternal life by the voice and covenant of the Father, He took every step required along the way. To "come, follow Him" includes doing likewise. If you do, you will find yourself adoring the Lamb of God. You will join a chorus of others who proclaim: "Worthy is the Lamb!"

Chapter 9

Parables

Except for the Sermon on the Mount (which I am not going to discuss in this book) Christ taught primarily in parables. (Even in that Sermon, He still used some metaphors and parables.) He explained His reason:

> All these things spake Jesus unto the multitude in parables; and without a parable spake he not unto them: That it might be fulfilled which was spoken by the prophet, saying, I will open my mouth in parables; I will utter things which have been kept secret from the foundation of the world. (Matt. 13: 34-35.)

In another place He said this:

> And when he had said these things, he cried, He that hath ears to hear, let him hear. And his disciples asked him, saying, What might this parable be? And he said, Unto you it is given to know the mysteries of the kingdom of God: but to others in parables; that seeing they might not see,

and hearing they might not understand. (Luke 8: 8-10.)

There is an interesting juxtaposition in these two statements. He intended to reveal things kept secret from the foundation of the world, but also wanted to keep most people from understanding Him. His intent was to leave an unworthy audience still uninformed. Only those who are prepared are allowed to "hear" the message He brought. No matter how great His desire was to share such things with all of us, only those who have the right heart are able to understand what He revealed. The Gospel of Jesus Christ becomes clear to those who are prepared to receive it, and remains concealed to the unprepared.

Christ and the true messengers He sends have messages which are clearest to those who are prepared for further truth and light. His true messengers know the boundaries of what is to be said, and therefore do not blurt out in plainness the sacred knowledge which the unworthy would reject. True messengers oftentimes do not warn the unworthy. They present their message in such a way that only the prepared understand what is taught. The worthy will draw closer to the Lord because of such teachings. The unprepared, however, will not associate anything significant with either the messenger or the message. As the final scene of God's strange act unfolds, there will be surprises for those who are regarded as the "wise" men among us.[52] In this chapter we will look at three examples of the Lord's use of parables. The first we consider is one of His greatest. It is a story about two lives, Lazarus and the rich

---

[52]D&C 101: 94-95: "That wise men and rulers may hear and know that which they have never considered; That I may proceed to bring to pass my act, my strange act, and perform my work, my strange work, that men may discern between the righteous and the wicked, saith your God."

man. The parable was given to an audience that included hostile lawyers and Pharisees. They were looking for ways to trap Christ and find an accusation which would allow them to discredit Him. The parable was told some months before the death of His friend Lazarus, whom He restored to life. It is likely the Lord deliberately chose the name Lazarus to foreshadow the events which would happen months later. The parable is recorded in these words:

> There was a certain rich man, which was clothed in purple and fine linen, and fared sumptuously every day: And there was a certain beggar named Lazarus, which was laid at his gate, full of sores, And desiring to be fed with the crumbs which fell from the rich man's table: moreover the dogs came and licked his sores. And it came to pass, that the beggar died, and was carried by the angels into Abraham's bosom: the rich man also died, and was buried; And in hell he lift up his eyes, being in torments, and seeth Abraham afar off, and Lazarus in his bosom. And he cried and said, Father Abraham, have mercy on me, and send Lazarus, that he may dip the tip of his finger in water, and cool my tongue; for I am tormented in this flame. But Abraham said, Son, remember that thou in thy lifetime receivedst thy good things, and likewise Lazarus evil things: but now he is comforted, and thou art tormented. And beside all this, between us and you there is a great gulf fixed: so that they which would pass from hence to you cannot; neither can they pass to us, that would come from thence. Then he said, I pray thee therefore, father, that thou wouldest send him to my father's house: For I have five brethren; that he may testify unto them, lest they also come into this place of torment. Abraham saith unto him, They have Moses and the prophets; let them hear them. And he said, Nay, father Abraham: but if one went unto them from the dead, they will repent. And he said

> unto him, If they hear not Moses and the prophets, neither will they be persuaded, though one rose from the dead. (Luke 16: 19-31.)

Using the two main characters, this parable gives a profound lesson about what matters most to God. At the beginning, the two characters are distinguished by their descriptions. The first character in this parable has no name, but the second one does. This implies God knows the one by name, but the other is given only the vaguest of notice. As to this "rich man" we know only that he was male and he was rich. The descriptor "rich man," is supposed to show the deceitfulness of riches.[53] The "certain rich man" was entirely deceived about his standing before God. He genuinely thought himself blessed, and therefore favored by God. His life was content. His circumstances were enviable. As the story unfolds, the rich man is surprised by the turn of events that show his true standing before God. By then, however, his life has ended and he can do nothing to change his lot.

On the other hand, the "beggar" is named. Anytime God speaks to His chosen disciples, He calls them by name.[54] Naming someone signifies that the person named belongs to or is intimate with the one naming him.

When the Lord enters into a covenant He will often confirm the covenant with a person by giving them a new name. Hence, Abram's name was changed to Abraham, Jacob's to Israel, Saul's

---

[53]This term ("deceitfulness of riches") was coined by Christ to illustrate how riches blind people to their true condition. See, e.g., Matt 13: 22 and Mark 4: 19.

[54]See, e.g., JS-H 1: 17, 49; Acts 9: 4; Exo. 3: 4; 1 Sam. 3: 3, among many others.

to Paul, and so on. The fact that there is a name used in the parable is of great significance and suggests intimacy between the outcast, downtrodden, sickly Lazarus, and heaven. Furthermore, the name used in the parable is one that is intimately associated with Christ. Lazarus was the brother to Mary and Martha. Their family was intimate with Christ. Lazarus is the name of the man who would later be notoriously raised from the dead.[55] The significance of the name would not be lost on those who heard the parable and understood Christ, for in all likelihood this was the name of His brother-in-law.

The rich man was clothed in the royal purple and fine linen which signified his high social standing in this life. He was noble. He was chosen. He was someone others would admire. Among his peers his name would have been recognized. But the story is being told from God's perspective and therefore does not include the name of this scion of society. Furthermore, to dress in the royal purple and fine linen was to proudly advertise his riches. This outward show of his wealth was shameful given the lack of charity he showed Lazarus. He dressed so as to call attention to himself. He would have expected people to notice him. He wanted the admiration of others. He wanted to be envied. He craved admiration from other damned souls. Since he did not have the attention of heaven, and God did not know his name, he needed worldly acclaim as a substitute.

---

[55]By the time of Christ's last Passover dinner, for example, both Lazarus and Christ could attract on-lookers: "Much people of the Jews therefore knew that he was there: and they came not for Jesus' sake only, but that they might see Lazarus also, whom he had raised from the dead." (John 12: 9.)

Christ's parable illustrates an unchanging condition of fallen man, where fame and fortune are envied by those who do not know God. But such worldly things do not fulfill those who have them. It leaves them empty and discontent. It is only those who know God who can say: "I have learned, in whatsoever state I am, therewith to be content." (Phillip. 4: 11.) The rich man was blessed with material things, but still wanted to be noticed because his possessions left him hollow.

The story continues by adding that the rich man fared sumptuously every day. His days were all filled with more than enough food, more than enough raiment, more than enough notice from his fellow man, and sumptuous portions of it all. From the shallow perspective of those who are damned, this was a great life. A life to be envied.

In contrast to this enviable state of the unnamed rich man, we learn the beggar named Lazarus was placed outside the rich man's home at his gate. The detail that Lazarus "was laid" suggests a lack of mobility. Lazarus was certainly physically infirm, because the story adds that he was full of sores. Being laid by others, and full of sores suggests that Lazarus had sunk to the depths of despair and humiliation. He was stripped of all pride. He was hungry, wanting the crumbs which fell from the rich man's table. He was infirm, covered in sores, a man of sorrows and acquainted with grief, and there is nothing in Lazarus that would make us desire him. He appeared for all the world to be cursed, rejected and hated by God.

The story goes on to say that dogs came and licked his sores. In this culture this made Lazarus both physically, and more importantly, ceremonially unclean. By stating that dogs licked his open sores Christ intended to make the character a complete outcast. Surely this unclean man would cause others to hide their faces from him so they would not have to look upon him.

The humiliated beggar named Lazarus is actually Christ. He is telling of His own life. He **is** Lazarus. And all those who choose to follow Him must take up their own crosses to understand what He wants us to learn. Anyone who is His must accept the direction He gave to Emma Smith: "And verily I say unto thee that thou shalt lay aside the things of this world, and seek for the things of a better." (D&C 25: 10.) You must despise worldliness, and find the beauty here which comes from blessing, helping, lifting and serving others.

Lazarus was sick and starving. He was covered with sores, and compassed by dogs licking his wounds (one of the great Messianic types[56]). Lazarus' condition inevitably lead to his death. But in the instant of his death, everything changes. Once released from the suffering of mortality, Lazarus is carried by the angels to Abraham. Previously, he "was laid" at the gate to beg; but now he is carried by angels. This suggests Lazarus has become royalty being carried about by servant angels as a royal soul in a canopy covered litter. He obtained an exalted post-mortal status. Now angels minister to him. Now his status is exalted. In death he is taken to associate with the Father of the Righteous himself, Abraham. Death has become sweet to Lazarus. He has entered into his kingdom at last.

In contrast, the rich man's death excites no similar greeting. He dies and "was buried." No acclaim, no angels, no royal litter, only torment. This torment is the regret he felt once he saw what his life had really been. "A man is his own tormenter and his own

---

[56]"For dogs have compassed me: the assembly of the wicked have inclosed me: they pierced my hands and my feet." (See Ps. 22: 16.)

condemner. Hence the saying, They shall go into the lake that burns with fire and brimstone. The torment of disappointment in the mind of man is as exquisite as a lake burning with fire and brimstone. I say, so is the torment of man." (*TPJS* p. 357.) Only in death does the rich man realize how he had squandered his mortality. When he recognizes who he really was, and the deceit caused by his riches while in mortality, he sees how unkind, uncharitable, ungodly, and unfit he was. His sore-covered spirit is exposed to view and he sees his damned state for what it really is. His soul is small, self-centered, and despicable.

Finally in death he sees things as they really are. He realizes that the one who was previously despised, rejected and acquainted with sorrow and grief all his days is really the close associate of Abraham. Abraham, the great symbol and mortal type of God the Father, is the one to whom the rich man now addresses his petition. He does not call upon Lazarus, but instead Abraham. But he asks for Lazarus to be the one sent back to give him relief. The relief he seeks is just a drop of water to be put upon his unclean tongue and relieve his suffering.

Christ deliberately chose the symbol of water for the rich man's relief. Water is intimately connected with baptism and the sacrament. Death confines the unconverted to the pit in which there is no water, or in other words where ordinances cannot be performed.[57] The rich man craves for the relief that baptism could bring him. But the relief he seeks cannot be given after mortality.

---

[57]Zech. 9: 11: "As for thee also, by the blood of thy covenant I have sent forth thy prisoners out of the pit wherein is no water." This Messianic prophecy is about Christ's atonement opening the door for those who were kept in the spiritual pit wherein there is no water, or where ordinances cannot be performed. Christ opened the door for such vicarious work. See D&C Section 138.

Abraham responds by explaining the rich man had a lifetime of good things, filled with all the world had to offer, but throughout he had chosen to ignore the suffering of others. His lack of charity toward his fellow man precluded charity for him in the afterlife. Now the saying: "Blessed are the merciful: for they shall obtain mercy," becomes clear. For only by showing mercy to others can we make claim on it for ourselves. (Matt. 5: 7.) Alma explained this doctrine to his son Corianton:

> And if there was no law given, if men sinned what could justice do, or mercy either, for they would have no claim upon the creature? But there is a law given, and a punishment affixed, and a repentance granted; which repentance, mercy claimeth; otherwise, justice claimeth the creature and executeth the law, and the law inflicteth the punishment; if not so, the works of justice would be destroyed, and God would cease to be God. But God ceaseth not to be God, and mercy claimeth the penitent, and mercy cometh because of the atonement; and the atonement bringeth to pass the resurrection of the dead; and the resurrection of the dead bringeth back men into the presence of God; and thus they are restored into his presence, to be judged according to their works, according to the law and justice. For behold, justice exerciseth all his demands, and also mercy claimeth all which is her own; and thus, none but the truly penitent are saved. What, do ye suppose that mercy can rob justice? I say unto you, Nay; not one whit. If so, God would cease to be God. And thus God bringeth about his great and eternal purposes, which were prepared from the foundation of the world. And thus cometh about the salvation and the redemption of men, and also their destruction and misery. Therefore, O my son, whosoever will come may come and partake of the waters of life freely; and whosoever will not come the same is

> not compelled to come; but in the last day it shall be restored unto him according to his deeds. If he has desired to do evil, and has not repented in his days, behold, evil shall be done unto him, according to the restoration of God. And now, my son, I desire that ye should let these things trouble you no more, and only let your sins trouble you, with that trouble which shall bring you down unto repentance. O my son, I desire that ye should deny the justice of God no more. Do not endeavor to excuse yourself in the least point because of your sins, by denying the justice of God; but do you let the justice of God, and his mercy, and his long-suffering have full sway in your heart; and let it bring you down to the dust in humility. And now, O my son, ye are called of God to preach the word unto this people. And now, my son, go thy way, declare the word with truth and soberness, that thou mayest bring souls unto repentance, that the great plan of mercy may have claim upon them. And may God grant unto you even according to my words. Amen. (Alma 42: 21-31.)

Mercy is unavailable to the unmerciful. Those who insist upon justice will merit only justice. Those who show mercy merit mercy. The rich man was unmerciful. Therefore, he could not obtain mercy.

In addition to the defect in the rich man's soul, the Gospel of repentance and vicarious baptism for those who had died was not established when Christ told the parable. Only upon His death would Christ open the door for the unredeemed dead to receive vicarious ordinances to free them from their confinement.[58]

---

[58]See, e.g., D&C 138: 30-34: "But behold, from among the righteous, he organized his forces and appointed messengers, clothed with power and authority, and commissioned them to go forth and carry

Therefore, in the parable Abraham speaks of a great gulf which divided those who died in their sins from those who died repentant.

On recognizing his own dismal fate, the rich man immediately showed mercy for his living siblings. He asked Abraham to send Lazarus as a witness to testify of what conditions would be in the afterlife. In response, Abraham tells the rich man that if his living siblings (the Jews) would not believe in the truth because of what is written in the law and the prophets, they would not believe "though one rose from the dead." Here Christ confronts His disbelieving audience of lawyers and Pharisees with a parable that foreshadows what was about to happen. He also confirms they would not believe Him even after His resurrection.

The parable is a direct confrontation between Christ and His critics. He is telling them His story. Their perception of Him as lowly, unworthy, unclean, un-credentialed, and without significance is all symbolized in Lazarus. They would ultimately compass Him about as dogs, and would inflict upon Him sores, cursing Him and hanging Him on a tree. All this was foretold in the parable. They thought themselves blessed of God. Symbolically (and some of

---

the light of the gospel to them that were in darkness, even to all the spirits of men; and thus was the gospel preached to the dead. And the chosen messengers went forth to declare the acceptable day of the Lord and proclaim liberty to the captives who were bound, even unto all who would repent of their sins and receive the gospel. Thus was the gospel preached to those who had died in their sins, without a knowledge of the truth, or in transgression, having rejected the prophets. These were taught faith in God, repentance from sin, vicarious baptism for the remission of sins, the gift of the Holy Ghost by the laying on of hands, And all other principles of the gospel that were necessary for them to know in order to qualify themselves that they might be judged according to men in the flesh, but live according to God in the spirit."

them literally) "dressed in purple," they thought they held priestly authority, they thought themselves worthy before God; holding down the chief seats, occupying the Temple of God, and collecting tithes and offerings, they "fared sumptiously." But all this only blinded them to their true condition. All this kept them from seeing God's true messenger. It would require them to die before they could see things as they really are.

Christ's parable is a testimony of His own life and ministry. He was direct and spoke candidly about the condition in which He lived and died. The confidence He had in His own calling, in His own fate, and in His own standing before God is the great message of this story. He knew He didn't look like someone God would raise up to save that generation of Jews. He knew they regarded Him as cursed. But He also knew the Father, and He was His Son. It was completely unnecessary for the world to recognize Him. His ministry was to find those who would "hear His voice;" it was not to compel anyone to recognize Him. The parable told them He knew who He was.[59]

Similarly, the parable warns the chief priests, lawyers, scribes and Pharisees about their perilous state. Christ was redefining for them what is valuable and will save. Although almost all those who lived at the time would see things just as did the rich man in the parable, Christ was teaching a radically different view. He wanted the listeners to consider how unkindness and uncaring toward their

---

[59]John records that Christ drew a direct connection between the "one raised from the dead" in this parable and the scribes and Pharisees' rejection of Him: "Do not think that I will accuse you to the Father: there is one that accuseth you, even Moses, in whom ye trust. For had ye believed Moses, ye would have believed me: for he wrote of me. But if ye believe not his writings, how shall ye believe my words?" (John 5: 45-47.)

fellow-man could become terrible burdens when carried into the next life. Christ was telling them to reconsider their values, and, in turn to reconsider who He was. If they changed how they saw what was important, they might then be able to see it was the Son of God who was teaching them.

The second parable is about the unjust judge. This parable was taught by Christ some months later, and came after He healed the ten lepers. He was making His way toward Jerusalem at the time. This would be His final trip, though months would pass between the time the parable was given and the time He finally arrived. The lesson of the story is for those who believe in the true God, who believe their cause is just, and who pray in faith for relief from afflictions. The parable is as follows:

> There was in a city a judge, which feared not God, neither regarded man: And there was a widow in that city; and she came unto him, saying, Avenge me of mine adversary. And he would not for a while: but afterward he said within himself, Though I fear not God, nor regard man; Yet because this widow troubleth me, I will avenge her, lest by her continual coming she weary me. And the Lord said, Hear what the unjust judge saith. And shall not God avenge his own elect, which cry day and night unto him, though he bear long with them? I tell you that he will avenge them speedily. Nevertheless when the Son of man cometh, shall he find faith on the earth? (Luke 18: 2-8.)

This tale puts God into the role of the "unjust judge." However, the story is not really about God's characteristics, but our own. It is told from the perspective of a widow, who represents all of us; or the church that awaits the return of the true Bridegroom.

From the widow's perspective, the judge from whom she needs relief is unjust. He has no regard for man and no fear of

God. However, because of her persistence, the judge is finally persuaded to grant her request.

This story illustrates the difference between man's perception of God who appears indifferent, and God's greater wisdom in timing His answers to our prayers. There are many reasons we are impatient with God. When we ask for something, we expect it to be granted sooner rather than later; on our timetable rather than His. But God is in control. He decides when we are ready to receive the things we request of Him.

We judge God. We think He delays, ignores or refuses us. This parable is teaching us to pray continually anyway. No matter what our perspective is, we should persist. Petition God until at last He delivers you. Never relent. Never stop asking. Even if you believe God to be unjust, and that your prayer should be answered more quickly, continue to petition Him. He does listen and He does answer. He not only controls the timing, but He also knows best when He should answer.

As the parable concludes, Christ asks: "shall not God avenge his own elect, which cry day and night unto him, though he bear long with them?" The question is rhetorical and the answer is implied. Certainly God avenges His elect. But they must remember to bear in patience, and be "willing to submit to all things which the Lord seeth fit to inflict upon [them], even as a child doth submit to his father." (Mosiah 3: 19.)

Joseph Smith was reminded as he suffered in a Missouri prison that timing was always left to God. The Lord put it to Joseph plainly: "if the very jaws of hell shall gape open the mouth wide after thee, know thou, my son, that all these things shall give thee experience, and shall be for thy good. The Son of Man hath descended below them all. Art thou greater than he? Therefore, hold on thy way, and the priesthood shall remain with thee; for their bounds are set, they cannot pass." (D&C 122: 7-9.)

When Joseph received that revelation, he had been in prison for months. His people were driven from Missouri in the dead of winter. They were impoverished, suffering and abused. Joseph petitioned the Lord from the dungeon where he was held, saying: "Let thine anger be kindled against our enemies; and, in the fury of thine heart, with thy sword avenge us of our wrongs. Remember thy suffering saints, O our God; and thy servants will rejoice in thy name forever." (D&C 121: 5-6.)

This petition went unanswered for months. The anxiety Joseph felt was multiplied by his own helplessness. He wanted to give relief to the saints, but he could do nothing. So he prayed. He asked God to avenge the wrongs of the saints. Joseph and the saints continued to languish. After months of this destitution and confinement, Joseph received letters from friends that provoked this response:

> We had been a long time without information; and when we read those letters they were to our souls as the gentle air is refreshing, but our joy was mingled with grief, because of the sufferings of the poor and much injured Saints. And we need not say to you that the floodgates of our hearts were lifted and our eyes were a fountain of tears, but those who have not been enclosed in the walls of prison without cause or provocation, can have but little idea how sweet the voice of a friend is; one token of friendship from any source whatever awakens and calls into action every sympathetic feeling; it brings up in an instant everything that is passed; it seizes the present with the avidity of lightning; it grasps after the future with the fierceness of a tiger; it moves the mind backward and forward, from one thing to another, until

> finally all enmity, malice and hatred, and past differences, misunderstandings and mis-managements are slain victorious at the feet of hope; and when the heart is sufficiently contrite, then the voice of inspiration steals along and whispers- (*TPJS* p. 134.)

The voice of inspiration which whispered to him said the following:

> My son, peace be unto thy soul; thine adversity and thine afflictions shall be but a small moment; And then, if thou endure it well, God shall exalt thee on high; thou shalt triumph over all thy foes. Thy friends do stand by thee, and they shall hail thee again with warm hearts and friendly hands. Thou art not yet as Job; thy friends do not contend against thee, neither charge thee with transgression, as they did Job. (D&C 121: 7-10.)

All of God's disciples experience this struggle in submitting their will to God's. All of us experience the exasperation that comes from petitioning the "unjust judge" whose patience and timing are beyond us. All are tempted to complain that God is unnecessarily delaying an answer to our needs. All of us will finally come to realize that God has always intended to avenge His people who cry to Him day and night, even though He may bear with us a long time first.

The final question in the parable asks: "Nevertheless when the Son of man cometh, shall he find faith on the earth?" Will men lose faith? Will they lose patience as they await the Lord's answer to their desperate pleas? He is showing us the struggle we will have in the last days before His return. Despite all He may have done to answers prayers before, it will seem He has abandoned those who are here waiting. Even though He has provided proof of His word to His disciples, His delay will not only try their faith, it will cause them to wonder if God is not this unjust judge who makes them wait. It will test them so completely the Lord asks whether at the Second Coming He will find faith left on the earth. It is a sobering question. It is a warning. Do **not** lose faith. He **does** listen, He **will** answer. But it will necessarily be on His timetable. "[S]eek the face of the Lord always, that in patience ye may possess your souls, and ye shall have eternal life." (D&C 101: 38.)

This parable is designed to forewarn us. Being forewarned should prepare us. Above all, the parable should instruct us to never lose faith. Never let your own impatience confuse you about God's love or His fairness. He will vindicate every word He has spoken. In modern revelation He has reiterated: "What I the Lord have spoken, I have spoken, and I excuse not myself; and though the heavens and the earth pass away, my word shall not pass away, but shall all be fulfilled." (D&C 1: 38.)

The final, short parable describes conditions immediately preceding the Second Coming. Christ told this parable a few days before the one of the unjust judge. I have inverted the order because of the message of these two parables. Concerning the day of His return, the Lord spoke this parable: "For wheresoever the carcase is, there will the eagles be gathered together." (Matt. 24: 28.) The message is short, but filled with meaning. In this parable the "carcase" should not be interpreted as something dead, but as a symbol communicating something about gathering found in nature. It is not negative. It is a symbol of the true body of believers. Around them, the "eagles" will gather. This is a reference to angelic visitation, or an angelic presence which hovers about the body of true believers in the last days.

The body of believers, the real body which has saving faith, will attract "the eagles" to gather with them. That is, angels minister to, fellowship with, and are looking over that small body of believers who will be prepared for the Second Coming. Any body of believers who do not have the heavenly eagles ministering to them is **not** prepared for His coming. Moroni explained the awful fate of people who claim to have the truth, but among whom angels have ceased to minister:

> God will show unto you, with power and great glory at the last day, that they are true, and if they are true has the day of miracles ceased? Or have angels ceased to appear unto the children of men? Or has he withheld the power of the Holy Ghost from them? Or will he, so long as time shall last, or the earth shall stand, or there shall be one man upon the face thereof to be saved? Behold I say unto you, Nay; for it is by faith that miracles are wrought; and it is by faith that angels appear and minister unto men; wherefore, if these things have ceased wo be unto the children of men, for it is because of unbelief, and all is vain. For no man can be saved, according to the words of Christ, save they shall have faith in his name; wherefore, if these things have ceased, then has faith ceased also; and awful is the state of man, for they are as though there had been no redemption made. (Moro. 7: 35-38.)

Christ intended for true, living faith to continue. The fullness of His Gospel will only continue at His coming among people who are patient, who trust in His deliverance, even if it seems He delays His coming. And the body of believers who will be prepared are those to whom angels will continue to minister. Every other group may claim to be the Lord's, but the true body will attract the gathering of eagles.

Christ taught many other parables. This book is not about all His works nor all His doings. It is about my testimony. Therefore only these three have been selected. They are enough to communicate my intent. He was the Great Teacher and His lessons were designed to elevate us, encourage us, clarify for us what is true and matters. Do not be misled by the things of this world. Riches deceive. Position does not matter. Lazarus' favor with heaven was completely undetected by those who saw him. But he was the symbol of Christ, the image in story of Christ's own mortal condition. Come, follow Him, and you will realize how great an illusion there is in success as the world defines it.

Petition God for relief. Do not grow impatient. Remember the Lord waited many years for the hour of His ministry to draw near, all the while waiting prepared. Never cease to believe and to ask. He does hear and He will answer.

Look for angels to mingle with the true body of believers. They are one of the great evidences that you have found God's people. When angels are no longer being seen, no longer ministering, no longer being heard from, then you must find your own connection to heaven and bring them back into your own life. The true body of Christ will always have "eagles" hovering over it.

Chapter 10

The Rich Young Man

There was an important incident involving a rich young man who came to Christ for guidance. The incident was recorded by Matthew:

> And, behold, one came and said unto him, Good Master, what good thing shall I do, that I may have eternal life? And he said unto him, Why callest thou me good? there is none good but one, that is, God: but if thou wilt enter into life, keep the commandments. He saith unto him, Which? Jesus said, Thou shalt do no murder, Thou shalt not commit adultery, Thou shalt not steal, Thou shalt not bear false witness, Honour thy father and thy mother: and, Thou shalt love thy neighbour as thyself. The young man saith unto him, All these things have I kept from my youth up: what lack I yet? Jesus said unto him, If thou wilt be perfect, go and sell that thou hast, and give to the poor, and thou shalt have treasure in heaven: and come and follow me. But when the young man heard that saying, he went away sorrowful: for he had great possessions. Then said Jesus unto his disciples,

> Verily I say unto you, That a rich man shall hardly enter into the kingdom of heaven. And again I say unto you, It is easier for a camel to go through the eye of a needle, than for a rich man to enter into the kingdom of God. (Matt. 19: 16-24.)

At the time of this event Christ had been preaching publicly for nearly three years and was entering the final few months of His life. News of Christ had undoubtedly reached this unnamed man who had great possessions. Although the specific place is not identified, we know it was somewhere between the borders of Judea beyond Jordan and the outskirts of Jerusalem. It may have been near Jericho.

The young man certainly knew about Christ, and may have heard Him preach before. The ready willingness to acknowledge Christ as "good" in his greeting tells us he had decided he wanted to follow Christ. This carefully planned encounter was the moment when he determined to bring himself to the attention of Christ. No doubt there was a great deal of thought that preceded the encounter and the words of his greeting were carefully chosen.

He addressed Christ as "Good Master." He was ready to receive Him as his Rabbi. He wanted to become a follower. So this was not just happenstance. He had rehearsed what he would say to Christ. He thought he was prepared for the answer.

In response to being called "Good Master" Christ responds: "Why callest thou me good? There is none good but one, that is, God." This may seem odd, but the comment was made within a context. To understand the comment we need to look at that context. The most important part of the Lord's mission was still incomplete. He was in His final trek into Jerusalem to confront that greatest of burdens. He knew what lay ahead for Him. Shortly after this incident, He would tell His disciples plainly: "Behold, we go up to Jerusalem; and the Son of man shall be betrayed unto the chief priests and unto the scribes, and they shall condemn him to death, And shall deliver him to the Gentiles to mock, and to scourge, and to crucify him: and the third day he shall rise again." (Matt. 20: 18-19.) Clearly, He knew beforehand what He faced, and even explained what lay ahead. He was going to be delivered, scourged, crucified, die and rise again from the dead. He also knew this was His final time to pass this way in mortality.

Although He would wait another few weeks before telling His disciples directly of His coming death, it must have been a great burden to Him during this encounter with the rich young man. He knew who He was and why He came into mortality. He would tell Pilate about His sentence to die: "To this end was I born, and for this cause came I into the world." (John 18: 37.)

Despite the clarity Christ had of His sacrificial suffering and necessary death, there were uncertainties until He completed the work. He knew He had to endure a great deal, and was familiar enough with the prophecies to have details of His coming ordeal weighing heavy on His mind. Until the suffering was underway, He could not know how well He would face it, nor could He know fully how difficult it would be to endure. He did not know, until the awful final hours were upon Him, whether He would be equal to His assignment. He had to entertain the possibility of failing, and the dread of that thought had to weigh upon Him.

On this final journey Christ increasingly looked to His Father for guidance, assistance and strength to face what lay ahead. Christ's reaction to the young man's greeting tells us about His mental state. As He contemplated His final journey to Jerusalem, where He would be sacrificed, He was unwilling to consider anything that might be flattery. He could not allow Himself to be vain. He knew the devil's methods. He knew how any hint of vanity, pride, weakness or arrogance could be turned against Him. He fought that battle before. Christ's response reveals that He knew His Father was good, but He was not yet sure He was. He was not certain He could measure up to the assignment His Father had given Him. He would rely upon the One who was good. He would trust in His Father and hope not to fail Him in the awful, certain fate which was shortly His. Until He met His burden, He refused to be called "good."

In answer to the young man's question about what he must do, Christ replied simply , "keep the commandments." All of us may have hope for eternal life by keeping the commandments. But the young man knew there had to be more. He knew that people who believed in Christ, and people who were critics of Christ, **all** tried in their own way to keep the commandments. To the credit of the young man he wanted more. He wanted the kind of spiritual certitude that comes from something more than mere outward obedience. He wanted his heart to be right before God. So he pressed the point with Christ and asked: "Which?" His question implies that if there were a commandment that could answer the awful need, the nagging uncertainty inside him, and if Christ would tell him what it was, he would readily conform to that key commandment. This was a sincere young man who genuinely wanted to find the missing key to true worship.

Christ quickly listed the fundamental commandments saying: "Thou shalt do no murder, Thou shalt not commit adultery, Thou shalt not steal, Thou shalt not bear false witness, Honour thy father and thy mother: and, Thou shalt love thy neighbour as thyself." The young man had not murdered, never committed adultery, had never stolen, nor borne false witness. He had honored his parents and loved his neighbor. So he replied to Christ: "And he answered and said unto him, Master, all these have I observed from my youth. Then Jesus beholding him loved him, and said unto him, One thing thou lackest: go thy way, sell whatsoever thou hast, and give to the poor, and thou shalt have treasure in heaven: and come, take up the cross, and follow me." (Mark 10: 20-21.) The confident response from the young man pleased Christ. Christ "beholding him loved him" because this eager young man really wanted eternal life. But, despite this, he knew he was lacking. He knew there had to be more. This was a young man who was prepared to receive more.

Christ's public ministry had shown to all those of Judah that there was another level to true faith. Unlike the chief priests and Pharisees, Christ's word came with power. Audiences had all been "astonished at his doctrine: for his word was with power." (Luke 4: 32.) The young man knew this. He saw how different Christ was from the teachers he experienced throughout his youth. He wanted to know more. He wanted a deeper understanding of the mysteries of God. He wanted what Christ was teaching, showing and living. He wanted eternal life. So he responded to Christ that he had kept these commandments all his life. Then he asked the question which each of us should, in all sincerity, ask the Lord. The great key to knowing what you must do is contained in the young man's next words: "what lack I yet?"

Christ took a careful inventory of the young man before responding further. It was a serious, humble request from a sincere young man. It deserved an inspired answer. So Christ considered the young man carefully before answering. He loved what He saw. This was a genuine, worthy young man. But he "had great possessions," therefore, his affluence must have been apparent. His demeanor and attire distinguished him as a person of privilege. His social circumstances were limited by that privilege. He needed to move beyond his circumstances, and come see the final weeks of Christ's life if he were to understand what eternal life meant, and the price he needed to pay to gain eternal life.

With the needs of the young man in mind, Christ gave the answer which would have in fact secured for him eternal life. The answer was twofold. First, it required the young man to sacrifice what he valued in order to obtain the faith which could save him. This is an eternal principle, and is as true of each of us as it was of Christ Himself. Joseph Smith explained it like this:

> Let us here observe, that **a religion that does not require the sacrifice of all things never has power sufficient to produce the faith necessary unto life and salvation**; for, from the first existence of man, **the faith necessary unto the enjoyment of life and salvation never could be obtained without the sacrifice of all earthly things. It was through this sacrifice, and this only, that God has ordained that men should enjoy eternal life; and it is through the medium of the sacrifice of all earthly things that men do actually know that they are doing the things that are well pleasing in the sight of God. When a man has offered in sacrifice all that he has for the truth's sake, not even withholding his life, and believing before God that he has been called to make this sacrifice because he seeks to do his will, he does know, most assuredly, that God does and will accept his sacrifice and offering, and that he has not, nor will not seek his face in vain.** Under these circumstances, then, he can obtain the faith necessary for him to lay hold on eternal life. **It is in vain for persons to fancy to themselves that they are heirs with those, or can be heirs with**

> **them, who have offered their all in sacrifice, and by this means obtained faith in God and favor with him so as to obtain eternal life, unless they, in like manner, offer unto him the same sacrifice, and through that offering obtain the knowledge that they are accepted of him.** It was in offering sacrifices that Abel, the first martyr, obtained knowledge that he was accepted of God. And from the days of righteous Abel to the present time, the knowledge that men have that they are accepted in the sight of God is obtained by offering sacrifice. And in the last days, before the Lord comes, he is to gather together his Saints who have made a covenant with him by sacrifice. Psalms 50:3-5: "Our God shall come, and shall not keep silence: a fire shall devour before him, and it shall be very tempestuous round about him. He shall call to the heavens from above, and to the earth, that he may judge his people. Gather my Saints together unto me; those that have made a covenant with me by sacrifice." **Those, then, who make the sacrifice, will have the testimony that their course is pleasing in the sight of God; and those who have this testimony will have faith to lay hold on eternal life, and will be enabled, through faith, to endure unto the end**, and receive the crown that is laid up for them that love the appearing of our Lord Jesus Christ. But **those who do not make the sacrifice cannot enjoy this faith, because men are dependent upon this sacrifice in order to obtain this faith: therefore, they cannot lay hold upon eternal life**, because the revelations of God do not guarantee unto them the authority so to do, and without this guarantee faith could not exist. (*Lectures*, Sixth, ¶ 7-10, emphasis added.)

Christ responded to the young man in the only way in which he could actually obtain what he sought. For the rich young man to develop the faith necessary for salvation, it required the sacrifice of all his earthly possessions. Although the young man had "great possessions," they were nothing when compared to eternal life. They were given to this young man as an opportunity for him to gain eternal life. This moment, on this day, with Christ as his personal tutor, the young man was given the chance to make the sacrifice; give up his earthly possessions, and gain faith through that sacrifice which would lead to eternal life. There was no other way for the young man to get what he sought. Therefore, Christ told him: "If thou wilt be perfect, go and sell that thou hast, and give to the poor, and thou shalt have treasure in heaven: and come and follow me." Christ wanted the young man to choose to follow Him.

Had the young man heeded the counsel, he would have lost his great possessions. But by sacrificing them he would have discovered for the first time how little they mattered. Those who trust in riches are always disappointed. The rich often learn how little good comes from fortune while still in mortality. Riches are hollow and do not fill the heart. They cannot buy peace of mind, freedom from guilt, or genuine affection. Whatever good may be derived from wealth always ends at death. Then the only things that matter are the character developed in mortality, the kindness shown others, the ordinances received in faith, and the light within the soul. Affluence often retards the development of character, resulting in unkindness because the wealthy feel entitled to make demands on others as a result of the power money gives them. Few rich people will humble themselves, submit in faith to the required ordinances, and make the sacrifices necessary to gather light within the soul.

Christ's answer had another part, as well. It invited the young man to come and follow Christ. In addition to providing the means for developing faith, Christ was inviting the young man to accompany Him during the last weeks of His mortal ministry. Had the young man accepted, he would have been present during the culmination of His ministry. He would have seen Christ's triumphant entry into Jerusalem, the cleansing of the Temple, the rebuke of the scribes and Pharisees, attended the Last Supper, and been in Gethsemene. He would have been a witness to the betrayal, followed the trial, seen the crucifixion, and been among those who saw the Risen Lord. Saving knowledge which would allow him to enter into eternal life would have been gained as an eye witness. He would have seen and participated in some of the greatest events of history, and the critical culmination of Christ's mortal ministry.

Had the young man accepted the invitation, he would not be known to us as a "young man" with "great possessions" but we would know his name. He would be the great example of those who came to labor late in the day, but earned a full day's pay.[60] Had

---

[60]He would have illustrated the parable of the laborers: "For the kingdom of heaven is like unto a man that is an householder, which went out early in the morning to hire labourers into his vineyard. And when he had agreed with the labourers for a penny a day, he sent them into his vineyard. And he went out about the third hour, and saw others standing idle in the marketplace, And said unto them; Go ye also into the vineyard, and whatsoever is right I will give you. And they went their way. Again he went out about the sixth and ninth hour, and did likewise. And about the eleventh hour he went out, and found others standing idle, and saith unto them, Why stand ye here all the day idle? They say unto him, Because no man hath hired us. He saith unto them, Go ye also into the vineyard; and whatsoever is right, that shall ye receive. So when even was come, the lord of the vineyard saith unto his steward, Call the labourers, and give them their hire, beginning from the last unto the first.

he accepted the Lord's counsel, he may well have been one of the authors of a book of the New Testament. His name may have been enshrined in history with Matthew, Mark, Luke, John, Peter, James, Jude and Paul. But the moment passed, the invitation was not accepted, and instead the young man "went away sorrowful."

Whatever sorrow the young man had on that day would pale in comparison to the sorrow he would feel later, when the inventory of his life was taken. He would eventually realize he walked away from the very Lord who came to save him. His regret at that day would be far greater than his disappointment when he declined Christ's invitation.

Often opportunity comes unexpectedly and requires us to respond quickly. It comes, bids us to do something inconvenient, then passes on when we hesitate. Joseph Smith taught that we should react to the very first instant of inspiration, and not hesitate: "A person may profit by noticing the first intimation of the spirit of revelation." (*TPJS* p. 151.) He went on to explain that it is "thus by learning the Spirit of God and understanding it, you may grow into the principle of revelation, until you become perfect in Christ Jesus." (Id.) Perfection comes from following the light. Light grows

---

And when they came that were hired about the eleventh hour, they received every man a penny. But when the first came, they supposed that they should have received more; and they likewise received every man a penny. And when they had received it, they murmured against the goodman of the house, Saying, These last have wrought but one hour, and thou hast made them equal unto us, which have borne the burden and heat of the day. But he answered one of them, and said, Friend, I do thee no wrong: didst not thou agree with me for a penny? Take that thine is, and go thy way: I will give unto this last, even as unto thee. Is it not lawful for me to do what I will with mine own? Is thine eye evil, because I am good? So the last shall be first, and the first last: for many be called, but few chosen." (Matt. 20: 1-16.)

only as we give heed to it. "That which is of God is light; and he that receiveth light, and continueth in God, receiveth more light; and that light groweth brighter and brighter until the perfect day." (D&C 50: 24.) When we walk away from the light, it is often a long time before the opportunity returns to receive it again, if it does not leave forever. In the case of the entire New Testament account, we have nothing to suggest the young man with great possessions ever returned to the faith offered him by Christ. Apart from this single encounter, we hear nothing further of him. We are left to conclude that his exaltation was forfeited as a consequence of the decision made on this day, outside Jericho when he encountered Christ and walked away sorrowful.

The challenge of the Gospel is that it requires the same from us all. Whether it is Abraham asked to sacrifice his beloved son Isaac; or Stephen being martyred and forfeiting his life; or Saul asked to repent and join the sect he was persecuting; or the father of King Lamoni giving away all his sins, it is always the same. To obtain the faith necessary for exaltation we are required to sacrifice all earthly things. What matters most to one is not what matters most to another. God will tell any honest soul who asks: "what lack I yet" the answer that is individual to them and their life. Although it may vary from person to person, the result is always the same. It will require whatever we value most to be sacrificed. This is the only way we can develop the faith necessary to save us. It is the same for everybody, including Christ. Faith is tied to sacrifice. Sacrifice is giving up what we value in this world. We must lay it on the altar.

The incident ends with Christ remarking to his followers: "Verily I say unto you, That a rich man shall hardly enter into the kingdom of heaven. And again I say unto you, It is easier for a camel to go through the eye of a needle, than for a rich man to enter into the kingdom of God." This is not because of inherent evil in wealth. Rather it is because those who trust in wealth are unable to trust in God.

The connotation of the words "rich man" are not limited to monetary wealth. There are many who are similarly " rich" as a result of position, reputation, fame, power, or authority to rule over others. The Gospel of Jesus Christ does not demand we walk away from these "riches." However, if asked, we should be willing to do so. We should treat each of our blessings as a stewardship entrusted to us as a gift from God, always subject to God's request to return it to Him.

Businessmen holding authority are blind to the significant power they hold over others. They often forget they will be judged on the basis of how they behaved toward their subordinates and those they dealt with in business. They can be distracted by the cares of this world and forget their obligation to seek first the kingdom of God. In that respect, business success can be just as compelling a reason to 'go away sorrowful' when the Lord would have you do otherwise.

Political leaders are controlled by public opinion. If they are subject to election, they must maintain their popularity. But popularity is just as deceitful as riches. Elected officials are always tempted to think of themselves as more than they are. They are often inevitably drawn to support popular causes even if they are unjust or worse. Political success can be just as tempting as riches, and can bring a person to decline the opportunity to "come, follow Christ" because of the cares of their position.

Whether it be popularity, fame, success in sports, entertainment professionals or community leaders, any of the cares of this world can conflict with the cares of eternity. The rich young man's struggle is all of ours. We must all be prepared to walk away from benefits in this life when they conflict with the pursuit of Christ. Nothing should distract us from the things which matter most.

When it comes to The Church of Jesus Christ of Latter-day Saints, the Lord has revealed that only a very few of those who ever receive even a little priestly authority will be saved.[61] It is easy for proud men to confuse position with favor from God. It is a terrible mistake, however, to be misled and trust that position or authority is a reflection of God's approval. It is by sad experience that we see almost universally that when men get a little authority (as they suppose), they begin to exercise unrighteous dominion.

---

[61]"Behold, there are many called, but few are chosen. And why are they not chosen? Because their hearts are set so much upon the things of this world, and aspire to the honors of men, that they do not learn this one lesson--That the rights of the priesthood are inseparably connected with the powers of heaven, and that the powers of heaven cannot be controlled nor handled only upon the principles of righteousness. That they may be conferred upon us, it is true; but when we undertake to cover our sins, or to gratify our pride, our vain ambition, or to exercise control or dominion or compulsion upon the souls of the children of men, in any degree of unrighteousness, behold, the heavens withdraw themselves; the Spirit of the Lord is grieved; and when it is withdrawn, Amen to the priesthood or the authority of that man. Behold, ere he is aware, he is left unto himself, to kick against the pricks, to persecute the saints, and to fight against God. We have learned by sad experience that it is the nature and disposition of almost all men, as soon as they get a little authority, as they suppose, they will immediately begin to exercise unrighteous dominion. Hence many are called, but few are chosen. No power or influence can or ought to be maintained by virtue of the priesthood, only by persuasion, by long-suffering, by gentleness and meekness, and by love unfeigned; By kindness, and pure knowledge, which shall greatly enlarge the soul without hypocrisy, and without guile." (D&C 121: 34-42.)

Ordination to the priesthood is referred to as "a little authority, as they suppose" in the revelation because the authority ends as soon as the person begins to exercise unrighteous authority. The temptation is to view priestly authority the same way we view worldly authority. Without a doubt, worldly authority can be and is abused. Priestly authority, however, cannot be abused. When it is attempted, the authority comes to an abrupt end. Then the man is left to himself to kick against the pricks, even though he may continue to hold an office and be sustained by a congregation.

Priesthood holders cannot actually compel others, or insist they have the right, by virtue of position alone, to be treated with respect. When men act that way, their authority comes to an immediate end. The real authority for any priest comes solely from heaven itself. Unless a man claiming priesthood has his commission from heaven, he has no authority. It may be conferred upon a person, but it has no power, no authority, and is entitled to no respect when it is divorced from the "powers of heaven."

Indeed, the only authority which can do anything on God's errand comes directly from heaven. We have many in The Church of Jesus Christ of Latter-day Saints whose pride in their "riches" is akin to the young man with great possessions. That is exactly what the revelations foretold. Therefore, it is exactly as it should be.

Receiving authority in the priesthood is like receiving the Holy Ghost. The ordinance requires the person receiving to accept the Spirit from heaven. The priesthood also requires the person who has it conferred upon him to recognize it is inseparably connected with the powers of heaven. The power of heaven cannot be handled with any degree of unrighteousness.

The priesthood is an opportunity to bless the lives of others. It is not and cannot be a means of controlling or exercising dominion over others. Those who think it gives them a right to exercise control, dominion or authority have no priestly authority. They are like the rich man who "trust in riches" but have no relationship with God.

This sobering incident involving the young man is instructive to all of us. He did not like the answer. He went away sorrowful. His opportunity faded.

We should not let the opportunity for our own exaltation pass us by. When the Lord asks something of you, anything of you, be prepared to give it. But do not give to unrighteous men. Give only to God. Indeed, what He is likely to ask of you will require you to resist unrighteousness. Be prepared. Do as He asks. Through it you will find eternal life.

Chapter 11
The Confrontation with the Scribes and Pharisees

In completing His mortal assignment, Christ came to the Temple two days before His arrest and delivered an unmistakable condemnation of the priestly leaders and their teachings. It was given on the Temple grounds, as the crowds were gathering for Passover. It was a verbal attack designed to provoke the decision to kill Him. He did not have His disciples with Him at this time. Though they were present, they were not nearby. Matthew records that the talk was given "to the multitude" first, "and to His disciples," second. They were in the background. (Matt. 23: 1.) They rejoined Him outside the Temple after the message concluded.

This message was delivered the day following His triumphant entry into Jerusalem. Throngs had greeted Him when He first entered the city, shouting, "Hosanna to the Son of David: Blessed is he that cometh in the name of the Lord; Hosanna in the highest." (Matt. 21: 9.) That "very great multitude" had spread their garments on the ground before Him as He rode into Jerusalem. (Id. v. 8.) They proclaimed Him, not only the "Son of David," but also explained to those who asked that "This is Jesus the prophet of Nazareth of Galilee." (Id. v. 11.) Jerusalem was swollen with visitors on the occasion. After His triumphant entry, He went to the Temple and ran out money-changers, then healed the lame and blind who were in the Temple. (Id. v. 12-14.) The praise of an admiring multitude attracted the ire of the Chief Priests, who demanded Christ correct the proclamations coming from the crowds of His followers: "And when the chief priests and scribes saw the wonderful things that he did, and the children crying in the temple, and saying, Hosanna to the Son of David; they were sore displeased, And said unto him, Hearest thou what these say? And Jesus saith unto them, Yea; have ye never read, Out of the mouth of babes and sucklings thou hast perfected praise?" (Id. vs. 15-16.) Not only did Christ accept their praise openly, He claimed it was inspired, indeed "perfected!" These events the day before this talk were provocative enough, but the sermon discussed in this chapter was even harder for the priestly leaders to endure.

For years the religious leaders had tried to discredit Him, but He had evaded or answered every trap they laid for him. After failing in the effort to discredit Him, they had decided it was necessary to have Him killed. The final decision had been made when Lazarus was raised from the dead.[62] Killing Him was only a

---

[62]"Then they took away the stone from the place where the dead was laid. And Jesus lifted up his eyes, and said, Father, I thank thee that thou hast heard me. And I knew that thou hearest me always: but because of the people which stand by I said it, that they may believe that thou hast sent me. And when he thus had spoken, he cried with a loud voice, Lazarus, come forth. And he that was dead came forth, bound

matter of timing. When Christ initiated the confrontation on this day, He decided the timing. The intent to kill Him was so well known that some asked the question openly, as Christ was teaching in Jerusalem: "Then said some of them of Jerusalem, Is not this he, whom they seek to kill?" (John 7: 25.) Christ knew it, and had even asked them a year earlier: "Why go ye about to kill me?" (Id. v. 19.) It wasn't His time then. But this was the time, the moment for His sacrifice. He came to bring about the necessary end.

This final public confrontation, at this location, where the Chief Priests held such power, was such a direct challenge and deliberate provocation to their power, they had to act. He knew this Passover was the right time, a Jubilee of Jubilees. The practice of forgiving debt, relieving the suffering of the poor, and resting from labor was instituted by a commandment to Moses on Sinai:

> And the Lord spake unto Moses in mount Sinai, saying, Speak unto the children of Israel, and say unto them, When ye come into the land which I give you, then shall the land keep a sabbath unto

---

hand and foot with graveclothes: and his face was bound about with a napkin. Jesus saith unto them, Loose him, and let him go. Then many of the Jews which came to Mary, and had seen the things which Jesus did, believed on him. But some of them went their ways to the Pharisees, and told them what things Jesus had done. Then gathered the chief priests and the Pharisees a council, and said, What do we? for this man doth many miracles. If we let him thus alone, all men will believe on him: and the Romans shall come and take away both our place and nation. And one of them, named Caiaphas, being the high priest that same year, said unto them, Ye know nothing at all, Nor consider that it is expedient for us, that one man should die for the people, and that the whole nation perish not. And this spake he not of himself: but being high priest that year, he prophesied that Jesus should die for that nation; And not for that nation only, but that also he should gather together in one the children of God that were scattered abroad. Then **from that day forth they took counsel together for to put him to death**." (John 11: 41-53, emphasis added.)

> the Lord. Six years thou shalt sow thy field, and six years thou shalt prune thy vineyard, and gather in the fruit thereof; But in the seventh year shall be a sabbath of rest unto the land, a sabbath for the Lord: thou shalt neither sow thy field, nor prune thy vineyard. That which groweth of its own accord of thy harvest thou shalt not reap, neither gather the grapes of thy vine undressed: for it is a year of rest unto the land. And the sabbath of the land shall be meat for you; for thee, and for thy servant, and for thy maid, and for thy hired servant, and for thy stranger that sojourneth with thee, And for thy cattle, and for the beast that [are] in thy land, shall all the increase thereof be meat. And thou shalt number seven sabbaths of years unto thee, seven times seven years; and the space of the seven sabbaths of years shall be unto thee forty and nine years. Then shalt thou cause the trumpet of the jubile to sound on the tenth day of the seventh month, in the day of atonement shall ye make the trumpet sound throughout all your land. And ye shall hallow the fiftieth year, and proclaim liberty throughout all the land unto all the inhabitants thereof: it shall be a jubile unto you; and ye shall return every man unto his possession, and ye shall return every man unto his family. (Lev. 25: 1-10.)

This was a Jubilee of Jubilees, the time to "proclaim liberty throughout all your land." The time of His sacrifice needed to come this year, and it needed to coincide with the Passover. Therefore, when He came to Jerusalem, He had already set His face "like flint" with the steady resolve to complete His assignment as the Pascal Lamb, the Savior, Redeemer, Lamb of God and Prince of Peace. He could not be confounded in His determination. (See Isa. 50: 7.)

Everything had been done to prepare for the moment. This Passover was the time the offering needed to be made. Most importantly, the timing of His resurrection needed to coincide with the already set timetable. John Pratt has reconstructed the calendar for those days: "The Resurrection of Jesus Christ was another of the most holy days discovered so far, also being holy on all seven sacred calendars hitherto published, with five of those seven dates corresponding to Easter on that calendar. With the advent of these two changes to being holy on eight of nine calendars. Sun[day] 3 Apr[il] AD 33 was the Firstfruits of Wheat on the Jubilee Fixed calendar (*gpp*), which is Easter, the Sunday after Passover week. Thus, on six of the nine calendars, it was the very day representing the Resurrection." (Pratt, *Meridian Magazine*, 17 November 2004.) He needed to insure the Chief Priests, scribes and Pharisees would play their role, and so this sermon was the final incident required to force them to act.

Before His talk began, the scribes and Pharisees confronted Him with questions about His authority. He deferred His answer, choosing first to ask them about John the Baptist's authority. When they refused to answer Him, He refused to answer them. (Matt. 21: 23-27.) Then He taught them two parables, both of which indicted them for their wickedness while in their stewardships over the people.

He had come to the Temple intending to deliver a message to rebuke and warn the corrupt priestly leaders. This skirmish involving parables was merely a prelude to the sermon.

Christ's address that day serves as a warning to all those who believe themselves to be God's chosen ministers. All who claim to have the truth would be well advised to study the Lord's indictment of these spiritual leaders who presided over Him. This chapter will deal with that sermon.

Anytime men try to control others, invariably the endeavor for control involves stifling dissent and criticism. Those who claim the right to rule over others try to reduce all disputes to a question of authority. The discussion about who has "the" authority makes the question of whether an idea is right or wrong inconsequential. If authority determines everything, then all you need to "win" is to control authority. For example, Rodrigo Borgia, who acquired the Papacy in 1492 by bribery and intrigue, was able to avoid all challenges to his actions because his position gave him control. He contracted syphilis from his sexual excesses with prostitutes. His reign as Pope Alexander VI was so marred that the name "Borgia" became a pseudonym for debased standards. But he did reign as Pope, and while in office no one questioned his absolute right to preside. The doctrine of infallibility applied to him despite his publicly recognized moral failings. Murders, robberies, prostitution and immorality all increased in Rome during his papacy because of his example, but no one doubted he had the "keys of Peter" and he could "bind on earth and in heaven" and therefore, his authority made him infallible.

When any social structure prohibits criticism, controls all dissent, and demands the authorities alone decide all questions facing them, the result is invariably evil. Monolithic thought arising from stifled ideas is Satanic. Christ not only understood this, He came to the social structure which best exemplified the problem. These were the only people who would have killed Him.[63] Christ

---

[63]"Wherefore, as I said unto you, it must needs be expedient that Christ--for in the last night the angel spake unto me that this should be his name--should come among the Jews, among those who are the more

broke social conventions throughout His ministry because they needed to be broken. On this occasion He went into the house controlled by the scribes and Pharisees, and directly attacked their pretended authority. He distinguished between their right to preside (which He did not challenge), and their assumed exclusive right to teach and interpret scripture (which He utterly rejected). He knew they would never allow this challenge.

To fully appreciate the perverse nature of the scribes' and Pharisees' errors, we need to keep in mind that this society was originally organized by God. These people were chosen to be His people, and included in a covenant with Him. Indeed, Christ came to spend His mortality with them precisely because they **were** His covenant people. Although they were chosen, ministered to by Christ, and under a covenant, they were utterly perverse. These sobering facts should warn any "chosen people" of God's ability to accomplish His purposes in choosing them whether or not His people choose to be damned.

His sermon began:

> Then spake Jesus to the multitude, and to his disciples, Saying, The scribes and the Pharisees sit in Moses' seat: All therefore whatsoever they bid you observe, that observe and do; but do not ye after their works: for they say, and do not. (Matt. 23: 1-3.)

Note that Christ addressed His remarks to the entire multitude. This was a public event with a large audience gathered for the coming high holy day. He began by recognizing the leaders

---

wicked part of the world; and they shall crucify him--for thus it behooveth our God, and **there is none other nation on earth that would crucify their God**." (2 Ne. 10: 3, emphasis added.)

as legitimate office holders. He did not challenge their right to direct all the affairs affecting believers. They "sat in Moses' seat," and therefore, were entitled to give instructions. He even told the crowd to observe and do what these leaders asked. However, He also clarified that the leaders were quick to command others, but slow to observe themselves. The public was advised to not imitate these serious shortcomings.

It is easy for religious leaders in any generation to pronounce rules for proper conduct. Anyone can give a list of "thou shalt's" and "thou shalt not's." Living them is another matter. These leaders could talk the talk, but could not walk the walk. Their lives were full of corruption.

He continued:

> For they bind heavy burdens and grievous to be borne, and lay them on men's shoulders; but they themselves will not move them with one of their fingers. But all their works they do for to be seen of men: they make broad their phylacteries, and enlarge the borders of their garments, And love the uppermost rooms at feasts, and the chief seats in the synagogues, And greetings in the markets, and to be called of men, Rabbi, Rabbi. But be not ye called Rabbi: for one is your Master, even Christ; and all ye are brethren. And call no man your father upon the earth: for one is your Father, which is in heaven. Neither be ye called masters: for one is your Master, even Christ. (Matt. 23: 4-10.)

These religious leaders were careless about the difficulties they imposed upon the rank and file follower. They were selfish, self-centered and incapable of identifying with the common man. They viewed their offices as opportunities to make demands, and impose burdens which they were heedless to follow themselves. They did not notice their own hypocrisy because they believed it was their right to command others. Not only were they out of touch with the common man, but more importantly, out of touch with the Spirit. They associated with each other, not the "little people." These plebeians were around to admire the scribes and Pharisees, certainly not to question them.

These leaders also wanted titles, recognition and acclaim. They desired celebrity status. Personal praise was expected. They would not brook criticism; but there was no limit to the praise or acclaim which they welcomed. The scribes and Pharisees, by the notice they received in mortality, already had their reward for their conduct. They should expect nothing further in the afterlife.[64]

The title they craved, "Rabbi," meant they demanded to be acknowledged as the teacher. They would not allow anyone to teach them, but required all to be subordinate to and ready to receive instruction from them. Criticism was unthinkable. Followers needed to be careful to dispense only praise about them. No matter how foolish, vain, unwise or wrong their conduct, they did not accept correction. Errors of course compound themselves, foolishness multiplies, and vanity grows whenever teachers are unchecked by constructive criticism. The only thing that grows in that kind of stifled, intellectual environment is false religion. In

---

[64]See, e.g., Matt. 6:2: "Therefore when thou doest thine alms, do not sound a trumpet before thee, as the hypocrites do in the synagogues and in the streets, that they may have glory of men. Verily I say unto you, They have their reward." Matt. 6: 5: "And when thou prayest, thou shalt not be as the hypocrites are: for they love to pray standing in the synagogues and in the corners of the streets, that they may be seen of men. Verily I say unto you, They have their reward." Matt. 6: 16: "Moreover when ye fast, be not, as the hypocrites, of a sad countenance: for they disfigure their faces, that they may appear unto men to fast. Verily I say unto you, They have their reward."

such a corrosive setting none of the participants were able to see how completely darkened their minds had become.

When they did something that demonstrated their piety, it was all for show. Their righteous acts were always calculated to be on conspicuous display. They staged their public appearances carefully. They craved admiration from the poor. Alms were offered only to be seen of men. They wanted only a veneer of virtue, and none of the inner fortitude required of the truly charitable soul.

They lavished upon themselves titles and long introductions. This gave them credibility. They wanted their pronouncements and declarations to be above question or criticism. In short, they wanted unquestioned authority. Holding unquestioned authority was critical for their success. It allowed them rule with impunity.

Christ identified the true "Master" as Himself. Respect was reserved for our Father in heaven. Men were nothing. No matter the authority, position or status men were not worthy of reverence. This is a sobering warning for all who seek to be respected for their religious knowledge, position or authority. It is perilous for anyone to do more than point to Christ and reverence the Father. Despite this peril, men have continued to march forth to the "chief seats," holding titles, and claiming the right to be acknowledged as "rabbi." Surely it has always been the case that as soon as men get a little authority, as they suppose, they will immediately exercise control, dominion and compulsion. These scribes and Pharisees were the example of this in Christ's time. There are examples to be found in every generation.

His comments on this day were repeating that which He had already taught by parable. The parable veiled the warning about poisonous teachings of uninspired priestly leaders. In an earlier sermon, Christ's reference to "leaven" confused His disciples. He had to clarify His meaning to the disciples so they would understand it was a reference to doctrine.[65] In this sermon, Christ made His warning unveiled, direct and into the ears of the very ones He condemned. Before He had used a parable. Now He spoke directly and plainly. He was no longer going to hide His rejection of them.

Christ continued:

> But he that is greatest among you shall be your servant. And whosoever shall exalt himself shall be abased; and he that shall humble himself shall be exalted. (Matt. 23: 11-12.)

The cure for the affliction that ailed these pretenders was well known to Christ. He could tell them how real greatness is achieved: it is always through service. On another continent, in an earlier generation, King Benjamin was inspired by Christ to coin the phrase: "when ye are in the service of your fellow beings ye are only in the service of your God." (Mosiah 2: 17.) It is only through service that men come to understand charity, and then become

---

[65]See, Matt. 16: 5-12: "And when his disciples were come to the other side, they had forgotten to take bread. Then Jesus said unto them, Take heed and beware of the leaven of the Pharisees and of the Sadducees. And they reasoned among themselves, saying, It is because we have taken no bread. Which when Jesus perceived, he said unto them, O ye of little faith, why reason ye among yourselves, because ye have brought no bread? Do ye not yet understand, neither remember the five loaves of the five thousand, and how many baskets ye took up? Neither the seven loaves of the four thousand, and how many baskets ye took up? How is it that ye do not understand that I spake it not to you concerning bread, that ye should beware of the leaven of the Pharisees and of the Sadducees? Then understood they how that he bade them not beware of the leaven of bread, but of the doctrine of the Pharisees and of the Sadducees."

charitable. Those who serve the most, gain the deepest understanding. Christ served mankind more than any other man. He understood perfectly what He was teaching.

But the Great Teacher also knew humility was absolutely essential to spiritual health. No matter what a man did otherwise, unless he kept his heart humble, he was vulnerable to the poison of pride. Pride is so toxic it precludes any growth. A broken heart and a contrite spirit both precede, and accompany spiritual maturity. It is so essential that "the Son of man came not to be ministered unto, but to minister, and to give his life a ransom for many." (Matt. 20: 28.) As we have seen, Christ's "humbling Himself" began at birth. He did not exalt Himself, but accepted a lowly position in society. He lacked formal rabbinical training. He was born in Nazareth, away from the center of influence. He lived an itinerant life, associated with outcast friends and followers, and was always willing to challenge social conventions. He had more association with prostitutes, lepers, publicans and sinners than with the leaders. He lived what He taught, and in turn He taught by how He lived.

After setting the stage, He moved on to pronounce "woes" upon these leaders because of how their example corrupted the whole of society:

> But woe unto you, scribes and Pharisees, hypocrites! for ye shut up the kingdom of heaven against men: for ye neither go in yourselves, neither suffer ye them that are entering to go in. Woe unto you, scribes and Pharisees, hypocrites! for ye devour widows' houses, and for a pretence make long prayer: therefore ye shall receive the greater damnation. (Matt. 23: 13-14.)

Because of their abhorrent practices, these men could never enter the kingdom of heaven. Neither they nor those who accepted their teachings could qualify. Their form of false religion was damning to them all.

They collected tithes from the poor, then used the property to support themselves in abundance. Their prayers were merely a pretense - necessarily long winded, trying to impress with oratory, rather than having their hearts drawn out to God. Not only does God not honor such prayers, but those who offer them are damned. Christ saw this all His life. His keystone Sermon on the Mount referred to this flawed, proud, vain way of praying. He had told them years earlier: "And when thou prayest, thou shalt not be as the hypocrites are: for they love to pray standing in the synagogues and in the corners of the streets, that they may be seen of men. Verily I say unto you, They have their reward. But thou, when thou prayest, enter into thy closet, and when thou hast shut thy door, pray to thy Father which is in secret; and thy Father which seeth in secret shall reward thee openly. But when ye pray, use not vain repetitions, as the heathen do: for they think that they shall be heard for their much speaking." (Matt. 6: 5-7.) He warned them before, they didn't cease their hypocrisy, and now He came to the Temple to pronounce "woes" upon them for rejecting what He had taught.[66]

He continued:

---

[66]This pattern is similar to Abinadi's, in which he came and delivered his message, then departed for two years, and returned to condemn the people who had rejected his message of repentance. See Mosiah 11: 20-12: 8. Abinadi also was killed for his testimony, and the society who killed him was judged and destroyed. The experience shared by Christ and Abinadi have many parallels.

> Woe unto you, scribes and Pharisees, hypocrites! for ye compass sea and land to make one proselyte, and when he is made, ye make him twofold more the child of hell than yourselves. (Matt. 23: 15.)

The length to which they would go to attract a convert knew no limits. They would "compass sea and land" to find a proselyte, but the effect of the conversion was damnation. The convert was indoctrinated into a false form of religion which lauded outward pretenses, but did nothing to change the heart.

These false teachers invited others to come practice the same kind of hypocrisy. A teacher cannot teach anything other than what they are. Therefore spreading their form of idolatry increased the population of hell.

> Woe unto you, ye blind guides, which say, Whosoever shall swear by the temple, it is nothing; but whosoever shall swear by the gold of the temple, he is a debtor! Ye fools and blind: for whether is greater, the gold, or the temple that sanctifieth the gold? And, Whosoever shall swear by the altar, it is nothing; but whosoever sweareth by the gift that is upon it, he is guilty. Ye fools and blind: for whether is greater, the gift, or the altar that sanctifieth the gift? Whoso therefore shall swear by the altar, sweareth by it, and by all things thereon. And whoso shall swear by the temple, sweareth by it, and by him that dwelleth therein. And he that shall swear by heaven, sweareth by the throne of God, and by him that sitteth thereon. (Matt 23: 16-22.)

The scribes and Pharisees supported the notion of sacred things, sacred space and the importance of the Temple. They studied these things, constructed elaborate, complex doctrines which gave the impression their teachings were well thought out.

It was a shell-game for the listener. The strategy was to distract their followers with complicated arguments to make them seem impressive. By giving plenty of details, and citing precedent, it appeared they taught substance. That is one of the beauties of a scholarly theology. There is always plenty to discuss. The distraction of false religion is almost always elaborate.

The blind guides preferred the gold, Christ preferred the Temple. They preferred the gift upon the altar, Christ preferred the altar. He not only insisted upon the primacy of the Temple, but also reminded them of Him "that dwelleth therein." This was, in Christ's view, His Father's house. In the scribes and Pharisee's view, it was a place of commerce. The gain they realized from the tithes and offerings was what really mattered to them.

How easy it is to become distracted by the things of this world. How easy it is for ministers claiming to be on God's errand to stray into being on their own errand. How easy it is for those who handle tithes and property to lose sight of the Lord and His house, and come to value only the property. Measurable things - numbers, growth charts, revenues collected, statistics on attendance, numbers of buildings built - everything which could evidence prosperity, overwhelms those who think succeeding in their stewardship depends on increasing that which can be measured.

Nephi warned that we would also succumb to this number-crunching mentality. And as we do, we will conclude, just like the scribes and Pharisees, that all is well: "And others will he pacify, and lull them away into carnal security, that they will say: All is well in Zion; yea, Zion prospereth, all is well--and thus the devil cheateth their souls, and leadeth them away carefully down to hell." (2 Ne. 28: 21.) Magnifying a calling has never been statistics-driven.

As Christ has shown throughout His ministry, claiming lost sheep and bringing them to the kingdom of heaven does not involve the acquisition of significant properties. Saving souls is quiet, personal, individual and often misunderstood by the kingdom-builders of this world. Indeed, Zion always flees when it is assembled.[67] The goals God would have us pursue are never temporal.

Christ not only insisted upon the primacy of eternal things, He made clear to all who were listening that the scribes and Pharisees were merely "blind guides," and not the spiritual leaders they claimed to be. He was cutting away layer after layer of falsehood, while exposing their moral weakness. Their teachings were wrong, and they were not worth following.

He continued:

> Woe unto you, scribes and Pharisees, hypocrites! for ye pay tithe of mint and anise and cummin, and have omitted the weightier matters of the law, judgment, mercy, and faith: these ought ye to have done, and not to leave the other undone. (Matt. 23: 23.)

Now the verbal assault escalates. Christ progresses from referring to them as "blind guides" to calling them "hypocrites." The language is stronger, the attack more complete, the condemnation more personal. His growing level of condemnation was in response to their reaction to the talk. As Luke recorded: "And as he said these things unto them, the scribes and the Pharisees began to urge him vehemently, and to provoke him to speak of many things: Laying wait for him, and seeking to catch something out of his mouth, that they might accuse him."(Luke 11:

---

[67]See, e.g., Moses 7: 69; D&C 38: 4; 76: 66; 84: 100; 97: 25; Psl. 48: 2 and JST-Gen. 7: 27.

53-54.) They were not listening for truth. They had their "truth" and could not be instructed. Instead they were looking to condemn Him. They wanted His rhetoric to increase until He lost control and said something they could use to condemn Him. Arrogance, pride, anger and foolishness were all that motivated them.

He condemned them for prizing only the outward observable practices, while missing entirely the underlying qualities of the heart, which matter and which save. The qualities of judgment, mercy and faith are the "weightier matters of the law." They cannot be measured, counted, seen or directly observed. They are of the inner man. Consequently, they cannot be faked. They are part of a person's heart. Christ looked upon the heart.

He added:

> Ye blind guides, which strain at a gnat, and swallow a camel. Woe unto you, scribes and Pharisees, hypocrites! for ye make clean the outside of the cup and of the platter, but within they are full of extortion and excess. Thou blind Pharisee, cleanse first that which is within the cup and platter, that the outside of them may be clean also. (Matt. 23: 24-26.)

Here Christ touches upon what occurs when religion is devoid of the Spirit. After losing the Spirit, the mind runs wild. It substitutes rationally developed theology for inspired direction. Indeed, after becoming blind, they believe their conclusions **are** inspired. All their followers fall in line once "authority" and "inspiration" have become conflated. The people then find it easy to "strain at a gnat, and swallow a camel." Everything is disproportionate. Since the light of the Spirit is gone, there is no way for them to tell the difference between the gnat and the camel. The whole of Christ's ministry was viewed by men whose judgment was so impaired that they could not distinguish between the goodness and charity of healing a man, and lifting the burden of physical distress from a suffering soul, and the idea that keeping the Sabbath holy prevented such kind acts because they were "labor." Christ had labored for three years to teach by precept and example the difference between the camel and the gnat, and they still refused to see. Worse, they insisted they had the authority to judge Him, and that His refusal to obey their teachings was rebellion against not only them, but God. Since they were God's chosen leaders of God's chosen people they had the authority, the right, and the power to insist everyone strain at gnats.

Those who have lost their bearings, cannot recognize the difference between mere ceremonial cleanliness and actual spiritual cleanliness. Ceremonial cleanliness has always been designed to teach a principle. But since these scribes and Pharisees had lost the deeper meaning, they were full of extortion and excess, rather than full of the weightier matters of judgment, mercy and faith. They believed wrongly that ceremonial cleanliness would make God delight in them. They believed that the Son of God's teachings on mercy and faith were utterly false. They believed the teaching of mercy and faith was not only false, but doing so made Christ rebellious and disrespectful of authority. Hypocrites who ceremonially washed their hands, sacrificed animals and refused to work on the Sabbath were extolled as virtuous. Their many internal sins were not important. What people could see in their outward conduct was enough to qualify them as "righteous" in that culture.

This darkness can take hold of any people. When it does they are inevitably led to take offense when the Lord (or any messenger sent by Him) walks in the light. Darkness and light are always two different paths. They are incompatible.

The people hearing Christ's sermon at this time were required to choose between everything they had been taught all their lives and what Christ was teaching. They were God's chosen people, led by leaders chosen by God. They were taught respect for the priestly authorities of their society by reading the scriptures, which assured them they were God's "chosen people," and by observing the traditions of their fathers. They were led by recognized leaders, chosen in an established system of succession, on the one hand, and then this Man from Nazareth, lacking any sort of credentials, on the other, asking them to "come follow" Him. Even though they had shouted "Hosanna!" at His arrival the day before, this sermon demanded they reject the established authorities in order to follow Him. It was an easy choice for them. Christ knew it would be. Indeed, He relied upon it being easy to reject Him. This sermon controlled the timing of their final rejection of Him. They would crucify Him.

He continued:

> Woe unto you, scribes and Pharisees, hypocrites! for ye are like unto whited sepulchres, which indeed appear beautiful outward, but are within full of dead men's bones, and of all uncleanness. Even so ye also outwardly appear righteous unto men, but within ye are full of hypocrisy and iniquity. (Matt. 23: 27-28.)

This comparison was particularly biting. Contact with the dead made a person ceremonially unclean. The High Priest was even forbidden contact with his own deceased parents.[68] Christ's analogy

---

[68]See Lev. 21: 10-11: "And he that is the high priest among his brethren, upon whose head the anointing oil was poured, and that is consecrated to put on the garments, shall not uncover his head, nor rend his clothes; Neither shall he go in to any dead body, nor defile himself

was more offensive because it did not suggest contact with the dead, but rather compared these deluded, religious leaders to the actual dead body. Not only were they unclean, but those who were coming into contact with them and their teachings were unclean.

Sepulchers were "whited" to make them visible. That way they could be avoided. Christ was saying they are like a conspicuous and unclean spot which was to be avoided in order to prevent contact. For any contact with their teachings brought about uncleanliness.

The hypocrisy and iniquity of these religious teachers was so toxic, so wrong, so dark that it made others unclean. This forced the audience to choose. There could be no middle ground. Either we trust in the traditions of our fathers, or we follow Christ. This sermon would allow for no other outcome.

This choice has always been required of God's people. Nephi assures us this will also be the case for our day. Only a very few will find the way, and it will require them to overcome bad teachings: "because of pride, and wickedness, and abominations, and whoredoms, they have all gone astray save it be a few, who are the humble followers of Christ; nevertheless, they are led, that in many instances they do err because they are taught by the precepts of men." (2 Ne. 28: 14.) The test will always be the same.

Next He added:

> Woe unto you, scribes and Pharisees, hypocrites! because ye build the tombs of the prophets, and garnish the sepulchres of the righteous, And say, If we had been in the days of our fathers, we would not have been partakers with them in the blood of the prophets. Wherefore ye be witnesses unto yourselves, that ye are the children of them which

---

for his father, or for his mother."

> killed the prophets. Fill ye up then the measure of your fathers. (Matt. 23: 29-32.)

This is the intractable problem of religion. True prophets, once deceased, are always used by the wicked to justify whatever the wicked teach. Therefore truth can never be distinguished from error because someone is quoting a deceased prophet. It takes something much finer. Without the Spirit of truth it is impossible to recognize the light. We cannot even be sure about who is and who is not a prophet without relying on the Spirit of truth. As I pointed out earlier, prophecy is a byproduct from the testimony of Christ.[69] But even coarse charlatans have claimed to testify of Christ while advancing their own agenda and satisfying their own appetites. The one universal truth is: once a man everyone acknowledges as a prophet is dead and his words can be parsed into support for the false teacher, the words **will** be used by false teachers for support.

This struggle between light and dark cannot be decided on the basis of the authorities quoted, scriptures cited or arguments made. Both sides will rely upon the same prophetic tradition to justify themselves. The only way to determine the truth is by the light inside you. That light cannot be borrowed. President Harold B. Lee quoted from Heber C. Kimball one of the most quoted statements from General Conferences over the years: "'Remember these sayings, for many of you will live to see them fulfilled. The time will come when no man nor woman will be able to endure on borrowed light. Each will have to be guided by the light within himself. If you do not have it, how can you stand?' *Life of Heber C. Kimball*, pp. 446, 449-450." (Lee, Harold B. *Conference Report*,

---

[69]See Rev. 19: 10.

October 1965, Afternoon Meeting, p. 128.) Accordingly, we will have to face the same dilemma that faced the crowd of God's chosen people in the Temple on the day Christ delivered this sermon. We are going to have to rely upon the light within us. Hopefully Christ's sermon will aid us when that moment comes.

Christ continued:

> Ye serpents, ye generation of vipers, how can ye escape the damnation of hell? Wherefore, behold, I send unto you prophets, and wise men, and scribes: and some of them ye shall kill and crucify; and some of them shall ye scourge in your synagogues, and persecute them from city to city: That upon you may come all the righteous blood shed upon the earth, from the blood of righteous Abel unto the blood of Zacharias son of Barachias, whom ye slew between the temple and the altar. (Matt. 23: 33-35.)

Christ's language took a profound turn here. Not only does He call them nasty names, He also consigns them to hell. First, the terms "serpents" and "generation of vipers" were well known slang words which were derisive and offensive. There can be no doubt Christ's words were far from gentle, intended to be an insult, and calculated to shock those who were respectful, deferential and polite to priestly authorities. This was derisive and divisive. Second, He condemns these false teachers to the damnation of Hell. Their pretensions to piety had been utterly condemned, and now they stand condemned to damnation as well. As His reproach was reaching its climax, the force of the language employed was also escalating.

In the same statement Christ takes ownership of the prophets by declaring "**I** send unto you prophets!" There can be no mistake about this claim of personal ownership. Christ identified Himself as Lord. All the prophets, wise men, and inspired scribes were sent by Him. He was identifying Himself as the Lord. He is taking personal credit for all Israel's sacred history, prophets and inspired leaders. From that vantage point He took upon Himself the right to judge these inferior leaders of His day against the standard of true prophets whom He had sent. After all, the scribes and Pharisees claimed they were inspired of God, entitled to lead, and possessing authority to rule over Israel. Since they made these claims, Christ judged them against the standard they claimed for themselves. As stated earlier in His Sermon on the Mount: "For with what judgment ye judge, ye shall be judged: and with what measure ye mete, it shall be measured to you again." (Matt. 7: 2.) Christ was merely using their standard, and at this point in His sermon, no doubt turning language upon them which they had been using for years toward Him. In that sense the Lord's words were not merely appropriate, but ironic. That, too, would not have been lost on the scribes and Pharisees.

With respect to slaying righteous men, Christ told them they would be accountable for all the lost, righteous blood. Christ's statement that the blood of these martyrs would "come upon you" was an expression which also would have been familiar to the audience. When an animal was slain for a sacrifice, the blood would have gushed out onto the stone ground of the Temple courtyard, and splashed onto the skirts of the priests and offerors. Animal sacrifice was messy. When practiced, the blood of the victim would almost invariably get all over the offeror. Christ's analogy, therefore, put these scribes and Pharisees in direct proximity of the slain righteous men of all past generations. He is saying it is as if they literally had done the killing. They had the same spirit as the murders from Able to Zacharias. In the case of Zacharias, they had actually stood by as the killing took place. As Joseph Smith explained: "When Herod's edict went forth to destroy the young children, John was about six months older than Jesus, and came under this hellish edict, and Zacharias caused his mother to take him into the mountains, where he was raised on locusts and wild honey. When his father refused to disclose his hiding place, and being the officiating high priest at the Temple that year, was slain by Herod's order, between the porch and the altar, as Jesus said." (*TPJS*, p. 261.)

> Verily I say unto you, All these things shall come upon this generation. O Jerusalem, Jerusalem, thou that killest the prophets, and stonest them which are sent unto thee, how often would I have gathered thy children together, even as a hen gathereth her chickens under her wings, and ye would not! Behold, your house is left unto you desolate. (Matt. 23: 36-38.)

If there were any doubt among the audience of Christ's claim to divine authority, He removed it here. "How often would **I** have gathered" puts Christ in the role of the divine gatherer. Christ would have gathered them, but they would not come. As a consequence of refusing to be gathered, He told them of the fateful judgment upon that generation: "Behold, your house is left unto you desolate." They were lost. Their "house" was "desolate." Neither they, nor their descendants would be gathered for many generations. The words are chilling to contemplate.

When the message ended, He departed the Temple grounds and His disciples rejoined Him. (Matt. 24: 1.) They met on the Mount of Olives where He discussed the future of the Jews and the end of the world. (See Matt. 24.)

Of all the moments in the Lord's ministry the one we have considered in this chapter gives us more of a look at His personality than any other. The ferocity of the language, the clarity of the subject matter, the deep implications for any people who claim to be "chosen" by God, and the risks of any religious leader attempting to teach while lacking the Spirit, which alone keeps things correctly aligned, are all covered. It is as offensive to proud leadership on the one hand, as it is gratifying to the humble truth seeker, on the other. Christ's beautiful command of expression also reveals something "great and terrible" about Him: He could cloak the greatest aspirations of man in language which was sublime; and He could condemn the works of darkness with guttural language suited to the subject of damnation itself. His prose was always proportionate. For the lofty, He raised them higher still. For the damned, He cut them with language they would employ themselves.

For us, perhaps there is no greater warning than the material in this sermon condemning the scribes and Pharisees. We also claim to be God's chosen people. Therefore we risk suffering the same result. Constant repentance, and continuing submission to direction from the Spirit are the only safe harbor for God's people. This sermon is a blueprint about how His people go awry.

For that generation, this sermon was a watershed. A choice had to be made - either Christ needed to assume the primary role in all of Judea to lead, preside and teach, or He had to be killed. There was little risk of the former. Since He had to be killed, this new turn of direct confrontation required the deed to be done quickly. The sermon was when Christ forced the issue. The decision could wait no longer.

Chapter 12
Gethsemene

I knew a man in Christ about four years ago, who, being overshadowed by the Spirit on the 26th of February, 2005, had the Lord appear to him again. And the Lord spoke to him face to face, in plain humility, as one man speaks to another, calling him by name.[70] As they spoke the Lord put forth His hand and touched the eyes of the man and said, "Look!"[71]

The man had opened before him a view of the Lord kneeling in prayer. It was in a dark place. The air was heavy and overcast with sorrow.[72] The man beheld the Lord praying in Gethsemene on the night of His betrayal and before His crucifixion.

All the Lord had previously done in His mortal ministry by healing the sick, rasing the dead, giving sight to the blind, restoring

---

[70]See, e.g., Alma 38: 7; Ether 12: 39 and D&C 50: 11.

[71]See, e.g., D&C 76: 19 and 1 Ne. 11: 8.

[72]See also Luke 22: 45.

hearing to the deaf, curing the leper and ministering relief to others as He taught was but a prelude to what the Lord was now to do on this dark, oppressive night.

As the Lord knelt in prayer, His vicarious suffering began. He was overcome by pain and anguish. He felt within Him, not just the pains of sin, but also the illnesses men suffer as a result of the Fall, and their foolish and evil choices.[73] The suffering was long and the challenge difficult.

The Lord suffered the afflictions. He was healed from the sickness. He overcame the pains, and patiently bore the infirmities until, finally, He returned to peace of mind, and strength of body. It took an act of will and hope for Him to overcome the affliction which had been poured upon Him. He overcame the separation caused by these afflictions and reconciled with His Father. He was at peace with all mankind.

He thought His sufferings were over, but to His astonishment another wave overcame Him. This one was much greater than the first. The Lord, who had been kneeling, fell forward onto His hands at the impact of the pain that was part of a greater, second wave.

This second wave was so much greater than the first that it seemed to entirely overcome the Lord. The Lord was now stricken with physical injuries, as well as spiritual affliction. As He suffered anew, His flesh was torn which He healed using the power of the charity within Him. The Lord had such life within Him, such power and virtue within Him, that although He suffered in His flesh, these injuries healed and His flesh restored. His suffering was

---

[73]See also Alma 7: 11-14.

both body and spirit, and there was anguish of thought, feeling and soul.

The Lord overcame this second wave of suffering, and again found peace of mind and strength of body; and His heart filled with love despite what He had suffered. Indeed, it was charity or love that allowed Him to overcome. He was at peace with His Father, and with all mankind, but it required another, still greater act of will and charity than the first for Him to do so.

Again, the Lord thought His suffering was over. He stayed on His hands and knees for a moment to collect Himself when another wave of torment burst upon Him. This wave struck Him with such force He fell forward upon His face.

He was afflicted by this greater wave. He was then healed only to then be afflicted again as the waves of torment overflowed. Wave after wave poured out upon Him, with only moments between them. The Lord's suffering progressed from a lesser to a greater portion of affliction; for as one would be overcome by Him, the next, greater affliction would then be poured out. Each wave of suffering was only preparation for the next, greater wave.

The pains of mortality, disease, injury and infirmity, together with the sufferings of sin, transgressions, guilt of mind, and unease of soul, the horrors of recognition of the evils men had inflicted upon others were all poured out upon Him; with confusion and perplexity multiplied upon Him.

He longed for it to be over, and thought it would end long before it finally ended. With each wave He thought it would be the last but then another came upon Him, and then yet another.

The one beholding this scene was pained by what he saw, and begged for the vision of the Lord's suffering to end. He could not bear to see his Lord suffering in this manner. The petition was denied and the vision did not end, for the Lord required him to witness it.

The man saw that the Lord pleaded again with the Father that "this cup may pass" from Him. But the Lord was determined to suffer the Father's will, and not His own. Therefore, a final wave came upon Him with such violence as to cut Him at every pore. It seemed for a moment that He was torn apart, and that blood came out of every pore.[74] The Lord writhed in pain upon the ground as this great final torment was poured upon Him.

All virtue was taken from Him. All the great life force in Him was stricken and afflicted. All the light turned to darkness. He was humbled, drained and left with nothing. It is not possible for a man to bear such pains and live,[75] but with nothing more than will, hope in His Father, and charity toward all men, He emerged from the final wave of torment, knowing He had suffered all this for His Father and His brethren. By His hope and great charity, trusting in the Father, the Lord returned from this dark abyss and found grace again, His heart being filled with love toward the Father and all men.

These great burdens were born by the Lord not only on behalf of mankind, but also as a necessary prelude to His death upon a Roman cross. Had He not been so physically weakened by these sufferings, and drained of power from within, the scourging and crucifixion He suffered at the hands of men could not have taken His life.

It was many hours after this vision closed before the one who witnessed this suffering could compose himself again. He wept

---

[74]See also Luke 22: 44.

[75]See also Mosiah 3: 7.

because of the vision shown him, and he wondered at the Lord's great suffering for mankind.

The witness reflected for many days upon this scene of the Lord's great suffering. He read many times the account of the Lord's agony given to Joseph Smith, which reads: "Therefore I command you to repent--repent, lest I smite you by the rod of my mouth, and by my wrath, and by my anger, and your sufferings be sore--how sore you know not, how exquisite you know not, yea, how hard to bear you know not. For behold, I, God, have suffered these things for all, that they might not suffer if they would repent; But if they would not repent they must suffer even as I; Which suffering caused myself, even God, the greatest of all, to tremble because of pain, and to bleed at every pore, and to suffer both body and spirit--and would that I might not drink the bitter cup, and shrink--Nevertheless, glory be to the Father, and I partook and finished my preparations unto the children of men." (D&C 19: 15-19.) He pondered and asked: Why were there waves of torment? Why did they increase in difficulty? How were they organized as they seemed to fit a pattern?

After long inquiring into the things which he had seen, the Lord, who is patient and merciful and willing to instruct those who call upon Him,[76] again appeared to the man on the 20th of December, 2007. He made known unto him that the waves of torment suffered by the Lord came in pairs which mirrored each other. The first of each wave poured upon the Lord those feelings, regrets, recriminations and pains felt by those who injured their fellow man. Then followed a second wave, which mirrored the first, but imposed the pains suffered by the victims of the acts

---

[76]See e.g., D&C 76: 5 and D&C 88: 63.

committed by those in the first wave. Instead of the pains of those who inflict hurt or harm, it was now the anger, bitterness and resentments felt by those who suffered these wrongs.

From each wave of suffering, whether as the one afflicting or as the victim of those wrongs, the Lord would overcome the evil feelings associated with these wrongs, and find His heart again filled with peace. This was why, in the vision of the suffering of the Lord it was in the second waves that there appeared oftentimes to be injuries to His body.

The greater difficulty in these paired waves of torment was always overcoming the suffering of the victim. With these waves, the Lord learned to overcome the victims' resentments, to forgive, and to heal both body and spirit. This was more difficult than overcoming the struggles arising from the one who committed the evil. This is because the one doing evil knows he has done wrong, and feels a natural regret when he sees himself aright. The victim, however, always feels it is their right to hold resentment, to judge their persecutor, and to withhold peace and love for their fellow men. The Lord was required to overcome both so that He could succor both.

In the pairing of the waves, the first torment was of the mind and spirit, and the second was torment of mind, spirit and body.

The Lord experienced all the horror and regret wicked men feel for their crimes when they finally see the truth. He experienced the suffering of their victims whose righteous anger and natural resentment and disappointment must also be shed, and forgiveness given, in order for them to find peace. He overcame them all. He descended below them all. He comprehends it all. And He knows how to bring peace to them all. He knows how to love others whether they are the one who has given offense or the one who is a victim of the offense.

In the final wave, the most brutal, most evil, most heinous sins men inflict upon one another were felt by Him as a victim of the worst men can do. He knew how it felt to wrongly suffer death. He knew what it was like to be a mother holding a child in her arms as they are both killed by those who delight in their suffering. He knew how it was for ambitious men to rid themselves of a rival by conspiracy and murder. He knew what it was to have virtue robbed from the innocent. He knew betrayal, treachery, and abuse in all its worst degrading horror. There was no cruelty, no offense, no evil that mankind has suffered or will suffer that was not put upon Him.

He knew what it is like for men to satisfy their ambition by clothing their hypocrisy in religious garb. He also felt what it was like to be the victim of religious oppression by those who pretend to practice virtue while oppressing others. He knew the hearts of those who would kill Him. Before confronting their condemnation of Him in the flesh, He suffered their torment of mind when they recognized He was the Lord, and then found peace for what they would do by rejecting Him. In this extremity there was madness itself as He mirrored the evil which would destroy Him, and learned how to come to peace with the Father after killing the Son of God, and to love all those involved without restraint and without pretense even before they did these terrible deeds. His suffering, therefore, encompassed all that has happened, all that did happen, and all that would happen in the future.

As a result of what the Lord suffered, there is no condition - physical, spiritual or mental - that He does not fully understand. He knows how to teach, comfort, succor and direct any who come to

Him seeking forgiveness and peace. This is why the prophet wrote: "by his knowledge shall my righteous servant justify many; for he shall bear their iniquities." (Isa. 53: 11.) And again: "Surely he hath borne our griefs, and carried our sorrows: yet we did esteem him stricken, smitten of God, and afflicted. But he was wounded for our transgressions, he was bruised for our iniquities: the chastisement of our peace was upon him; and with his stripes we are healed." (Id. v. 4-5.) He obtained this knowledge by the things he suffered. He suffered that we might avoid sin by being obedient to His commandments. None of us need harm another, if we will follow Him. He knows fully the consequences of sin. He teaches His followers how to avoid sin.

The prophet Alma taught and understood our Lord's sufferings as he wrote: "And he shall go forth, suffering pains and afflictions and temptations of every kind; and this that the word might be fulfilled which saith he will take upon him the pains and the sicknesses of his people. And he will take upon him death, that he may loose the bands of death which bind his people; and he will take upon him their infirmities, that his bowels may be filled with mercy, according to the flesh, that he may know according to the flesh how to succor his people according to their infirmities." (Alma 7: 11-12.)

He can bring peace to any soul. He can help those who will come to Him love their fellow man. He alone is the Perfect Teacher because He alone has the knowledge each of us lack to return to being whole and at peace with the God and Father of us all after our transgression of His will. He is wise to what is required for each man's salvation.[77]

---

[77]See Isa. 53: 11.

As the Lord made these terrible things known to the man he cried out: "Hosanna to the Lamb of God! He has trodden the winepress alone! Glory, honor and mercy be upon the Chosen One forever and ever! I will submit unto anything you see fit to require of me! I will bend my knee in obedience to you! Let thy will, not mine be done! For worthy is the Lamb!" Then, thinking upon how trifling his difficulties and disappointments had been in comparison with the suffering he saw imposed upon his Lord, the man added: "Surely goodness and mercy have been mine all the days of my life!"[78]

And the Lord responded: "And you shall dwell in the house of the Lord forever."[79]

Then the man wept.

I write these things with permission, and not on my own.[80] For those who receive a knowledge of these things are not always permitted to make them known, nor should they do so.[81] But the Lord requires that some must bear testimony so that others may read or hear, and be edified by them, that faith may increase among mankind. If none of those who receive these things were ever permitted to make them known, then mankind could not come to their Lord and be healed. It is not important to know why the Lord chooses to make these things known to some and then instructs them to testify of them to another. It is only necessary to understand that the Lord is the One to whom all should look in

---

[78]See Psalms 23: 6.

[79]Id.

[80]See, e.g., 2 Ne. 33: 11 and 3 Ne. 26: 12.

[81]See, e.g., D&C 76: 115.

their trials and afflictions for succor. He is mighty and able to save.[82] You do not and will not suffer from any affliction, any dilemma, disap-pointment or pain which He does not already understand. He has overcome it all.[83] He is worthy to be trusted with your burdens. Come to Him and be healed! Come to Him and be understood! When all others move away, He will come to you! There is nothing wretched that you must confront that He did not first confront and overcome! Take your burdens to Him!

The great Atonement of the Lord allowed Him to know our weaknesses and troubles, and to understand how to bring us back to peace.[84] Christ, as the Atoning One, knows how to bring every troubled soul back to peace. The Lord can tutor us and help us lay down any burden we may be bearing. We are all required to come to peace with our sins and with the offenses we have suffered. To be fully redeemed, we must leave this life having peace through a clear conscience before God and all mankind. This can only be obtained by forgiving others their trespasses. As was recorded about Joseph Smith, before his death: "When Joseph went to Carthage to deliver himself up to the pretended requirements of the law, two or three days previous to his assassination, he said: 'I am going like a lamb to the slaughter; but I am calm as a summer's morning; **I have a conscience void of offense towards God, and towards all men.**'" (D&C 135: 4, emphasis added.) He was able to do this because Joseph had forgiven in advance, those who he expected would kill him. It was by these means he was able to have

---

[82]See, e.g., 2 Ne. 31: 19; Alma 7: 14 and D&C 133: 47.

[83]See, e.g., Alma 42: 15 and 3 Ne. 11: 11.

[84]See, e.g., Alma 7: 12.

a clear conscience, void of any offense toward all men. Though others would cry revenge for Joseph's death, Joseph himself obtained the fullness of his reconciliation to God through the act of forgiving those who would kill him.

Christ taught His followers to forgive, that they may in turn merit forgiveness. He said: "For if ye forgive men their trespasses, your heavenly Father will also forgive you: But if ye forgive not men their trespasses, neither will your Father forgive your trespasses." (Matt. 6: 14-15.) He taught this because of the atoning power of forgiving others. As a result of the things He suffered, He understood that men must forgive others in order to be able to obtain forgiveness. There are many things men do that they lack the capacity to make amends. The price they must pay for their own transgressions are paid by forgiving all others of their offenses.

Christ was asked by Peter how often men ought to forgive one another. "Then came Peter to him, and said, Lord, how oft shall my brother sin against me, and I forgive him? till seven times?" (Matt. 18: 21.) In response Christ taught this, saying:

> Jesus saith unto him, **I say not unto thee, Until seven times: but, Until seventy times seven**. Therefore is the kingdom of heaven likened unto a certain king, which would take account of his servants. And when he had begun to reckon, one was brought unto him, which owed him ten thousand talents. But forasmuch as he had not to pay, his lord commanded him to be sold, and his wife, and children, and all that he had, and payment to be made. The servant therefore fell down, and worshipped him, saying, Lord, have patience with me, and I will pay thee all. Then the lord of that servant was moved with compassion, and loosed him, and forgave him the debt. But the

> same servant went out, and found one of his fellowservants, which owed him an hundred pence: and he laid hands on him, and took [him] by the throat, saying, Pay me that thou owest. And his fellowservant fell down at his feet, and besought him, saying, Have patience with me, and I will pay thee all. And he would not: but went and cast him into prison, till he should pay the debt. So when his fellowservants saw what was done, they were very sorry, and came and told unto their lord all that was done. Then his lord, after that he had called him, said unto him, O thou wicked servant, I forgave thee all that debt, because thou desiredst me: **Shouldest not thou also have had compassion on thy fellowservant, even as I had pity on thee?** And his lord was wroth, and delivered him to the tormentors, till he should pay all that was due unto him. So likewise shall my heavenly Father do also unto you, if ye from your hearts forgive not **every one his brother their trespasses**. (Matt. 18: 22-35, emphasis added.)

He taught this to show how offering forgiveness was in turn obtaining forgiveness. His disciples continued to misunderstand how these two are related. They did not understand that forgiveness is the means by which the Lord enables men to take advantage of His "preparations unto the children of men." (D&C 19: 19.) To forgive is to atone.

The Lord taught elsewhere: "And when ye stand praying, forgive, if ye have ought against any: that your Father also which is in heaven may forgive you your trespasses. But if ye do not forgive, neither will your Father which is in heaven forgive your trespasses." (Mark 11: 25-26.) The Father cannot give to men what they ask of Him until they first forgive all offenses among one another.

The voice of the Lord came to Alma, also, and said unto him: "And ye shall also forgive one another your trespasses; for verily I say unto you, he that forgiveth not his neighbor's trespasses when he says that he repents, the same hath brought himself under condemnation." (Mosiah 26: 31.) Alma taught this to the people of Mosiah, so they might abide the conditions to obtain forgiveness for their own sins.

When instructing those who assembled in the land of Bountiful, Christ taught: "For, if ye forgive men their trespasses your heavenly Father will also forgive you; But if ye forgive not men their trespasses neither will your Father forgive your trespasses." (3 Ne. 13: 14-15.) He said this so they may understand the means by which men are redeemed. All mankind must redeem themselves by permitting others to escape condemnation for the offenses they have committed against them. In this way men are no longer their brother's accuser; and the Accuser of Mankind is without means to keep men from redemption. For justice cannot have hold on those who have claim on mercy. Mercy comes to those who give mercy, and men are restored to that which they have become. The merciful are entitled to mercy.

In revelations to Joseph Smith the Lord has commanded: "Verily, verily, I say unto you, my servants, that inasmuch as you have forgiven one another your trespasses, even so I, the Lord, forgive you." (D&C 82: 1.) And, again: "Wherefore, I say unto you, that ye ought to forgive one another; for he that forgiveth not his brother his trespasses standeth condemned before the Lord; for there remaineth in him the greater sin." (D&C 64: 9.)

To enter into the kingdom of heaven, all men must lay down their sins. But this they cannot do when they claim the right to restitution for any offense from their brother. All claims must be set aside, the greater and more difficult being the righteous claim against another for their deliberate offense. Yet in asking for justice for yourself, you always require justice be answered in turn for all of your offenses A man will not be given mercy if he is not merciful. Alma taught this plainly to his son, Corianton, so he might be redeemed. Mormon preserved this teaching that all men who read the Book of Mormon may be redeemed and have claim on mercy:

> Now, there was a punishment affixed, and a just law given, which brought remorse of conscience unto man. Now, if there was no law given--if a man murdered he should die--would he be afraid he would die if he should murder? And also, if there was no law given against sin men would not be afraid to sin. And if there was no law given, if men sinned what could justice do, or mercy either, for they would have no claim upon the creature? But there is a law given, and a punishment affixed, and a repentance granted; which repentance, mercy claimeth; otherwise, justice claimeth the creature and executeth the law, and the law inflicteth the punishment; if not so, the works of justice would be destroyed, and God would cease to be God. But God ceaseth not to be God, and mercy claimeth the penitent, and mercy cometh because of the atonement; and the atonement bringeth to pass the resurrection of the dead; and the resurrection of the dead bringeth back men into the presence of God; and thus they are restored into his presence, to be judged according to their works, according to the law and justice. For behold, justice exerciseth all his demands, and also mercy claimeth all which is her own; and thus, none but the truly penitent are saved. What, do ye suppose that mercy can rob justice? I say unto you, Nay; not one whit. If so, God would cease to be God. And thus God bringeth about his great and eternal purposes,

> which were prepared from the foundation of the world. And thus cometh about the salvation and the redemption of men, and also their destruction and misery. Therefore, O my son, whosoever will come may come and partake of the waters of life freely; and whosoever will not come the same is not compelled to come; but in the last day it shall be restored unto him according to his deeds. If he has desired to do evil, and has not repented in his days, behold, evil shall be done unto him, according to the restoration of God." (Alma 42: 18-28.)

Now I know these things to be true, and the Lord has permitted them to be made known to anyone who will believe so they may repent and forgive one another, and may in turn have claims on mercy for themselves. It is certain Christ is able to heal us of any affliction which this life may visit upon any of us, but only if we will forgive one another and come to Him. He can teach all how to forgive. No matter how terrible the offense, He has the knowledge to lead us to peace.

When men come to the Lord seeking forgiveness, He will prepare the means for each of them to obtain forgiveness. The way will be opened for them to forgive so they in turn may be forgiven. In this way all may come to know their Lord.

Do not depart this life while still harboring resentment against any person. It does not matter how just the claim may be, we must surrender our claims for justice to merit mercy. Find a way to forgive all those who transgress against you before leaving mortality and, by showing mercy to them, you will find mercy for yourself. As Joseph Smith put it:

> I charged the Saints not to follow the example of the adversary in accusing the brethren, and said, "If you do not accuse each other, God will not accuse

> you. If you have no accuser you will enter heaven, and if you will follow the revelations and instructions which God gives you through me, I will take you into heaven as my back load. If you will not accuse me, I will not accuse you. If you will throw a cloak of charity over my sins, I will over yours-for charity covereth a multitude of sins." (*TPJS* p. 193.)

This path to knowing God's goodness has been made known to every people in every generation. It can be felt whenever any man has shown mercy to his fellowman. Christ taught this, but the light of Christ leads all those who seek wisdom to find this truth. God is no respecter of persons. Blessed are the merciful, for they will always obtain mercy. More blessed are those who love, for God is love.

To obtain perfect charity, however, a man must make intercession for those who offend him. Christ taught: "I say unto you, Love your enemies, bless them that curse you, do good to them that hate you, and pray for them which despitefully use you, and persecute you; That ye may be the children of your Father which is in heaven[.]" (Matt. 5: 44-45.) He wants us to go beyond merely forgiving others. He wants us to become like Him, and atone or cover the sins of others. Through intercession on behalf of our enemies, we not only learn to understand Him, we also learn to be like Him. This is what Christ did. This is what Stephen did. All those who have the hope of Christ within them will do likewise. I testify these things are true, Christ being my witness.

Chapter 13
Crucifixion

Crucifixion was a brutal way to die. It may have been the most cruel way ever used by government to execute a criminal. It combined prolonged torture and public humiliation for the victim, together with intimidation of all who saw it.

For a Jew, this form of death was "cursed" under the Law of Moses. In Deuteronomy it is written:

> And if a man have committed a sin worthy of death, and he be to be put to death, and thou hang him on a tree: His body shall not remain all night upon the tree, but thou shalt in any wise bury him that day; (for he that is hanged is accursed of God;) that thy land be not defiled, which the Lord thy God giveth thee for an inheritance. (Deut. 21: 22-23.)

The cruelty of this awful form of punishment was necessary for Christ to suffer. His purpose was to deliberately "descend below all things." (D&C 122: 8.) A pain-free, dignified death would not do. It had to be such an ordeal that any of us thinking about what He endured would be convinced He did not spare Himself. He suffered to the limits all that He could endure. He proved His love for us beyond any doubt. The price was necessarily high.

Crucifixion was also destined to become the symbol of God's salvation. This type of death for Israel's Messiah was foreshadowed by earlier events. Moses led his people through a wilderness infested with poison adders. Israelites were stung by the deadly snakes, whose venom felt like fire to the victims. The cure came through a symbol which pointed to Christ's sacrifice on the cross. Those who looked in faith at the brass serpent hung upon a pole would live:

> And the Lord sent fiery serpents among the people, and they bit the people; and much people of Israel died. Therefore the people came to Moses, and said, We have sinned, for we have spoken against the Lord, and against thee; pray unto the Lord, that he take away the serpents from us. And Moses prayed for the people. And the Lord said unto Moses, Make thee a fiery serpent, and set it upon a pole: and it shall come to pass, that every one that is bitten, when he looketh upon it, shall live. And Moses made a serpent of brass, and put it upon a pole, and it came to pass, that if a serpent had bitten any man, when he beheld the serpent of brass, he lived. (Num. 21: 6-9.)

The serpent that hung on the pole healed the stricken Israelites. The sign behind the cure symbolized the future healing of all mankind through Christ. In this particular event involving Israel, there were two opposing serpents. One serpent brought death and the other serpent restored life. Although traditional Christianity has come to regard the serpent exclusively as a symbol of Satan, it was originally the symbol of Christ. Satan appropriated it in the Garden of Eden, when, pretending to be the son of God, he lied to Eve and convinced her to partake of the forbidden fruit. Satan supplanted Christ as the "serpent." Moses restored the serpent as a symbol of Christ when he made the brass image and hung it on a pole to save those stung by the fiery poison of the serpents.

The fiery serpents symbolized Satan, and had no power to kill those who looked with faith upon the brass serpent hung on the pole symbolizing Christ. The whole event was used by the Lord to foreshadow the true Son of God ultimately prevailing over the fallen son of the morning. The Israelites were like all mankind, in-between these two opposing parties. Satan, as serpent, seeks to cause suffering and death to all mankind. The true Serpent, who would hang on a tree for our salvation, is the One through whom enduring life is offered to anyone who will "look to Him." The plight of mortality is on display in this juxtaposition. Men are stung by Satan's destructive poison. But Christ has the final power to save. Therefore look to Him for salvation.

Christ's crucifixion was at the same time the symbol of cursing and redemption. Christ being accursed and us being redeemed. It was the culminating event in Christ's triumph as the true Son of God over the liar who claimed to be the son of God.

His final act of devotion to the Father was also the final act of perfecting His love for mankind. He could develop and show "greater love" in no other way than to "lay down his life for his friends." (John 15: 13.) For Christ, this final altar upon which He offered His body and shed His blood, was so that in turn men may have every reason to "always remember him, and keep his commandments which he hath given them, that they may always have his Spirit to be with them." (Moroni 4: 3; 5: 2.) The crucifixion was the moment of His Sacramental sacrifice of His flesh and blood.

Christ was weakened before the crucifixion by the ordeal in Gethsemene. He had been beaten, abused and scourged. Between blood loss and the cumulative effect of torture, Christ physically broke down while carrying the cross to Golgotha. He was weak, dehydrated and already dying by the time they nailed Him to the tree.

There are four different accounts of the crucifixion in the Gospels. This chapter will select from each, but not rely on any of them in full. The first excerpt is taken from Matthew and begins with the treatment of Christ by the Roman soldiers in the common hall:

> Then the soldiers of the governor took Jesus into the common hall, and gathered unto him the whole band of soldiers. And they stripped him, and put on him a scarlet robe. And when they had platted a crown of thorns, they put it upon his head, and a reed in his right hand: and they bowed the knee before him, and mocked him, saying, Hail, King of the Jews! And they spit upon him, and took the reed, and smote him on the head. And after that they had mocked him, they took the robe off from him, and put his own raiment on him, and led him away to crucify him. (Matt. 27: 27-31.)

Here in very deed is the event which the ancient ceremonial humiliation of the king foretold.[85] They first stripped Him,

---

[85]See, e.g., Hugh Nibley, *Nibley on the Timely and the Timeless*, p.142: "[A. R.] Rosenberg has shown that the title of Suffering Servant was used in the Ancient East to designate 'the substitute king' - the noble victim. Accordingly, the 'new Isaac' mentioned in Maccabees 13:12 must be 'a "substitute king" who dies that the people might live.' The starting

preparatory to adorning Him in the mocking ceremonial robe of royalty. Then, after dressing Him in a scarlet robe, emblematic of nobility, they crowned Him with a mock crown of braided thorns. Having clothed and crowned Him, they then "anointed" Him with spittle, while striking His head with a reed-stick. They unknowingly finished the cruel mimic of ordinances that were designed to bless and honor those who follow Him. Here, instead of laying hands upon His head to confer a blessing, He was struck by a hand wielding a stick to inflict pain and humiliation. Everything these abusive soldiers did to degrade Him has a counterpart in ordinances designed to bless and elevate His followers. The abuse was "inspired" mimicry, whose inspiration came from that fallen son of the morning who has always opposed God and exalted himself.[86] There should be little astonishment he would inspire this abuse to mimic and mock God. Isaiah said it best: "we did esteem him stricken, smitten of God, and afflicted. But he was wounded

---

point in Rosenberg's investigation is Isaiah 52: 13 to 53: 12, which 'seems to constitute a portion of a ritual drama centering about a similar humiliation, culminating in death, of a "substitute" for the figure of the king of the Jews.' If we examine these passages, we find that they fit the story of Abraham's sacrifice even better than that of Isaac." Also, Hugh Nibley, *Abraham in Egypt*, p.207 - 208, which we will omit here, and Hugh Nibley, *The World and the Prophets*, 3rd ed., p. 233 - 234: "The schools of Wellhausen and Gressmann, though diametrically opposed, were each convinced that it had blasted the supernatural element out of religion forever by demonstrating that there were everywhere in the ancient world close ritual parallels to the crucifixion. The now well-known Year Drama, a ritual found throughout the whole world, presents everywhere, though with a great variety of local variations, substantially the same ritual pattern: the humiliation and sacrifice of the king, his rising from the tomb after three days to be proclaimed as the god victorious over death and worthy to rule forever."

[86]See, e.g., 2 Thes. 2: 3-4.

for our transgressions, he was bruised for our iniquities: the chastisement of our peace was upon him; and with his stripes we are healed." (Isa. 53: 4-5.) For us, when our street clothing is replaced by white garments we are symbolically covered by His body which He gave for us. When we don a Temple bonnet, it symbolizes a future crown given by God to those who follow Him. When anointed and washed, we receive blessings of infinite duration. For Him, the cruelty of His Roman guards was a bitter mockery of the ordinances of eternal life.

Matthew's account continues:

> And as they came out, they found a man of Cyrene, Simon by name: him they compelled to bear his cross. And when they were come unto a place called Golgotha, that is to say, a place of a skull, They gave him vinegar to drink mingled with gall: and when he had tasted thereof, he would not drink. (Matt. 27: 32-34.)

Matthew tells us Simon's name and where he came from. Mark adds: "they compel one Simon a Cyrenian, who passed by, coming out of the country, the father of Alexander and Rufus, to bear his cross." (Mark 15: 21.) These details let us know Simon was no stranger to Christ's disciples who wrote the Gospels. Luke adds that Simon was "a Cyrenian, coming out of the country," a detail which tells us Simon was on his way to the Passover when he overtook the crucifixion assembly, and was enlisted to carry the cross. (Luke 23: 26.) Only John does not mention Simon on the walk to Golgotha.

Simon's involvement was because of Christ's physical distress. Not only had He suffered infinite, debilitating agony in Gethsemene, but the Roman abuse and scourging that followed had also taken a terrible toll. He struggled as He tried to carry the cross on which He would die.

The drink of vinegar and gall was a sedative designed to dull the pain of crucifixion. It was the one tiny mercy given by Romans to their condemned victims. However, when Christ "had tasted thereof, he would not drink." He would do nothing to mitigate His suffering.

Matthew continues:

> And they crucified him, and parted his garments, casting lots: that it might be fulfilled which was spoken by the prophet, They parted my garments among them, and upon my vesture did they cast lots. And sitting down they watched him there; And set up over his head his accusation written, THIS IS JESUS THE KING OF THE JEWS. Then were there two thieves crucified with him, one on the right hand, and another on the left. And they that passed by reviled him, wagging their heads, (Matt. 27: 35-39.)

The first time the Roman guards stripped Him they replaced His clothing with a scarlet robe of mock royalty. This time they left Him naked. His clothing was divided among them as the normal payment given to those who served in this grim duty. Once the clothing had been distributed, they watched "**[H]im**" even though "two thieves crucified with him, one on the right hand, and another on the left" were also present. Christ compelled their attention. His demeanor, countenance and presence made Him the central figure on that day. Even in this dreadful circumstance He was kingly.

As was customary, Christ's "accusation" was set over his head. This served as reminder to anyone who saw the indictment, and the malefactor's sentence of crucifixion, to remain obedient. In the case of the Lord, however, the accusation was a proclamation that Christ was "KING OF THE JEWS," a charge which the chief priests and scribes disputed. John recorded their attempt to change the writing:

> And Pilate wrote a title, and put it on the cross. And the writing was, JESUS OF NAZARETH THE KING OF THE JEWS. This title then read many of the Jews: for the place where Jesus was crucified was nigh to the city: and it was written in Hebrew, and Greek, and Latin. Then said the chief priests of the Jews to Pilate, Write not, The King of the Jews; but that he said, I am King of the Jews. Pilate answered, What I have written I have written. (John 19: 19-22.)

Pilate would not change the title. It was, in fact, correct.

We have already discussed in the chapter titled "Bookends" the taunting directed at Christ while He hung on the cross. The public shame of this form of death always inspired critics to abuse the condemned criminal. In Christ's case, there was also the self-righteous anger from an offended, religious hierarchy which motivated their cruel remarks. The mob-mentality spread to other spectators who decided to add to the mockery.

In the midst of this chorus of insults the Lord did something remarkable. After enduring three hours of their abuse He cried out in a loud voice, to be heard above the voices of the ignorant crowd:

> Now from the sixth hour there was darkness over all the land unto the ninth hour. And about the ninth hour Jesus cried with a loud voice, saying, Eli, Eli, lama sabachthani? that is to say, My God, my God, why hast thou forsaken me? (Matt. 45-46.)

This statement by Christ has been long misunderstood and the subject of endless speculation. What Christ shouted, however, was unmistakable to those present. After all He had endured, it would have required a great effort for Him to cry out with a loud voice. His hoarse cry from the cross still rang out in the familiar words and tune from the great Messianic Psalm. His cry called attention to the prophecy which was at that very moment being fulfilled. Christ was bearing testimony that He was the Messiah, and that this sacrifice and suffering was necessary. Those who heard the first words of the Psalm would have been able to complete it in their own minds. He did not need to go any further than the opening line. The Psalm He shouted out to the crowd says, among other things:

> **My God, my God, why hast thou forsaken me?** why art thou so far from helping me, and from the words of my roaring? O my God, I cry in the daytime, but thou hearest not; and in the night season, and am not silent. But thou art holy, O thou that inhabitest the praises of Israel. Our fathers trusted in thee: they trusted, and thou didst deliver them. They cried unto thee, and were delivered: they trusted in thee, and were not confounded. But **I am a worm, and no man; a reproach of men, and despised of the people. All they that see me laugh me to scorn: they shoot out the lip, they shake the head, saying, He trusted on the Lord that he would deliver him: let him deliver him, seeing he delighted in him.** But thou art he that took me out of the womb: thou didst make me hope when I was upon my mother's breasts. I was cast upon thee from the womb: thou art my God from my mother's belly. **Be not far from me; for trouble is near; for there is none to help.** Many bulls have compassed me: strong bulls of Bashan have beset me round.

> **They gaped upon me with their mouths**, as a ravening and a roaring lion. **I am poured out like water, and all my bones are out of joint**: my heart is like wax; it is melted in the midst of my bowels. **My strength is dried up like a potsherd; and my tongue cleaveth to my jaws; and thou hast brought me into the dust of death. For dogs have compassed me: the assembly of the wicked have inclosed me: they pierced my hands and my feet.** I may tell all my bones: **they look and stare upon me. They part my garments among them, and cast lots upon my vesture.** But be not thou far from me, O Lord: O my strength, haste thee to help me. Deliver my soul from the sword; my darling from the power of the dog... **I will declare thy name unto my brethren: in the midst of the congregation will I praise thee.** Ye that fear the Lord, praise him; all ye the seed of Jacob, glorify him; and fear him, all ye the seed of Israel. For he hath not despised nor abhorred the affliction of the afflicted; neither hath he hid his face from him; but when he cried unto him, he heard. My praise shall be of thee in the great congregation: I will pay my vows before them that fear him... **They shall come, and shall declare his righteousness unto a people that shall be born, that he hath done this**. (Ps. 22: 1-20, 22-25, 31, emphasis added.)

These were familiar words of a well-known Psalm. Christ reminded those who heard Him that this terrible scene was foreknown and foretold. When He cried out in a loud voice, He knew who He was. He knew the importance of this sacrifice. More importantly, He knew His public shame, the reproach, "laughter to scorn," "shooting out the lip," "shaking of the head," and declaration that "He trusted God to deliver Him so let God now deliver Him," was all part of His messianic burden.

Those who heard His cry also knew from the Psalm they were acting the part of the ungodly, the unrighteous persecutors of the Messiah. Christ's shout: "My God, my God, why hast thou forsaken me?" was perhaps His single greatest declaration of His true identity. If the chief priests and scribes wondered whether Christ believed in His messiahship, they got their answer. He knew who He was. He shouted it out even as He finished His suffering.

Luke records shortly after this first shout, Christ cried out again in a loud voice, but he does not report what was said. (Luke 23: 46.) John tells us what He said. He shouted: "It is finished!" (John 19: 30.)

The Roman guards would have known what these words meant. It was the cry of triumph. It was the declaration of victory. When battles were won, "It is finished!" was the victor's shout. It signaled the time for killing had ended and surrender was secured. It was Christ's declaration that the battle was over, and victory secured!

These loud declarations by the crucified and suffering Lord tell us there was absolutely no confusion, no doubt, no uncertainty by Him as He completed the final agony of His assigned ministry. He knew full well who He was, even if those present doubted. He proclaimed His status as Messiah, the necessity of His suffering, and His victory loudly, boldly, and without any hint of doubt or regret. Here was a God indeed. Here was victory by a noble, determined, suffering God.

Then, having won the greatest victory of the ages, sensing at last the end of His ordeal, He quietly spoke His final words to His Father: "Father, into thy hands I commend my spirit." (Luke 23: 46.) The Romans, and a few close by heard the quiet comment to His Father then saw Him die. Those present would never be able to erase their memory of that day. Even those responsible for His crucifixion had to be awed by what He did and said at the end. Even in death, He remained certain, even in control, as He voluntarily permitted them to abuse Him. He put the whole ordeal into the scriptural context of the suffering Messiah foretold in the 22nd Psalm. He shouted out His vision of the role He played, never doubting the rightness of all He did, all He was doing, all He was suffering. The Roman guards could not contain their admiration of this great soul. They knew this was no ordinary man. The Jewish crowd was filled with regret:

> Now when the centurion saw what was done, he glorified God, saying, Certainly this was a righteous man. And all the people that came together to that sight, beholding the things which were done, smote their breasts, and returned. (Luke 23: 47-48.)

Matthew described it in these words:

> Now when the centurion, and they that were with him, watching Jesus, saw the earthquake, and those things that were done, they feared greatly, saying, Truly this was the Son of God. And many women were there beholding afar off, which followed Jesus from Galilee, ministering unto him: Among which was Mary Magdalene, and Mary the mother of James and Joses, and the mother of Zebedee's children. (Matt. 27: 54-56.)

Those who saw the grace of Christ on the cross, who heard Him cry out the beginning of the 22nd Psalm, who heard Him shout the victory shout, "It is finished!", and who then witnessed His quiet passing from life, marveled at this King of the Jews. They smote their breasts. The Roman centurion concluded this was the Son of God. Because we know of His subsequent resurrection, we fail to notice the power of His testimony and example on the cross. He was certain of His calling to pass through this ordeal. He knew exactly the prophecy which described best the manner of His suffering. He reminded all who were present of that prophetic Psalm that foretold this very hour of His suffering. It foretold the details of piercing His hands and feet, the taunting that He had saved others, let Him save Himself, parting His garments, and looking upon Him as accursed. To those present, or to us if we can take it in, this was all intended as a powerful testimony to us that He was our Messiah, our Savior, the Lamb of God. Whenever we ignore the power of this Man's example and words while in the extremity of this dying sacrifice, we miss some of the greatest evidence of His true identity. The centurion was right: "of a truth, He was the Son of God."

His death was followed immediately by an earthquake in Jerusalem, and a much greater disturbance of the land on the American continent.[87] Truly the God of Nature suffered death that day. (See, 1 Ne. 19: 12.)

A significant result of the earthquake at Jerusalem was that the veil inside the Temple was torn. This opened the view of the Holy of Holies. The only time the Holy of Holies was visited was once a year, on the Day of Atonement. On that occasion the blood of the Atonement sacrifice was sprinkled before the symbolic presence of God. On this day, however, was the real atoning sacrifice; it was no longer just ritual. No priest would take His blood into the Holy of Holies and sprinkle it there. Instead, at the moment Christ completed the sacrifice, the Holy of Holies opened to acknowledge His blood. Matt. 27: 51reports: "And, behold, the veil of the temple was rent in twain from the top to the bottom;

---

[87] See 3 Ne. 8, beginning at verse 5 for an account.

and the earth did quake, and the rocks rent[.]"[88] Symbolically, this completed the ceremony on the Day of Atonement, as God acknowledged the blood of the slain sacrifice. On this day, however, the symbol of the ritual inside the Holy of Holies was the lesser event. God the Father had already openly witnessed the sacrifice of His Son, and had openly accepted His sacrifice. Opening up the veil of the Temple was yet another Divine witness that Christ was the true sacrifice to which the Day of Atonement ceremony had always pointed.

Although the Jewish leaders were willing to have Him crucified, they did not want His body to remain on the cross overnight. It would be a religious offense, because as we saw in Deuteronomy at the beginning of this chapter, the body of one killed on a tree was required to be buried "that day; (for he that is hanged is accursed of God;) that thy land be not defiled."(Deu. 21: 22-23.) So even those who were unable to see He was the Son of God, were still controlled by their religious beliefs to take His body down on the same day. They were willing to reject their Lord, but did not want His death to defile their land. Clearly they were devoted to their false religion. As John explains:

> The Jews therefore, because it was the preparation, that the bodies should not remain upon the cross on the sabbath day, (for that sabbath day was an high day,) besought Pilate that their legs might be broken, and that they might be taken away. Then came the soldiers, and brake the legs of the first, and of the other which was crucified with him. But when they came to Jesus, and saw that he was dead

---

[88] Luke also records the veil being rent: "And it was about the sixth hour, and there was a darkness over all the earth until the ninth hour. And the sun was darkened, and the veil of the temple was rent in the midst." (Luke 23: 44-45.)

> already, they brake not his legs: But one of the soldiers with a spear pierced his side, and forthwith came there out blood and water. And he that saw it bare record, and his record is true: and he knoweth that he saith true, that ye might believe. For these things were done, that the scripture should be fulfilled, A bone of him shall not be broken. And again another scripture saith, They shall look on him whom they pierced. And after this Joseph of Arimathaea, being a disciple of Jesus, but secretly for fear of the Jews, besought Pilate that he might take away the body of Jesus: and Pilate gave him leave. He came therefore, and took the body of Jesus. (John 19: 31-38.)

To avoid profaning the high holy day associated with Passover, the bodies of all three condemned men needed to come down from their crosses. It was the Jewish leaders who, for religious reasons, asked for the legs of them all to be broken.

There is something more sinister here, however. Given John's reference to the scripture that required not a bone of his body to be broken,[89] the request from the leaders was likely made as a pretext to deny that Christ was the one foreshadowed by the ritual of the Pascal lamb. Christ had just shouted out the beginning words of the 22nd Psalm. These leaders may not have believed on Him, but they certainly understood the scriptures and what they foretold about Him. Therefore the request to break the legs to avoid profaning the high holy day was a ruse to break the bones of the Son of God. By doing so, they could distinguish Jesus in death from the requirements for a Pascal lamb. They needed His bones to be broken.

---

[89]See the description of the Pascal Lamb in Ex 12: 46 and Num. 9: 12 which required Israelites to not break a bone of the sacrifice.

When the order came to break the legs, Christ was already dead. The other two victims were not so fortunate. The Roman guards bludgeoned their shins to break the lower bones. Breathing was difficult for the crucified. It was necessary to push up with the legs to free the constriction of the chest in order to inhale. When the Roman guards broke the two thieves' legs, it stopped them from straightening upward using the cross' support, to gasp for more breath. After the legs were broken, the thieves would have expired from suffocation in just a few minutes.

Christ was already dead. His arms were up-stretched, His head was bowed, His knees bent as if kneeling. The resting position into which His lifeless body settled looked to all who saw it as if He were in the act of worship of His Father. It not only looked so, it was so: He suffered the will of the Father in all things from the beginning. (3 Ne. 11: 11.) His final mortal act was an act of devotion, and when His lifeless body appeared to be worshiping, it was not merely a sign, but also His dying testimony. It should make us adore Him all the more for what He did and who He was. Throughout the ordeal He was proclaiming with confidence who He was. By what He suffered He was declaring how very much He loves us.

There was no need to break His legs, but to make certain He was dead His side was speared. Roman soldiers were well enough acquainted with their tools of combat to know how to strike a fatal blow. With a single thrust the spear-tip penetrated into the heart. Were He still alive that stab would have killed Him. His lifeless body did not react to the spear. Blood and water ran out of the wound. His broken heart was no longer beating. What little blood remained was already coagulating in His corpse.

When His death was certain and known, Joseph of Arimathaea, a member of the Sanhedrin, and a secret disciple, asked for Christ's body. Pilate consented, and Joseph took Christ's body for burial. In Luke's account we are informed that Joseph had not consented to the council's decision to have Christ killed (indeed he had been excluded from the decision):

> And, behold, there was a man named Joseph, a counsellor; and he was a good man, and a just: **(The same had not consented to the counsel and deed of them;)** he was of Arimathaea, a city of the Jews: who also himself waited for the kingdom of God. This man went unto Pilate, and begged the body of Jesus. And he took it down, and wrapped it in linen, and laid it in a sepulchre that was hewn in stone, wherein never man before was laid. (Luke 23: 50-53, emphasis added.)

Joseph carried the body to the unused tomb. There the tortured, lifeless body of the Lamb of God was placed in the earth. A proper preparation would be delayed until after the Sabbath, but by that time it became unnecessary.

From Gethsemene to Golgotha, Christ paid a dreadful price to redeem mankind. We are the beneficiaries. The events of those terrible hours are humbling to ponder. When the scriptures finally record His death, we are relieved. The agony, intentional brutality, public humiliation and insults He endured are shocking no matter how familiar we are with the story. This awful price purchased our resurrection and opened the door for our return to the Father. Surely He is worthy not only of our gratitude, but also our adoration.

Chapter 14

Resurrection

I hope you will pardon the personal nature of this chapter. When it comes to a discussion of the resurrection, I cannot avoid bearing personal testimony of Christ.[90] When I saw His resurrection, I was surprised to see it was still dark. I had always thought it occurred at sun up, as the return of daylight symbolized the return of life. But it was dark. The Gospel of John is the only one which records the darkness of that morning.[91] Even so, it never registered with me that Christ rose in the darkness of that early morning.

---

[90]All of this book is a personal testimony. However some comments are so obviously personal that they can interrupt the flow. It is the obvious personal nature of parts of this chapter for which I make an apology to the reader. By the time you get to the end of the chapter you will see this is about you, as the reader, and not me, as the writer.

[91]John 20: 1: "The first day of the week cometh Mary Magdalene early, when it was yet dark, unto the sepulchre, and seeth the stone taken away from the sepulchre."

In the spring of 2009, I went in the early morning while it was still dark to the Jordan River Temple to attend a session for one of my ancestors. As I walked from the parking lot toward the front of the building I noticed how the birds were all singing. It was dark, so they remained on their nighttime perches inside the trees providing them cover. It would have been dangerous for them to attempt flight in the dark, so they remained motionless. But they sang. All of them were chirping, whistling, singing out with such a combined chorus that I had to stop and listen. It was striking. They seemed so joyful, even enthusiastic.

I stood there on the northern sidewalk adjacent to the Jordan River Temple and took in this loud, joyful sound. I wondered why they were so filled with song while it was still dark and they were still confined to their trees.

"Perhaps," I thought, "it is because they knew another day was coming. And, after all, if I could fly every time daylight returned I would be happy to awake and contemplate the coming flight." As I mused over the birds it struck me - this was the time of morning when the Lord rose from the dead! This was the moment, when it is yet dark, but the day will soon break forth, when He returned to life! This morning chorus coincided with that event. I thought it is certainly true that, as Moses wrote and Joseph Smith restored:

> And behold, ... all things are created and made to bear record of me, both things which are temporal, and things which are spiritual; things which are in the heavens above, and things which are on the earth, and things which are in the earth, and things which are under the earth, both above and beneath: all things bear record of me. (Moses 6: 63.)

Since that morning outside the Jordan River Temple, I have not heard the birds sing out in an early morning, while it is yet dark, without the instant recognition and conviction they are bearing witness to the moment at which the Lord arose from the dead. He did rise from the dead. We rejoice because it is true. As so many others have done before, I can add my own witness that He rose from the dead. I was shown it. It happened. He who died on the cross rose from the dead and He lives still.

The witnesses of Christ's resurrection have been plentiful. Some of them will be discussed in this chapter. If they were all discussed it would take a book devoted to that subject alone. I will not mention more than a few. The earliest witnesses of Christ's resurrection are described in the Four Gospels of the New Testament. Matthew's account says the following:

> In the end of the sabbath, as it began to dawn toward the first day of the week, came Mary Magdalene and the other Mary to see the sepulchre. And, behold, there was a great earthquake: for the angel of the Lord descended from heaven, and came and rolled back the stone from the door, and sat upon it. His countenance was like lightning, and his raiment white as snow: And for fear of him the keepers did shake, and became as dead men. And the angel answered and said unto the women, Fear not ye: for I know that ye seek Jesus, which was crucified. He is not here: for he is risen, as he said. Come, see the place where the Lord lay. And go quickly, and tell his disciples that he is risen from the dead; and, behold, he goeth before you into Galilee; there shall ye see him: lo, I have told you. And they departed quickly from the sepulchre with fear and great joy; and did run to bring his disciples word. And as they went to tell his disciples, behold, Jesus met them, saying, All hail. And they came and held

> him by the feet, and worshipped him. Then said Jesus unto them, Be not afraid: go tell my brethren that they go into Galilee, and there shall they see me. (Matt. 28: 1-10.)

This description includes physical events which happened at the moment of Christ's rising. The earthquake, stone door of the sepulchre moved, an angelic presence whose countenance was "like lightning," intimidated the guards, and a message stated Christ has risen from the dead all occurred. We know that the Lord's resurrection was not limited to the verbal report from believers, but also included these physical events as well. The movement of the stone door was so incontestible an event that the Jewish leadership paid a bribe to the disabled guards so they would accuse Christ's followers of having moved the stone.[92] The payment of the bribe is evidence the stone was actually moved and the body of Christ was actually missing. Through this act the chief priests and scribes inadvertently also bear witness of Christ's resurrection.

Two women were the first witnesses to learn He had risen from the dead. The news spread quickly, and many other witnesses joined in before that day ended.

Mark wrote this account:

> And when the sabbath was past, Mary Magdalene, and Mary the mother of James, and Salome, had bought sweet spices, that they might come and

---

[92]See Matt. 28: 11- 15: "Now when they were going, behold, some of the watch came into the city, and shewed unto the chief priests all the things that were done. And when they were assembled with the elders, and had taken counsel, they gave large money unto the soldiers, Saying, Say ye, His disciples came by night, and stole him away while we slept. And if this come to the governor's ears, we will persuade him, and secure you. So they took the money, and did as they were taught: and this saying is commonly reported among the Jews until this day."

> anoint him. And very early in the morning the first day of the week, they came unto the sepulchre at the rising of the sun. And they said among themselves, Who shall roll us away the stone from the door of the sepulchre? And when they looked, they saw that the stone was rolled away: for it was very great. And entering into the sepulchre, they saw a young man sitting on the right side, clothed in a long white garment; and they were affrighted. And he saith unto them, Be not affrighted: Ye seek Jesus of Nazareth, which was crucified: he is risen; he is not here: behold the place where they laid him. But go your way, tell his disciples and Peter that he goeth before you into Galilee: there shall ye see him, as he said unto you. And they went out quickly, and fled from the sepulchre; for they trembled and were amazed: neither said they any thing to any man; for they were afraid. Now when Jesus was risen early the first day of the week, he appeared first to Mary Magdalene, out of whom he had cast seven devils. And she went and told them that had been with him, as they mourned and wept. And they, when they had heard that he was alive, and had been seen of her, believed not. (Mark 16: 1-11.)

In this account the two women wondered how they could anoint the body since the stone door was in place. But as they arrived they saw it had been opened. Looking inside they saw a "young man" who was clothed in "a long white garment." His assignment was apparently to greet the women, testify to them that Christ was risen and show them the place from which He arose. Mark clarifies that Mary Magdalene was the first to see Him.

In Luke we read:

> Now upon the first day of the week, very early in the morning, they came unto the sepulchre, bringing the spices which they had prepared, and

> certain others with them. And they found the stone rolled away from the sepulchre. And they entered in, and found not the body of the Lord Jesus. And it came to pass, as they were much perplexed thereabout, behold, two men stood by them in shining garments: And as they were afraid, and bowed down their faces to the earth, they said unto them, Why seek ye the living among the dead? He is not here, but is risen: remember how he spake unto you when he was yet in Galilee, Saying, The Son of man must be delivered into the hands of sinful men, and be crucified, and the third day rise again. And they remembered his words, And returned from the sepulchre, and told all these things unto the eleven, and to all the rest. It was Mary Magdalene, and Joanna, and Mary the mother of James, and other women that were with them, which told these things unto the apostles. And their words seemed to them as idle tales, and they believed them not. Then arose Peter, and ran unto the sepulchre; and stooping down, he beheld the linen clothes laid by themselves, and departed, wondering in himself at that which was come to pass. (Luke 24: 1-12.)

Again we see the women who came first to the sepulchre were the first witnesses. The Apostles initially learned second-hand that He had arisen.

> The first day of the week cometh Mary Magdalene early, when it was yet dark, unto the sepulchre, and seeth the stone taken away from the sepulchre. Then she runneth, and cometh to Simon Peter, and to the other disciple, whom Jesus loved, and saith unto them, They have taken away the Lord out of the sepulchre, and we know not where they have laid him. Peter therefore went forth, and that other disciple, and came to the sepulchre. So they ran both together: and the other disciple did outrun

> Peter, and came first to the sepulchre. And he stooping down, and looking in, saw the linen clothes lying; yet went he not in. Then cometh Simon Peter following him, and went into the sepulchre, and seeth the linen clothes lie, And the napkin, that was about his head, not lying with the linen clothes, but wrapped together in a place by itself. Then went in also that other disciple, which came first to the sepulchre, and he saw, and believed. For as yet they knew not the scripture, that he must rise again from the dead. Then the disciples went away again unto their own home. But Mary stood without at the sepulchre weeping: and as she wept, she stooped down, and looked into the sepulchre, And seeth two angels in white sitting, the one at the head, and the other at the feet, where the body of Jesus had lain. And they say unto her, Woman, why weepest thou? She saith unto them, Because they have taken away my Lord, and I know not where they have laid him. And when she had thus said, she turned herself back, and saw Jesus standing, and knew not that it was Jesus. Jesus saith unto her, Woman, why weepest thou? whom seekest thou? She, supposing him to be the gardener, saith unto him, Sir, if thou have borne him hence, tell me where thou hast laid him, and I will take him away. Jesus saith unto her, Mary. She turned herself, and saith unto him, Rabboni; which is to say, Master. Jesus saith unto her, Touch me not; for I am not yet ascended to my Father: but go to my brethren, and say unto them, I ascend unto my Father, and your Father; and to my God, and your God. Mary Magdalene came and told the disciples that she had seen the Lord, and that he had spoken these things unto her. (John 20: 1-18.)

In this account Peter and John, two of the Apostles, ran to the tomb after hearing He has risen. They see it is empty, but the Lord did not appear to them. Christ does not appear to Mary until after the Apostles left.

The accounts differ in the details. All four are set out to allow us to consider their similarities and differences. They are universal in the fact that Christ was seen by the women (or woman) first, and not by His Apostles. The last account, quoted immediately above, records that Christ told Mary: "Touch me not." In the Joseph Smith translation the words are changed to read: "Hold me not." (JST-John 20: 17.) Joseph's change of the text was warranted.

When Mary realized it was Jesus, she embraced Him joyfully. She did not timidly reach out her hand, but she readily greeted Him with open arms, and He, in turn, embraced her. It is difficult to describe what I saw of the incident, apart from saying the Lord was triumphant, exultant, overjoyed at His return from the grave! She shared His joy. I was shown the scene and do not have words to adequately communicate how complete the feelings of joy and gratitude were which were felt by our Lord that morning. As dark and terrible were the sufferings through which He passed, the magnitude of which is impossible for man to put into words, these feelings of triumph were, on the other hand, of equal magnitude in their joy and gratitude. I do not think it possible for a mortal to feel a fullness of either. And, having felt some of what He shares with His witnesses, I know words are inadequate to capture His feelings on the morning of His resurrection. He had the deep satisfaction of having accomplished the most difficult assignment given by the Father, knowing it was a benefit to all of His Father's children, and it had been done perfectly.

Mary and Christ embraced. There was nothing timid about the warm encounter she had with Him. Then He said to her, "Hold me not" because He had to ascend, return and report to His Father.

Joseph Smith was correct when he revised this language. I then saw Him ascend to heaven. I saw the golden heavenly light glowing down upon Mary as she watched His ascent. All this happened while it was yet dark on the morning He rose from the dead. He has shown this to me and I can testify to it as a witness.

On the morning of the resurrection Christ appeared in this order: First, to Mary adjacent to the Garden Tomb. (Mark 16: 9-10; John 20: 14.) Next, He appeared to His mother, who was in company with several other women at the time. (Matt. 28: 9.)

Later in the day He spent several hours in the company of two disciples (Cleopas and likely Luke) and walked with them from Jerusalem to Emmaus. After the walk, He joined them for the blessing of the evening meal, and then He departed. (Mark 16: 12; Luke 24: 13-33.)[93] Next, He appeared to Peter at Jerusalem. (Luke 24: 34.) Then He appeared to a gathering of ten of the Twelve Apostles and an unidentified group of others who were assembled with them in Jerusalem. (Luke 24: 33-45.)

A week after this, He appeared to all eleven of the surviving Twelve Apostles in Jerusalem as they were eating the dinner meal together. (Mark 16: 14; John 20: 26-29.) He told the Apostles to go to Galilee and meet Him there, where He then met with them beside the Sea of Galilee. (John 21: 1-24.) The eleven were told to go to a nearby mountain top where He visited with them again. (Matt. 28: 16.) Next, He appeared to a larger group numbering more than five-hundred on a hilltop near Jerusalem. The Apostle Paul reported of this appearance in a letter written more than two

---

[93] I have written about this incident at length in the Appendix to *Eighteen Verses*. None of that material will be repeated here. If interested, an explanation of what this event revealed about the Risen Lord, can be found in that discussion.

decades later. (1 Cor. 15: 6.) Then He was seen by James at an unspecified place and time. (1 Cor. 15: 7.) Next, at the time of His final ascension, He appeared to a gathering that included eleven of the Twelve Apostles. (Mark 16: 19; Luke 24: 50-51.)

Months after this, at some unspecified time, He appeared to Stephen as he was being stoned for his testimony of Christ as the Son of God. Stephen saw the Father in the same vision, and was so filled with love by the experience that he forgave his killers while they were in the act of stoning him. (Acts 7: 54-60.)

Weeks later, He appeared to Saul of Tarsus, an enemy of the Church He had founded, as Saul was on a road leading to Damascus. (Acts 9: 1-9.) Christ's final appearance in the New Testament came many decades later, to John while on the Isle of Patmos. (Rev. 1: 10-18.)

His appearances probably had an order and purpose. It is likely they reflected relationships in their order of importance. Since the family is eternal, and Church callings are only temporary, and of this world, His first appearances were to members of His own, immediate family. After His immediate family, He then appeared to two disciples, neither of whom were one of the Twelve Apostles. We do not know why they were given that priority, but the fact they were should not be ignored. It suggests that Church office may not establish the priority some of us may think it does. Although He arose early in the morning, these first three visits lasted until late in the evening, did not include any of the Twelve Apostles, and clearly demonstrate to all who understand the scriptures that there has never been a time when the Lord honored any hierarchy to the exclusion of others who believe in and follow Him. All are equal before Him.

It was well into the evening of the first day before any member of His surviving Apostles saw Him. When He did appear, He first came to Peter, the Chief Apostle. This shows that inside the hierarchy the Lord does respect the order of priority He has established. After appearing to Peter, He soon appeared at a meeting in which ten of the Twelve (again including Peter) were present, along with several other unidentified individuals which likely included both women and men.

Over the forty days of His post-resurrection ministry, He clearly made an effort to teach His Twelve Apostles in repeated meetings with them. The mountain top ministry, in which sacred rites were likely communicated, included sessions with both the Twelve (on two occasions) and others, including one company of over five-hundred.

When Stephen saw the resurrected Christ, he also saw the Father with Him. The fact that he saw Christ and the Father at the time of his martyrdom as he was dying for the testimony of Christ was significant. The Father appearing is also in itself important. The Father has limited involvement with mankind, but when He does appear it is oftentimes connected with accepting someone as His son.[94] With Stephen, the vision was accompanied by an outpouring of love which allowed him to offer genuine forgiveness and make an intercessory prayer for his executioners. Considered as a whole, it compels the conclusion that Stephen was given the promise of eternal life in that vision. Although not fully recorded,

[94]The Messianic Psalm referring to the Father's confession of Christ as Son, found in Psalms 2: 7, is something which is not limited to Christ, but also includes "many sons" of God. (See John 1: 12; Rom. 8: 14 and Heb. 2: 10.) These are all sons of God who "can cry: Abba, Father!" (*TPJS*, p. 374.)

it contains elements which are clear enough to make this an appropriate, if not inevitable, conclusion.[95]

The appearance to Saul of Tarsus, later known as the Apostle Paul, reveals yet another profound truth about the Lord's appearances. Christ did not consult with, or give any warning to His Chief Apostle Peter, or any of the Twelve when He visited with Saul. They were genuinely surprised to learn of Saul/Paul's conversion. They initially feared him and had to have Barnabas vouch for him before they would allow him into their presence. (Acts 9: 26-28.) It is clear the Lord independently appears and ministers to people who have absolutely no association with the leadership of His Church. Indeed, in the case of Saul/Paul He chose to appear to a person the Church found repugnant, an enemy, a zealous persecutor and an unbeliever. The man He chose, however, would in time produce two-thirds of the books of the New Testament to document Christ's Dispensation of the Meridian of Time, more than any other single writer. Therefore, only in hindsight can we see the wisdom of the Lord in making His appearance to this unlikely witness.

From all the above it should also be clear the Lord is not only "no respecter of persons," and is willing to appear to any, but that efforts to confine His New Testament appearances and post-resurrection work to a hierarchical structure simply is not true. Because He is the same yesterday, today and forever, we should never limit the Lord's prerogative to appear to whomever He decides. When we presume to limit the Lord's ability to act as He will, call witnesses who please Him, appear to women as He

---

[95]The elements referred to are discussed in *Beloved Enos* for any reader who would like to understand this subject more fully.

wishes, or reveal great truths to any who seek Him, we are contradicting His clear pattern of past conduct. We know He honors those who have sacrificed for Him. These people have qualified to see both the Father and the Son. Since the Lord is always the same, we should not attempt to circumscribe His hand.

After the appearances around Jerusalem and Galilee[96] comprising His forty-day ministry, He departed. Even though He would make other appearances as noted above, His Apostles were given the burden of carrying forward the work of His Church. He had other forty-day ministries among other chosen sheep. We do not know the number, nor the locations of all the "other sheep" He went to visit after His ascension in the land of Jerusalem. Although we have no record to confirm His other visits, it is likely one of the places He visited first was the land from which the "wise men" came, approximately two years travel distance from Jerusalem.

We do know that approximately eleven months after His resurrection, He came to minister to the Nephites who kept a record of His visit. That record was restored to us through the Prophet Joseph Smith. From the Nephite record, we learn a great deal about the Lord's teachings during His forty-day ministry. We also learn that He continues to make appearances throughout the world to scattered bodies of believing Israelites. These Israelites were lost to the knowledge of those in Jerusalem. Although "lost sheep" may be unknown to each other, they were always known to God.

Concerning this worldwide duty to make appearances, Christ explained to the Nephites:

---

[96]See Acts 1: 3.

Ye are my disciples; and ye are a light unto this people, who are a remnant of the house of Joseph. And behold, this is the land of your inheritance; and the Father hath given it unto you. And not at any time hath the Father given me commandment that I should tell it unto your brethren at Jerusalem. Neither at any time hath the Father given me commandment that I should tell unto them concerning the other tribes of the house of Israel, whom the Father hath led away out of the land. This much did the Father command me, that I should tell unto them: That other sheep I have which are not of this fold; them also I must bring, and they shall hear my voice; and there shall be one fold, and one shepherd. And now, because of stiffneckedness and unbelief they understood not my word; therefore I was commanded to say no more of the Father concerning this thing unto them. But, verily, I say unto you that the Father hath commanded me, and I tell it unto you, that **ye were separated from among them because of their iniquity**; therefore it is because of their iniquity that they know not of you. And verily, I say unto you again that the other tribes hath the Father separated from them; and it is because of their iniquity that they know not of them. And verily I say unto you, that **ye are they of whom I said: Other sheep I have which are not of this fold; them also I must bring, and they shall hear my voice; and there shall be one fold, and one shepherd**. And they understood me not, for they supposed it had been the Gentiles; for they understood not that the Gentiles should be converted through their preaching. And they understood me not that I said they shall hear my voice; and they understood me not that the Gentiles should not at any time hear my voice--that I should not manifest myself unto them save it were by the Holy Ghost. But behold, ye have both

> heard my voice, and seen me; and ye are my sheep, and ye are numbered among those whom the Father hath given me. **And verily, verily, I say unto you that I have other sheep, which are not of this land, neither of the land of Jerusalem, neither in any parts of that land round about whither I have been to minister. For they of whom I speak are they who have not as yet heard my voice; neither have I at any time manifested myself unto them. But I have received a commandment of the Father that I shall go unto them, and that they shall hear my voice, and shall be numbered among my sheep, that there may be one fold and one shepherd; therefore I go to show myself unto them.** (3 Ne. 15: 12-16: 3, emphasis added.)

The post-resurrection ministry of the Lord continued for at least a year. His crucifixion occurred on the first month, fourth day, as the Nephites reckoned their calendar. (3 Ne. 8: 5.) But it was not until "the ending of the thirty and fourth year" that Christ appeared to the Nephites. (3 Ne. 10: 18.) Assuming the Lord's ministry was more or less continuous, He could have visited as many as eight bodies of believing Israelites or "other sheep" during this time, before coming to the Nephites. This would make ten bodies of His sheep, including Jerusalem and the Nephites. We are left to wonder if His use of the number ten in the parable of the woman and her silver (Luke 15: 8-10), the ten servants (Luke 19: 12-27), which included the reference to "ten cities" (Luke 19: 17) were intended to give us a hint of the number of His bodies of "lost sheep." We will know for certain when their records are finally restored to us. We are promised these records have been kept and will be restored in the due time of the Lord:

> For I command all men, both in the east and in the west, and in the north, and in the south, and in the islands of the sea, that they shall write the words which I speak unto them; for out of the books which shall be written I will judge the world, every man according to their works, according to that which is written. For behold, I shall speak unto the Jews and they shall write it; and I shall also speak unto the Nephites and they shall write it; and I shall also speak unto the other tribes of the house of Israel, which I have led away, and they shall write it; and I shall also speak unto all nations of the earth and they shall write it. And it shall come to pass that the Jews shall have the words of the Nephites, and the Nephites shall have the words of the Jews; and the Nephites and the Jews shall have the words of the lost tribes of Israel; and the lost tribes of Israel shall have the words of the Nephites and the Jews. And it shall come to pass that my people, which are of the house of Israel, shall be gathered home unto the lands of their possessions; and my word also shall be gathered in one. And I will show unto them that fight against my word and against my people, who are of the house of Israel, that I am God, and that I covenanted with Abraham that I would remember his seed forever. (2 Ne. 29: 11-14.)

We can safely assume, however, that the records of all these "lost sheep" will agree with each other. We can also know there are many witnesses of Christ's resurrection beyond those identified in the New Testament.

In our own day there have been witnesses of the resurrected Christ. The most notable witnesses and their words of testimony include Joseph Smith, who said in part:

> I retired to the woods to make the attempt. It was on the morning of a beautiful, clear day, early in

> the spring of eighteen hundred and twenty. It was the first time in my life that I had made such an attempt, for amidst all my anxieties I had never as yet made the attempt to pray vocally. After I had retired to the place where I had previously designed to go, having looked around me, and finding myself alone, I kneeled down and began to offer up the desires of my heart to God. I had scarcely done so, when immediately I was seized upon by some power which entirely overcame me, and had such an astonishing influence over me as to bind my tongue so that I could not speak. Thick darkness gathered around me, and it seemed to me for a time as if I were doomed to sudden destruction. But, exerting all my powers to call upon God to deliver me out of the power of this enemy which had seized upon me, and at the very moment when I was ready to sink into despair and abandon myself to destruction--not to an imaginary ruin, but to the power of some actual being from the unseen world, who had such marvelous power as I had never before felt in any being--just at this moment of great alarm, I saw a pillar of light exactly over my head, above the brightness of the sun, which descended gradually until it fell upon me. It no sooner appeared than I found myself delivered from the enemy which held me bound. When the light rested upon me I saw two Personages, whose brightness and glory defy all description, standing above me in the air. One of them spake unto me, calling me by name and said, pointing to the other--This is My Beloved Son. Hear Him! (JS-H 1: 14-17.)

Both Joseph Smith and Oliver Cowdrey were present during the appearance of the Resurrected Christ in the Kirtland Temple on April 3, 1836, and reported in part:

> The veil was taken from our minds, and the eyes of our understanding were opened. We saw the Lord standing upon the breastwork of the pulpit, before us; and under his feet was a paved work of pure gold, in color like amber. His eyes were as a flame of fire; the hair of his head was white like the pure snow; his countenance shone above the brightness of the sun; and his voice was as the sound of the rushing of great waters, even the voice of Jehovah, saying: I am the first and the last; I am he who liveth, I am he who was slain; I am your advocate with the Father. Behold, your sins are forgiven you; you are clean before me; therefore, lift up your heads and rejoice. Let the hearts of your brethren rejoice, and let the hearts of all my people rejoice, who have, with their might, built this house to my name. For behold, I have accepted this house, and my name shall be here; and I will manifest myself to my people in mercy in this house. (D&C 110: 1-7.)

Joseph Smith and Sidney Rigdon testified of an appearance of Christ to them on February 16, 1832, their testimony included in part:

> And now, after the many testimonies which have been given of him, this is the testimony, last of all, which we give of him: That he lives! For we saw him, even on the right hand of God; and we heard the voice bearing record that he is the Only Begotten of the Father--That by him, and through him, and of him, the worlds are and were created, and the inhabitants thereof are begotten sons and daughters unto God. (D&C 76: 22-24.)

Joseph F. Smith testified of seeing Christ in a vision given to him on October 3, 1918, which included among other things, the following description:

As I pondered over these things which are written, the eyes of my understanding were opened, and the Spirit of the Lord rested upon me, and I saw the hosts of the dead, both small and great. And there were gathered together in one place an innumerable company of the spirits of the just, who had been faithful in the testimony of Jesus while they lived in mortality; And who had offered sacrifice in the similitude of the great sacrifice of the Son of God, and had suffered tribulation in their Redeemer's name. All these had departed the mortal life, firm in the hope of a glorious resurrection, through the grace of God the Father and his Only Begotten Son, Jesus Christ. I beheld that they were filled with joy and gladness, and were rejoicing together because the day of their deliverance was at hand. They were assembled awaiting the advent of the Son of God into the spirit world, to declare their redemption from the bands of death. Their sleeping dust was to be restored unto its perfect frame, bone to his bone, and the sinews and the flesh upon them, the spirit and the body to be united never again to be divided, that they might receive a fulness of joy. While this vast multitude waited and conversed, rejoicing in the hour of their deliverance from the chains of death, the Son of God appeared, declaring liberty to the captives who had been faithful; And there he preached to them the everlasting gospel, the doctrine of the resurrection and the redemption of mankind from the fall, and from individual sins on conditions of repentance. But unto the wicked he did not go, and among the ungodly and the unrepentant who had defiled themselves while in the flesh, his voice was not raised; Neither did the rebellious who rejected the testimonies and the warnings of the ancient prophets behold his presence, nor look upon his face. Where these were, darkness reigned, but

> among the righteous there was peace; And the saints rejoiced in their redemption, and bowed the knee and acknowledged the Son of God as their Redeemer and Deliverer from death and the chains of hell. Their countenances shone, and the radiance from the presence of the Lord rested upon them, and they sang praises unto his holy name. (D&C 138: 11-24.)

There have been other appearances of Christ to His followers in this Dispensation, the accounts of which are both recorded and unrecorded. All these witnesses have been given to us so that we may believe. There are many living witnesses whose own testimonies are not public. Although I have disclosed some of what I have been shown I cannot tell all. I am merely a lay member of The Church of Jesus Christ of Latter-day Saints, with no authority or position of any significance. If I have a witness of the Lord's resurrection, certainly you can have the same. There is nothing significant about me. Further, I cannot compel you to believe me, but can truthfully testify of Him. Believe His promise to come to you and comfort you, and take up His abode with you. (John 14: 18-23.) Believe Him, because everybody is equally dependent upon Him for their hope of salvation. Never put your eternal salvation in the hands of anyone other than Jesus Christ, who paid to ransom you.

Belief based upon the testimony or witness of another should never satisfy you. You should press forward and obtain your own witness of your Risen Lord. Move into action, grow beyond belief, act in conformity to the things He has asked you, and develop faith. Use that faith to develop knowledge of Him. We proceed from belief to faith, and from faith to knowledge, by following the pattern of everyone who has seen Him. The conditions are no different for any of them and are no different for you.

My earlier book *The Second Comforter: Conversing With the Lord Through the Veil* is a description of the path these others have followed. If you are interested in taking that same journey, that book describes it.

Let me end this brief retelling of His resurrection with my own witness: He lives! I have seen Him. These testimonies of those who have had the opportunity to see Him are not fables, they are all true. I do not ask you to merely believe my account. Instead, I invite you to go obtain your own directly from Him. You, like the many witnesses referred to in this chapter, are entitled to come and know these things for yourself. Then you will not be dependent upon anyone else for knowledge which will both save you and assure you eternal life.

Chapter 15

Love: The Sign of Christ

Christ's love for us was apparent in everything He did. He lived, served, taught and died in an extended labor of love. What He did taught us how we should love one another.

Without charity we are nothing. (See 2 Ne. 26: 30; Moroni 7: 46; and 1 Cor. 12: 2-3.) Charity is the kind of love Christ has for us. It is the purest kind of love. (Moroni 7: 47.) Christ lived the highest form of love. All He did from the moment His public ministry began was love on display. His greatest sermon (The Sermon on the Mount) was devoted to love. (See Matt. Chapters 5-7; 3 Ne. Chapters 12-14.) In it, He spoke of the poor in spirit inheriting the kingdom of heaven; and promised those who mourn they will be comforted. He promised the meek they will inherit the earth; and told the hungry and thirsty they will be filled. For the merciful, He promised mercy. He said the pure in heart would see God. He told the peacemakers they were the children of God. To those who are persecuted He promised the kingdom of heaven. He told those who were reviled and had evil spoken about them because they followed Him to be exceedingly glad. They were following in the footsteps of the prophets. Their reward would be infinite.

For all the suffering men endure, He offered hope. For all they sacrificed in their pursuit of righteousness, He promised a reward.

He admonished mankind to return love for hate. It is not enough to refrain from retaliation, He said to purge anger from our hearts. He required us to forgive people quickly, before they even ask to be forgiven. He said men should not offer anything to God at an altar without first reconciling and forgiving all ill-will toward their fellow-man.

He said men should not just avoid adultery, but they should remove lust from their hearts. We should love our enemies and love those who hate us. He pointed out that even the wicked love those who love them. Even the worldly and hypocritical religious leaders of His time loved those who loved them. But those who follow Him should determine instead to love those who despise, hate, persecute and afflict them.

He requires us to be better than we think even possible. He requires us to be perfect. No matter how unlikely that may seem, He speaks with such authority about it that it inspires confidence in us to at least try to live His commandments.

In rapid succession He tells us: Show charity in secret. Pray in secret. Do good in secret. Our Father in Heaven will recognize these things openly, but only if we keep them from the attention of others as we do them in this life.

He told us not to judge others. He told us not to correct others. Instead, He said to be self-critical, remove our own faults, and be tolerant and forgiving of the faults of others.

He said that there would be many who choose damnation, and only a few who choose salvation.[97] Not everyone who wants will be permitted to enter into the kingdom of heaven. Only those who were willing to do the things He said would be allowed to enter.

It is an astonishing sermon, which if it were followed would bring about a world of peace. He tells us how to love. He tells us how to change a fallen Telestial world into a Millennial Terrestrial Kingdom. It is a sermon which goes right to the heart of man. In it He explains how all may love their fellow-man. The sermon explains who He was, what was in His heart, and how He lived and acted throughout His life.

The great triumph of Christ is His love. There is no power which can separate us from His love. He has overcome all that divides us, and is able to reach across any gulf, overcome any distance and meet any challenge. Paul wrote about the power of Christ's love in a remarkable letter to the Romans in which he stated: "Who shall separate us from the love of Christ? shall tribulation, or distress, or persecution, or famine, or nakedness, or peril, or sword? As it is written, For thy sake we are killed all the day long; we are accounted as sheep for the slaughter. Nay, in all these things we are more than conquerors through him that loved us. For I am persuaded, that neither death, nor life, nor angels, nor principalities, nor powers, nor things present, nor things to come, Nor height, nor depth, nor any other creature, shall be able to separate us from the love of God, which is in Christ Jesus our Lord." (Rom. 8: 35-39.) I think Paul was right. I believe he had

---

[97]"Enter ye in at the strait gate: for wide is the gate, and broad is the way, that leadeth to destruction, and many there be which go in thereat: Because strait is the gate, and narrow is the way, which leadeth unto life, and few there be that find it." (Matt. 7: 13-14.)

enough of an opportunity to observe Christ that he was able to see the greatest victory gained by Christ was His infinite ability to love. His love is so compelling it would require us to walk away, to reject what He offers, before we can lose what He freely gives.

In one exchange with His disciples, Christ explained: "And I, if I be lifted up from the earth, will draw all men unto me. This he said, signifying what death he should die." (John 12: 32-33.) In one brief statement Christ summarized the power of His love. He does not compel men to come, instead He will "draw all men unto [Himself]." Without compulsory means, men come to Him. They are attracted to Him. Men want to be with Him. He is pleasant, appealing, inviting and positive. Men seek Him out when they realize who He is.

Christ leaves it to each of us to choose between Him and all He offers, or to reject Him. He invites. He does not demand. In one exchange with a doubting critic, He patiently explained to His interrogator that only those who belong to Him will follow Him. Others are free to wander off. Those who follow, however, would be protected eternally through His enduring love. As He explained: "But ye believe not, because ye are not of my sheep, as I said unto you. **My sheep hear my voice, and I know them, and they follow me: And I give unto them eternal life; and they shall never perish, neither shall any man pluck them out of my hand.**" (John 10: 26-28.)

When explaining priesthood power to Joseph Smith in Liberty Jail, Christ revealed a great deal about Himself. Explaining priestly power is explaining Christ's power. The revelation is worth repeating at length:

> Behold, there are many called, but few are chosen. And why are they not chosen? Because their hearts are set so much upon the things of this world, and

aspire to the honors of men, that they do not learn this one lesson--That **the rights of the priesthood are inseparably connected with the powers of heaven, and that the powers of heaven cannot be controlled nor handled only upon the principles of righteousness**. That they may be conferred upon us, it is true; but when we undertake to cover our sins, or to gratify our pride, our vain ambition, or **to exercise control or dominion or compulsion upon the souls of the children of men, in any degree of unrighteousness, behold, the heavens withdraw themselves; the Spirit of the Lord is grieved; and when it is withdrawn, Amen to the priesthood or the authority of that man**. Behold, ere he is aware, he is left unto himself, to kick against the pricks, to persecute the Saints, and to fight against God. We have learned by sad experience that it is the nature and disposition of **almost all men, as soon as they get a little authority, as they suppose, they will immediately begin to exercise unrighteous dominion**. Hence many are called, but few are chosen. **No power or influence can or ought to be maintained by virtue of the priesthood**, only by persuasion, by long-suffering, by gentleness and meekness, and by love unfeigned; By kindness, and pure knowledge, which shall greatly enlarge the soul without hypocrisy, and without guile--Reproving betimes with sharpness, when moved upon by the Holy Ghost; and then showing forth afterwards an increase of love toward him whom thou hast reproved, lest he esteem thee to be his enemy; That he may know that thy faithfulness is stronger than the cords of death. **Let thy bowels also be full of charity towards all men**, and to the household of faith, and let virtue garnish thy thoughts unceasingly; then shall thy confidence wax strong in the presence of God; and

> the doctrine of the priesthood shall distill upon thy soul as the dews from heaven. The Holy Ghost shall be thy constant companion, and thy scepter an unchanging scepter of righteousness and truth; and thy dominion shall be an everlasting dominion, and **without compulsory means it shall flow unto thee forever and ever.** (D&C 121: 34- 46.)

Taken literally, these words contain shocking limits on what comprises "priesthood" power. They negate any idea that it is possible to abuse priestly authority. When abuse is present, the authority vanishes. Then the abuser is alone, without God, and acting to his condemnation. When viewed in absolute terms, the priesthood of God does not amount to anything other than an invitation to get one's heart aligned with heaven. It is an invitation to love. Since the revelation about priesthood is a revelation about how Christ's love is a form of power, we should consider it carefully. Here is another way to restate the revelation:

> Although the Lord invites all to come to Him, only a few will accept the invitation to come. You may wonder why; but it is because men are unwilling to accept what is offered. They want authority in this world. They want praise and honor from men. They cannot accept His invitation until they lay all such things aside and realize that any honor, any authority, any power comes only from heaven. Without a connection to heaven there is no power, no authority and no honor. Heavenly power or authority can only be exercised by fully mirroring the will of heaven, and never by acting independent of that will. Man's own will cannot, does not, and never will be allowed to govern. Even though someone may be ordained to hold priesthood, called to an office, or given the right to decide matters in the Church, that does not empower them to contradict the will of heaven.

Men cannot substitute their desire for heaven's; because whenever they do that, the acts they perform while only pretending to follow heaven will condemn them. They use the name of God in vain anytime they follow their own desire, while falsely claiming they are doing heaven's will. Men who try to conceal their sins, who in their pride claim authority over others, who claim the right to control or manipulate others, whose ambitions set their agenda, cannot and do not conform to heaven's will. Heaven itself withdraws from such men, and when it does they have absolutely no priesthood authority or power. Such men are left to themselves, and oftentimes they seek to exercise yet more control, more authority, and more feigned priesthood rights over the humble who suffer under their claimed presiding authority. When such ambitious men subjugate these humble Saints, they are fighting against God. They will come to learn too late for their own salvation that they have been on their own errand all along, and not the Lord's. Unfortunately almost all men fall victim to this false illusion of control over others. As soon as someone believes they have been given the authority of heaven, they almost immediately begin to abuse their fellow man with claims about the right to control, manipulate or coerce them. This is why so very few have ever really accepted His invitation to come unto Him. There really is no authority in the priesthood He gives to men. The priesthood is an invitation to come and learn to persuade others by the power of example, to convince others by the things which you will endure for their sake, to show love without pretense and without calling attention to yourself. It is an invitation to service. It is an invitation to seek after heaven itself. When someone accepts that invitation, and meekly submits to the gentle influence of the Holy Spirit, they will learn more by

> showing kindness to their fellow man than they can ever learn through any other means. Such men will rebuke others only on those occasions when heaven would rebuke; but even then they will immediately show increased love. They will not fail to show unceasing love, even to those who required a sharp word. Such men always show love to others as the most important part of their example. Such men will convince those to whom they minister that they would give their lives to save them because their love is so strong. Anyone who is in contact with heaven will love all their fellow men. They will meditate night and day upon the things of heaven. They will be able to enter into God's own presence because their lives are so lived that heaven willingly accompanies them. They will deserve residence in heaven, and therefore heaven will take up residence with them. God will be their companion. Love will be theirs because they will never try to control, dominate or subdue others. Because of their love, the power of heaven (which is love) will be with them forever and ever. (Paraphrase of D&C 121: 34- 46.)

The power of love inspires all that is or all that ever will be. Love is creative. Everything else is subject to entropy. Love alone renews, creates, empowers and overcomes. Without love there is defeat, disarray, disintegration and dissolution.

It is significant how often Christ referred to love in His ministry. It was the great commandment. It was the reason for His coming. It is how He and His Father related to each other. It was what He expected as the great sign of His followers. It was the duty of those who claimed to follow Him. Here are only a few of the comments Christ made about love in the New Testament:

"Ye have heard that it hath been said, Thou shalt love thy neighbour, and hate thine enemy. But I say unto you, Love your enemies, bless them that curse you, do good to them that hate you, and pray for them which despitefully use you, and persecute you;" (Matt. 5: 43-44).

"For if ye love them which love you, what reward have ye? do not even the publicans the same?" (Matt. 5: 46.)

"Thou shalt love thy neighbour as thyself." (Matt. 19: 19.)

When asked by an inquisitor what the great commandment was "Jesus said unto him, Thou shalt love the Lord thy God with all thy heart, and with all thy soul, and with all thy mind. ... And the second [is] like unto it, Thou shalt love thy neighbour as thyself." (Matt. 22: 37, 39.)

"But I say unto you which hear, Love your enemies, do good to them which hate you," (Luke 6: 27.)

"But love ye your enemies, and do good, and lend, hoping for nothing again; and your reward shall be great, and ye shall be the children of the Highest: for he is kind unto the unthankful and [to] the evil." (Luke 6: 35.)

"Jesus said unto them, If God were your Father, ye would love me:" (John 8: 42).

"Therefore doth my Father love me, because I lay down my life, that I might take it again." (John 10: 17.)

"A new commandment I give unto you, That ye love one another; as I have loved you, that ye also love one another. By this shall all men know that ye are my disciples, if ye have love one to another. (John 13: 34-35.)

"If ye love me, keep my commandments." (John 14: 15.)

"He that hath my commandments, and keepeth them, he it is that loveth me: and he that loveth me shall be loved of my Father, and I will love him, and will manifest myself to him." (John 14: 21.)

"Jesus answered and said unto him, If a man love me, he will keep my words: and my Father will love him, and we will come unto him, and make our abode with him." (John 14: 23.)

"As the Father hath loved me, so have I loved you: continue ye in my love. If ye keep my commandments, ye shall abide in my love; even as I have kept my Father's commandments, and abide in his love." (John 15: 9-10.)

"This is my commandment, That ye love one another, as I have loved you." (John 15: 12.)

"Greater love hath no man than this, that a man lay down his life for his friends." (John 15: 13.)

"So when they had dined, Jesus saith to Simon Peter, Simon, son of Jonas, lovest thou me more than these? He saith unto him, Yea, Lord; thou knowest that I love thee. He saith unto him, Feed my lambs. He saith to him again the second time, Simon, son of Jonas, lovest thou me? He saith unto him, Yea, Lord; thou knowest that I love thee. He saith unto him, Feed my sheep. He saith unto him the third time, Simon, son of Jonas, lovest thou me? Peter was grieved because he said unto him the third time, Lovest thou me? And he said unto him, Lord, thou knowest all things; thou knowest that I love thee. Jesus saith unto him, Feed my sheep." (John 21: 15-17.)

Love is the great lesson. Love is the great commandment. Love is what defines those who follow Him.

Christ's example of leadership followed the terms set out in Section 121. His authority was entirely based upon invitation, gentle persuasion and example. He did not dictate nor compel. It was left to each hearer to decide how he would respond. When His detractors asked for a demonstration of His power, He declined. When confronted by threatening ecclesiastical power, He submitted. When threatened with death, He did not resist. When His hands were nailed to the cross, He forgave the executioners. His example was always submissive and meek.

His disciples were taught both by His example and His words to also be submissive and meek. He was repulsed by the way the Gentile "leaders" would exercise authority, control and dominion over others. He was given the opportunity to teach how true leaders should act when Zebedee's wife confronted Him in company with her sons:

> Then came to him the mother of Zebedee's children with her sons, worshipping him, and desiring a certain thing of him. And he said unto her, What wilt thou? She saith unto him, Grant that these my two sons may sit, the one on thy right hand, and the other on the left, in thy kingdom. But Jesus answered and said, Ye know not what ye ask. Are ye able to drink of the cup that I shall drink of, and to be baptized with the baptism that I am baptized with? They say unto him, We are able. And he saith unto them, Ye shall drink indeed of my cup, and be baptized with the baptism that I am baptized with: but to sit on my right hand, and on my left, is not mine to give, but it shall be given to them for whom it is prepared of my Father. And when the ten heard it, they were moved with indignation against the two brethren. But Jesus called them unto him, and said, **Ye know that the princes of the Gentiles exercise dominion over them, and they that are great exercise authority upon them. But it shall not be so among you: but whosoever will be great among you, let him be your minister; And whosoever will be chief among you, let him be your servant: Even as the Son of man came not to be ministered unto, but to minister, and to**

> **give his life a ransom for many**. (Matt. 20: 20-28, emphasis added.)

The only proper way to lead is to serve. The only way to be greater than another is to bend lower, raise them up, and let your good works speak for you.

He did not tolerate praise, and rebuked the attempt to flatter Him. When called "good" He refused the compliment and said: "Why callest thou me good? there is none good but one, that is, God" (Matt. 19: 17.) He meant everything He said about being subordinate, meek, gentle and inviting. His life of service was lived among the common, the downtrodden, the outcasts who engaged in tax-collection, prostitution, and the ceremonially unclean. He did not need, and never sought for credentials, position or authority among men. He was only concerned with setting an example, teaching truth and living meekly.

Christ's opposite can be found among those who seek authority, honor, credentials, position and recognition. Paul wrote about those who would come after Christ, and change the faith taught by Him into an instrument for their unrighteous control of others. He wrote about that day: "Let no man deceive you by any means: for that day shall not come, except there come a falling away first, and that man of sin be revealed, the son of perdition; Who opposeth and exalteth himself above all that is called God, or that is worshipped; so that he as God sitteth in the temple of God, shewing himself that he is God." (2 Thes. 2: 3-4.) This is the great sign of the apostate - one who claims to have God's own authority given to him, and seeks to exalt himself. The contrast between such a "leader" and Christ's true messengers could not be greater. These false men do not show the power of the Spirit in what they do and teach. Instead they claim their right to act "as God" while sitting "in the temple of God."

We saw this unfold in Historic Christianity. The Holy Spirit ceased to show itself, and men lost the extraordinary gifts which were once common in the Church established by Christ. As John Wesley explained it:

> It does not appear that these extraordinary gifts of the Holy Spirit [speaking of I Cor. xii] were common in the church for more than two or three centuries. We seldom hear of them after that fatal period when the Emperor Constantine called himself a Christian; and from a vain imagination of promoting the Christian cause thereby heaped riches, and power, and honor upon Christians in general, but in particular upon the Christian clergy. From this time they [the spiritual gifts] almost totally ceased; very few instances of the kind were found. The cause of this was not (as has been supposed) because there was no more occasion for them, because all the world was become Christians. This is a miserable mistake; not a twentieth part of it was then nominally Christian. The real cause of it was the love of many, almost all Christians, so-called, was waxed cold. The Christians had no more of the Spirit of Christ than the other heathens. The Son of Man when he came to examine his church, could hardly find faith upon the earth. This was the real cause why the extraordinary gifts of the Holy Ghost were no longer to be found in the Christian Church-because the Christians were turned heathens again and only had a dead form left. (*John Wesley's Works.* 7 vols., Vol. vii, Sermon 89, pages 26, 27. Grand Rapids: Baker Publishing, 1996.)

Although the Spirit had abandoned the Historic Christian Church, it would be unthinkable to them to admit it. And so in place of the authentic gifts which came from the Spirit, the Historic Christians accepted the decisions of ecumenical councils as *de facto* pronouncements of the Holy Spirit. It was impossible, they thought, for the Holy Spirit to abandon them. "Thus Bishop John Kaye of Lincoln, *Ecclesiastical History*, 276: '**The promise of the Holy Spirit, made by Christ to the Church, precludes the possibility of an universal defection from the true faith.**' Apparently the good bishop is oblivious to the fact that the promise of the spiritual gifts to accompany the Holy Spirit-prophecy, tongues, etc.-precludes the possibility of any modern church possessing it. **The fact that the scripture is the sole source of 'revelation' in all the synods and councils of the Christian church cancels any claim it might make to being the recipient of the promised Paraclete** [Holy Spirit]." (Nibley, Hugh. *Mormonism and Early Christianity*,. Edited by Todd M. Compton and Stephen D. Ricks. Salt Lake City: Deseret Book, 1987, footnote 185 appearing at p. 162, emphasis added.) Meaning that when prophecy ended, revelations ceased, and seership was no longer in existence, it was impossible for them to credibly assert the Holy Spirit was with them. Yet they continued (and continue) to make the claim.

As one Catholic (former Jesuit) writer explained the Historic Christian definition of "revelation:"

> **Christianity and Judiasm are religions of revelation. But how, exactly, is the content of our beliefs revealed? It is a long time since we took for granted the idea of theophany, a sudden and dramatic unveiling of mystery – an experience like that of Moses before the burning bush, or Moses coming down from the mountaintop with the tablets of the Law.** One of the assumptions I make in a work like this,

> however, is that **the truth of our beliefs is revealed in history, with the contours of the mundane, and not through cosmic interruptions in the flow of time. Revelation comes to us gradually, according to the methods of human knowing. And so revelation comes to us ambiguously. Certitude and clarity are achieved only in hindsight, and even then provisionally**. That is the work of memory, which is the arrangement of incident and experience into a meaningful narrative with a beginning, middle, and end. The theophany of Moses is less a matter of what happened to him on Mount Sinai than it is of the story told by those who came after him. (Carroll, James. *Constantine's Sword.* New York: Houghton Mifflin Company, 2001; p. 172, emphasis added.)

This is what the Historic Christian movement **must** do, unless they are willing to admit their apostasy. Since they can never make that admission, they are forced to redefine "revelation" so as to claim the right to inherit the tradition founded by Christ and His Apostles. If there is no open vision, no angelic ministers, no "burning bush" with clarity and direction, then things become "ambiguous" and require reflection and rationalization. Their true "revelation" requires hindsight and generations of scholarly rumination before God's hand becomes clear. This is how Historic Christianity decides it is still in favor with God and receiving revelation.

Oddly, as the Holy Spirit wanes, men's claims to have authority increase. They no longer really need the gifts of the Spirit because they own the authority delegated from Christ to act "as God" while occupying the chief seats. They exercise authority exactly as the Gentiles have always done: They claim it their right to control, coerce and hold dominion. So, as the Spirit slips out the back door, through the front door comes the claims of power to control, to demand and to exercise God's own authority.

Since this is how Historic Christianity killed and supplanted the Primitive Church, we Latter-day Saints would be wise to not only note the historic failing, but to guard carefully against repeating it. The revelation in Section 121 demands that Latter-day Saints notice how many are called but how few are chosen, because those who hold authority fail to recognize the only authority to act on God's behalf must necessarily come from heaven. It requires the saints reject all claims that revelation does not need to continue, or that revelation is ambiguous and God's dealings can only be understood in hindsight after scholars have studied for generations the decisions of councils.

On this subject the Book of Mormon is even more candid, and alarming. As Nephi warned, speaking about latter-day Zion:

> Therefore, wo be unto him that is at ease in Zion! Wo be unto him that crieth: All is well! Yea, **wo be unto him that hearkeneth unto the precepts of men, and denieth the power of God, and the gift of the Holy Ghost! Yea, wo be unto him that saith: We have received, and we need no more**! And in fine, wo unto all those who tremble, and are angry because of the truth of God! For behold, he that is built upon the rock receiveth it with gladness; and he that is built upon a sandy foundation trembleth lest he shall fall. **Wo be unto him that shall say: We have received the word of God, and we need no more of the word of God, for we have enough**! For behold, thus saith the Lord God: I will give unto the children of men line upon line, precept upon precept, here a little and there a little; and blessed are those who hearken unto my precepts, and lend an ear unto my

> counsel, for they shall learn wisdom; for **unto him that receiveth I will give more; and from them that shall say, We have enough, from them shall be taken away even that which they have. Cursed is he that putteth his trust in man, or maketh flesh his arm, or shall hearken unto the precepts of men, save their precepts shall be given by the power of the Holy Ghost**. (2 Ne. 28: 24-31, emphasis added.)

Moroni also cautioned us to take care to keep the gifts of the Spirit among us. If we let them slip away, then we will all be lost. As he explained:

> And Christ truly said unto our fathers: If ye have faith ye can do all things which are expedient unto me. And now I speak unto all the ends of the earth--that **if the day cometh that the power and gifts of God shall be done away among you, it shall be because of unbelief. And wo be unto the children of men if this be the case; for there shall be none that doeth good among you, no not one. For if there be one among you that doeth good, he shall work by the power and gifts of God. And wo unto them who shall do these things away and die, for they die in their sins, and they cannot be saved in the kingdom of God; and I speak it according to the words of Christ; and I lie not**. (Moro. 10: 23-26, emphasis added.)

Latter-day Saints must resist the idea that we can redefine "revelation" to be something gradual, subtle and ambiguous. We must fight against the notion that whatever happens in one of our councils is necessarily the result of the Holy Spirit, because we are reduced, with Bishop John Kaye of Lincoln, *Ecclesiastical History*, p. 276, to the circular argument: "**The promise of the Holy Spirit,**

made by Christ to the Church, precludes the possibility of an universal defection from the true faith." In effect, he is saying what happens in the Historic Christian churches must be with the Holy Spirit's approval, because to ever admit otherwise is unthinkable. Christ's promise of the Holy Spirit "precludes the possibility" of apostasy! Really? Humility, meekness, unfeigned love and obedience to Christ's Gospel are all irrelevant! Historic Christians can relax, because Christ "promised" the Spirit to them! This is so transparently foolish that no one should be deceived by the false notion. We are also at risk of the same failing as Historic Christianity. Nothing is guaranteed us, and no human failing is precluded. Everything is always at risk. The Book of Mormon's warnings make it clear that Latter-day Zion has no pass on these things.

We must fight against the arguments that would equate a consensus among Church councils with a revelation from the Holy Spirit. We must never accept the rationalization of Historic Christianity that Christ's commission to an original leader somehow "precludes the possibility of an universal defection from the truth" because the Book of Mormon warns us repeatedly that this possibility remains a risk which we also face. We should recoil in distress when we read the argument made recently in a well-received scholarly work (considered by some to be the best history written of Latter-day Saint origins), which said: "After the organization of the Twelve Apostles, the frequency of canonical revelations dropped precipitously. The commandments to particular people, included among the revelations in the early years, were omitted from later compilations. Instead, Joseph's **history was filled with the minutes of the Twelve Apostles' meetings, as if they had become the source of inspiration**. The Acts of the Apostles from the New Testament – **a history of their activities – became the pattern for revelation rather than the visions of Moses on Sinai**. At a moment when Joseph's own revelatory powers were at their peak, he divested himself of sole responsibility for revealing the will of God and **invested that gift in the councils of the Church, making it a charismatic bureaucracy**." (Bushman, Richard L. *Rough Stone Rolling*. New York: Alfred A. Knopf, 2005, p. 257-58, emphasis added.) Brother Bushman's argument is similar to Bishop John Kaye's above. Revelation is sudden, unexpected, interrupts time and space and is unequivocal. When we have it, we know it. When we have mere agreement among men, well, we have an agreement.[98]

The way to avoid all these grave errors can be found only through Christ's example. He loved. He did not demand. He persuaded, He did not control. He showed only meekness to His followers. He did not coerce, but showed pure love, which "greatly enlarged the souls" of those who listened to Him. He warned about trying to become great, holding authority over others, and seeking to occupy chief seats. This is the way of the Gentiles, but should never be the way of His followers.

How then might we recognize His true messengers? How can we know something comes from Him and not from those who

---

[98]Of course an agreement through an inspired council is a revelation. But the participants will know when that is the case. A good example is shown by the various accounts given by those present when Official Declaration No. 2, found in the Doctrine and Covenants, was received. But, in that example, the Declaration itself proclaims that God "has heard our prayers, and **by revelation has confirmed** that the long-promised day has come[.]" (D&C O.D. 2.) The question is not solved by the presence or absence of a council, but entirely by whether a revelation has been received or not. That comes from heaven alone.

merely pretend to be His messengers? We should look for a sign to distinguish His true messengers from those who falsely claim to be sent by Him. We should remember how He supplicates with gentleness, and never compels or demands we follow Him. President Spencer W. Kimball described the beggar's petition in these words: "I have seen your cathedrals with altars of gold and silver and your beggars on the cold floors of such edifices, with their skinny arms extended and **their bony hands cupped and raised** to those who come to see or to worship." (*Teachings of Spencer W. Kimball, The.* Edited by Edward L Kimball. Salt Lake City: Deseret Book, 1982, p. 214, emphasis added.) This sign of entreaty from the beggar, whose petition invites those who can to give them alms, is surely a sign for how He beckons for us. He entreats. He implores. He invites. But He does not proceed with a clenched fist, a harsh gesture, an insistent demand. His cupped hand beckons us to give Him our attention. Surely those who are His true messengers will do likewise. Surely one sign they have been sent by Him is this gentle entreaty, and not a call which relies on status. Since no power or authority can or ought to be maintained by virtue of His priesthood, His true messengers will never claim people should follow them because of their pretended authority. They will use, instead, pure knowledge which will greatly enlarge the souls of His sheep. They hear His voice in these gentle words of truth. For them the status of the teacher is irrelevant, and only the message is important.

Among the ordinances Christ has given mankind, water is used to baptize and to wash. Consecrated oil is used to anoint and to bless. These are the ceremonial symbols of Christ's love. His love cleanses us. His oil anoints us to glory. These liquids signify the removal of sin and stains. They cleanse us and renew us spiritually. They are symbols of the Holy Ghost and the Spirit of Christ. They signify holiness and spirituality. Both are preeminent symbols of love.

Liquid cannot be grasped nor held in the hand. The tighter the hand closes, the more liquid is forced out. Indeed, the only way to hold water or oil in our hand is to cup our palm. Only by making the hand open can these symbolic liquids be held. In the ordinances and liquids employed to show the cleansing power of His love, He reminds us of the true sign of His messengers. They, like Him, will petition. They will never come with a clenched hand, but only an open, cupped hand, inviting the follower and beckoning him to come.

Is not the cupped hand recognized everywhere as the beggar's petition? Is it not a symbol of beseeching? Does it not remind us of how we look to our Father in Heaven for all that we have? In this simple physical symbol we see how Christ's power to ordain and control power, principalities, thrones, dominions under His almighty hand is linked inevitably to the openness, the uncontrolling, and petitioning hand which has been lovingly extended in cupping shape. His hand is never clenched, tight, controlling. An open hand is a sign of both Christ and His true messengers. They, like Him, will show forth love, openness, and the kind of gentle petitioning and beckoning that is seen in the beggar's cupped hand for us to follow. They will never claim authority except to bless or ordain.

Of all that can be said of Our Lord, it is His love which distinguishes Him the most. He is the greatest because He loves more than any of us. He is the greatest, but He acts as the least. His message is delivered by entreaty. When we finally see Him as He is, we will all recognize Him as the very definition of Love; for God is Love. (1 Jn. 4: 8.) In turn, His followers will learn to love.

Chapter 16
Conclusion

Now, after the many testimonies which have been given of Him, this is the testimony, latest of all which I give of Him: That He lives. For I saw Him. He has ministered to me. I know He lived, died and rose the third day, early in the morning while it was yet dark - as a thief in the night. After rising from the dead He ministered to His family, friends and Apostles in the land of Jerusalem, ascended to heaven, and appeared in turn to other lost sheep of Israel. Among those to whom He ministered were the Nephites on the American continent. These people kept a faithful record, which we now know as the Book of Mormon. He visited other lost sheep as well, who kept faithful records which are yet to come forth. When they do, they will also bear witness of Him.

This book has been written by another witness of Him. Its contents have been approved by the Spirit, and were necessary to be written. Under guidance from the Spirit, I am responsible for this book, not an organization. If there are errors, they are my responsibility alone.

At the beginning of this book I asked: "What think ye of Christ?" This was the question posed by Christ to His inner circle of disciples. It remains the question that is still relevant to salvation for each of us. Hopefully this book has given us reason to believe in and trust Christ and the message He brought to mankind. If it has, we ought to press forward seeking to know more of Him, and ultimately come to know Him in word, in power and in very deed.[99]

He promised to come to those who follow Him: "I will not leave you comfortless: **I will come to you... ye see me: because I live, ye shall live also**... he that loveth me shall be loved of my Father, and **I will love him, and will manifest myself to him**." (John 14: 18, 19, 21, emphasis added.) If we follow Him, obey His commandments, remain faithful to His ordinances, we create the conditions in which it is possible for Him to keep these promises. We allow Him to come to us. When He does, He will teach us the peaceable things of His kingdom. As Joseph Smith explained these verses from John: "It is no more nor less than the Lord Jesus Christ Himself; and this is the sum and substance of the whole matter; that when any man obtains this last Comforter, **he will have the personage of Jesus Christ to attend him, or appear unto him from time to time, and even He will manifest the Father unto him, and they will take up their abode with him, and the visions of the heavens will be opened unto him, and the Lord will teach him face to face, and he may have a perfect knowledge of the mysteries of the Kingdom of God**;

---

[99]See 1 Ne. 14: 1: "And it shall come to pass, that if the Gentiles shall hearken unto the Lamb of God in that day that he shall manifest himself unto them in word, and also in power, in very deed, unto the taking away of their stumbling blocks--"

and this is the state and place the ancient saints arrived at when they had such glorious visions-Isaiah, Ezekiel, John upon the Isle of Patmos, St. Paul in the three heavens, and all the saints who held communion with the general assembly and Church of the Firstborn." (*TPJS,* p. 150, emphasis added.[100]) The process can be taught. The things which are learned from the process, however, are reserved for the Lord alone to teach.

I have been writing to explain the complete Gospel of Jesus Christ in a total now of six books. The witness of Christ set out in this book is given to bring hope, to secure faith, and to give confidence to the follower of Christ. He is real. What He taught is true. He is worthy of our trust.

The ordinances administered through The Church of Jesus Christ of Latter-day Saints have been authorized by Christ and established by the ministering of angels sent by Him. His work today is no different than the work He initiated during His mortal ministry. Then and now He requires faith, repentance and baptism preliminary to the Gift of the Holy Ghost. The Gift of the Holy Ghost is given by the laying on of hands of properly ordained priesthood holders. He restored these covenant-making rites as part of this Dispensation of the Fullness of Times. It is all available again.

There is no perfect human organization. His Church in the New Testament and His Church today are both manned by flawed men and women. That is as it must be, and as it should be. If we cannot show charity to the honest and sincere efforts of flawed

---

[100]See also, D&C 130: 3: "John 14:23--The appearing of the Father and the Son, in that verse, is a personal appearance; and the idea that the Father and the Son dwell in a man's heart is an old sectarian notion, and is false."

fellow-servants, then we are no true disciple of His. His teachings **presume** there will be offenses given. We are supposed to take no notice of them, and to refuse to be offended by them. He will make all things right in the end. For us, in the meantime, we should endure the flaws, errors, pride and foolishness of others charitably. His Church cannot function if we are not tolerant of one another.

If we see flaws in His Church, we are noticing only the weaknesses of men. We all have weaknesses. If we pass over the sins of others without condemning them, we, in turn, will not be condemned for our own sins. As Joseph Smith taught: "I charged the Saints not to follow the example of the adversary in accusing the brethren, and said, 'If you do not accuse each other, God will not accuse you. If you have no accuser you will enter heaven, and if you will follow the revelations and instructions which God gives you through me, I will take you into heaven as my back load. If you will not accuse me, I will not accuse you. If you will throw a cloak of charity over my sins, I will over yours-for charity covereth a multitude of sins.'" (*TPJS*, p. 193.)

For those who have read my books, I would suggest the first book, *The Second Comforter: Conversing With the Lord Through the Veil*, is not merely an extended discussion of a sacred subject. Rather it is a manual, describing the actual process by which any person may come to have the experience which Joseph Smith described. Just as Joseph said, you also can have the personage of Jesus Christ to attend you or appear to you from time to time. When He does, He will eventually manifest the Father to you, after He has prepared you by what He teaches in His continuing personal ministry. They (the Father and Son), will "take up their abode with you," and when that happens it inevitably is accompanied by the visions of the heavens opening to you. Then, just as happened to Joseph Smith, the Lord will teach you face to face.

This is the point that Jeremiah prophesied would happen, and which the Lord, by covenant, promised would come when He said: "But this shall be the covenant that I will make with the house of Israel; After those days, saith the Lord, I will put my law in their inward parts, and write it in their hearts; and will be their God, and they shall be my people. And **they shall teach no more every man his neighbour, and every man his brother, saying, Know the Lord: for they shall all know me, from the least of them unto the greatest of them**, saith the Lord: for I will forgive their iniquity, and I will remember their sin no more." (Jer. 31: 33-34, emphasis added.) This day will only come when we assume the responsibility for seeking Him by following His ways. We should stop waiting for someone else to cause it to happen. It was never their responsibility in the first place. It is and always has been ours.

The answer to the question of what you think of Christ is really answered by what you do about Him. You need not say a thing. Your answer is the life you live. If you think Him the Son of God, then you will follow Him. That, of course, cannot be done without obeying His commandments.

He does not love any of us more than another. But the conditions under which He may come to one are the same as those under which He may come to another. We cannot reject those conditions and then expect to receive what He offers. His gifts are free. But the manner in which we take delivery is through accepting His ordinances and abiding His teachings. When we do, the gifts flow as naturally as sunlight comes on a cloudless day. It is natural, and without compulsion in any degree.

I hope the rigors of Christ's life have become more clear as you read this book. More importantly, I hope the reality of who He was and what He did and taught have become more real to you as a result of what you've read here. Admiration will turn to adoration if you know Him.

He is the Living God. Let us all be faithful to Him. Let us come to sing new words to an old Hymn:

Oh, come, all ye faithful, Joyfully before Him!
Oh, come ye, oh, come ye to Zion's God.
Come and behold Him, Still the King of heaven;
Oh, come, let us adore Him; Oh, come, let us adore Him;
Oh, come, let us adore Him, Christ, the Lord.

Sing, choirs of angels, Sing royal anthems;
Sing, all ye citizens of heav'n and earth!
Glory to God, Glory in the highest;
Oh, come, let us adore Him; Oh, come, let us adore Him;
Oh, come, let us adore Him, Christ, the Lord.

Yea, Lord, we greet thee, On this very morning;
Jesus, to thee we give all glory.
Son of the Father, Now to flesh appearing;
Oh, come, let us adore Him; Oh, come, let us adore Him;
Oh, come, let us adore Him, Christ, the Lord.

No person can understand what He has done for him and fail to adore this living God. He is our Tree of Life.

He is the garment with which we can cover our nakedness.

He is the One who became a serpent, hung on a tree, upon whom if we cast our eyes in faith, will heal us.

He is the One who with a touch can heal a leper and with His word can raise the dead. His ministry was to bring hope for all mankind.

Do not refuse to eat of that tree, cover yourself with Him, look upon Him in faith, receive His touch, be healed from sin and sickness, and accept the hope which is in Him. Let us all together come, and adore Him.

There are some clarifications which I need to make before concluding. I make them as the final statement of my testimony. First, with respect to Christ's suffering in Gethsemene, all waves of torment which overflowed Him came in pairs. The first wave imposed upon Him the feelings, guilt and suffering that those who commit the offenses must endure because of their sins. The second imposed the suffering of those who are victims of these offenses. After He had endured the first pair of waves, He understood that subsequent waves would follow the same pattern; the first being for the offender, the second would be a mirror, but it would be the suffering of the offended. He did not know how many times the cycle would repeat. He thought it would be over long before it was. He knew only that when another wave hit Him from the guilty offender's burden that He would also suffer a mirrored burden of the non-guilty offended's burden.

It was by faith the Lord accomplished His great works. Faith brought Him to Gethsemene. It was through **hope** that He was able to bear the burden of the guilty offender. His hope in the Father's promises made it possible for Him to return to peace, shed the guilt, and become right with the Father despite feeling the shame of their disobedience.

For the burdens He felt as the victim; whose suffering was caused by the unjust, even deliberate wrongdoing of others, He was able to overcome by **charity** the heavy burden of resentment and anger naturally flowing from the wrongs done by others. He perfected charity by the things which He suffered in innocence. It was through charity that, after suffering in Gethsemene, He healed the High Priest's servant Malchus' ear after Peter cut if off. (See John 18: 10-11, Luke 22: 50-51.) Through charity He endured the trial, insults and pains of His crucifixion while pronouncing forgiveness upon those who carried out the decision to kill Him. (See Luke 23: 33-34.)

The waves of suffering in Gethsemene seemed to occur as time stood still. While the suffering was over in a single night, there seemed to be no time to the event. That is, the time involved for each wave seemed without limits fixed by a clock. He struggled for so long as was necessary to complete the process of becoming whole again, despite what had been poured out upon Him. He was given the cup to drink. It was left to Him to overcome, and for each allotment He had as long as it took to overcome. During that struggle, time seemed not to move.

The darkness of that night was both spiritual and physical. It overcame those who were in attendance, who were also affected by the burden of suffering on that night. As Luke put it: "[W]hen He rose up from prayer, and was come to His disciples, He found them sleeping for sorrow[.]" (Luke 22: 45.) Mark says: " And he taketh with him Peter and James and John, and began to be sore amazed, and to be very heavy; And saith unto them, My soul is exceeding sorrowful unto death: tarry ye here, and watch." (Mark 14: 33-34.) Matthew wrote: "And he took with him Peter and the two sons of Zebedee, and began to be sorrowful and very heavy. Then saith he unto them, My soul is exceeding sorrowful, even unto death: tarry ye here, and watch with me." (Matt. 26: 37-38.)

John did not feel at liberty to discuss it at all. This was a description of the heaviness, the burden, the great evils that hovered about the Lord that evening which would be fully poured upon Him. Those who were present felt it. It was palpable. It was real. Others there were overcome with sorrow, exhaustion and stupor. He alone remained equal to the confrontation of the terrible presence and overcoming it with full faculties despite the heaviness of that night.

Second, there are things I believe about Luke that are not shared by scholars. For example, many who have studied him believe he was a convert to Christ after Christ's ascension into heaven. I believe otherwise. My conclusion is that Luke was a follower of the Lord sometime approximately midway through His ministry, and remained faithful to the Lord's instructions thereafter. He is the only one who records the early events involving Gabriel's visits to Zacharias and to Mary. He alone records the intimate family details of the early life of Christ, including the visit of Mary to Elisabeth before the birth of John. He records the details of Christ's family visiting the Temple when He was twelve. This level of intimate knowledge of family history that all three other Gospel writers leave untouched, tells us Luke had direct, open and intimate discussions with Mary. She would not have shared these things with a stranger, or a Gentile convert to her Son's status as Messiah. She knew that Luke was familiar with, and trusted by her Son.

Luke gives us an explanation of the extent of his personal involvement in Christ's life as he began his Gospel. He is no pretender to knowledge, no second-hand scribe. He tells us who he is and what his qualifications are to write:

> Forasmuch as many have taken in hand to set forth in order a declaration of those things which are most surely believed among us, Even as they

> delivered them **unto us,**[101] **which from the beginning were eyewitnesses**, and ministers of the word; It seemed good to me also, **having had perfect understanding of all things from the very first**, to write unto thee in order, most excellent Theophilus, That thou mightest know the certainty of those things, wherein thou hast been instructed. (Luke 1: 1-4; emphasis added.)

Luke asserts he was an "eyewitness" whose knowledge was "from the beginning" of his account. If Luke is to be trusted on other matters in his Gospel, then he ought to be trusted as he asserts his status as an eyewitness from the beginning. He knew Christ. He associated with Him. He gathered details which others either did not see or were not told. He was a convert of gentile parentage. His gentile status may have disqualified him from being called as an Apostle, but it did nothing to prevent him from associating with the other followers and, in turn, becoming intimate with Christ and His surviving family members.

Scholars rely upon the use of first person pronouns in Acts 16: 10 to determine Luke's first appearance in the narrative. When scholars detect that he has written himself into the story, they conclude that is the first he arrives on the scene of the New Testament events. That conclusion presumes Luke was entirely deliberate and consistent in the use of the first person throughout all he wrote, but ignores Luke's opening verses of his Gospel. As a writer who is deliberate about words, I know how difficult it is, even using the most forgiving, modern word processing

---

[101]Scholars use the wording of Luke in Acts which adopt "we" or "us" as marking the time of his involvement. However, those arguments ignore Luke's opening verses of his Gospel in which the same first person account is found.

equipment, editors and proof readers to keep the first and third person consistent while writing even a short chapter. Therefore, from personal experience, I would acknowledge personal pronoun mistakes are inevitable. I put his entrance into the events mid-way into the Lord's ministry and allow him to be an "eyewitness" of his account. I distrust the scholars' conclusion that Luke was a late arrival to the New Testament era. I believe it was Luke who acquired the details of the walk on the road to Emmaus by participating with Cleopas in that day's journey alongside the Risen Savior. It is only from Luke's Gospel that the conversational details of that day's events are reported. (See Luke 24: 13-35.) Mark merely affirmed that the incident happened. Mark's brief mention is two verses in length: "After that he appeared in another form unto two of them, as they walked, and went into the country. And they went and told it unto the residue: neither believed they them." (Mark 16: 12-13.)

The scholars who believe Luke came late to the events of the New Testament must discredit him even as they accept him as a Gospel writer. They must also assert that the gentile-born convert was a confidant of Mary's, learning details of her's and Christ's early life, but never knew Christ, nor followed Him while He ministered. He must also be the confidant of either the mystery person, or the unknown Cleopas whose sole mention in the New Testament account comes from Luke's 24th Chapter.[102] The only people present, besides the Lord, during that seven mile walk were the unnamed witness and Cleopas. Accordingly, it takes more effort to remove Luke from that conversation and yet have him

---

[102]Very few people think this was the same person as "Cleophas" mentioned in John 19: 25 as wife to a woman also named "Mary" to distinguish her from the other two Marys in the story.

preserve it, than it does to admit he was the second, unnamed participant. I believe he was one of those who were visited by Christ the day of the resurrection and were personally instructed by Him for hours about the necessity of His sacrifice.[103] This was a good foundation from which Luke built a sound understanding of Christ. An understanding which informed all he wrote in Luke and Acts.

Thirdly, it is important to understand how Christ works with an established hierarchy. He set in motion the structure that endured from Moses to His own day. He respected that hierarchy, worshiped at the Temple controlled by it, paid tithes and offerings to it, and did not rebel against it. But He also acted independently from it in teaching the fullness of His Gospel.

He established another hierarchy to endure after His ascent into heaven. However, from the morning of the resurrection through the time of Paul, He always acted independent of the Twelve Apostles when it came to revealing Himself to His "sheep." Indeed, He did not even inform His Twelve Apostles in Jerusalem about the ministry He would undertake among other "lost sheep," because they didn't ask.[104] We referred to His delay on the day of His resurrection in visiting with ten of the remaining eleven Apostles. First He visited with others, including Luke and Cleopas, spending about two hours teaching them. When He finally visited with the ten of the Apostles, He spent only a short time confirming

---

[103]There is an extended discussion of this event in the Appendix to my book *Eighteen Verses*, from pages 336-367. I took no position there about the identity of the second, unidentified witness. I have decided to go ahead and admit here that I believe it was Luke.

[104]I have treated this subject at length in *The Second Comforter*, pages 92-100. I will not repeat it again here.

visually and physically His return to life and rebuking them for not believing the others' reports of His rise from the dead.[105] When He appeared to all eleven, Mark records: "Afterward he appeared unto the eleven as they sat at meat, and upbraided them with their unbelief and hardness of heart, because they believed not them which had seen him after he was risen." (Mark 16: 14.) John attempts to explain the reason for this failing: "For as yet they knew not the scripture, that he must rise again from the dead." (John 20: 9.) The picture in this record shown to us is that of a hierarchy of very ordinary men, who struggle before they can grasp the meaning of Christ's life and ministry. It is clear that these ordinary men were called to undertake a ministry that was far greater than any of them were qualified to perform. If other ordinary disciples were better prepared for Him to visit, both men and women, He visited with them.

Despite any shortcomings among His chosen hierarchy of Apostles, Christ was able to make witnesses of Him from among all His believers. Whether they were women, gentile converts or persecutors of the faith; the hierarchy was never intended to stand between Christ and His followers. He chose witnesses from diverse backgrounds. Some of them were never going to be chosen to fill positions in His church.[106] Women, for example, were barred from holding religious offices. But being barred from office did not

---

[105]Luke 24: 11 records the Apostles' reaction to the first reports from the women who visited the tomb: "And their words seemed to them as idle tales, and they believed them not."

[106]Today divorced men are disqualified from serving in positions such as Bishop, Stake President or General Authority. But disqualification from such service by the institution has no effect upon the Lord's willingness to make such a man His witness - nor to have borne his burdens.

disqualify the women from being witnesses of His resurrection, nor excuse His Apostles from treating lightly their witness. He expected the Apostles to believe Mary. He upbraided them when they did not.

They had a ministry entrusted to them to declare the word of His Gospel: "And he said unto them, Go ye into all the world, and preach the gospel to every creature. He that believeth and is baptized shall be saved; but he that believeth not shall be damned." (Mark 16: 15-16.) Their ministry is authoritative, approved, and indeed commissioned by Him. They are His Apostles. But they are not all of His witnesses. Neither in the New Testament, nor today, does the Lord confine His witnesses to any office, calling, group or special families. He never has. He still does not.[107] But there will never be a true witness of Him who rejects the established authorities of His Church. Paul wrote: " Let every soul be subject unto the higher powers. For there is no power but of God: the powers that be are ordained of God. Whosoever therefore resisteth the power, resisteth the ordinance of God: and they that resist shall receive to themselves damnation." (Rom. 13: 1-2.) Paul's comment was much more comprehensive. He was speaking of all authorities, even those in the Roman Empire that would eventually kill him, just as they had killed Christ and Peter. Yet Paul saw no reason to rebel, condemn or reject. He saw the established authorities as ordained of God, and therefore, there is a duty to support them. The Lord alone will determine when it is time to take the fullness of the Gospel from the latter-day Gentile church. (See 3 Ne. 16:

---

[107] I have written about this in *The Second Comforter*, and illustrated the individual path back in the parable titled *The Missing Virtue* in the book *Ten Parables.*

10.) Until He does, it is the Gentile leaders who should be sustained.

Even when it came to Annas and Caiaphus, this burden to support the established authorities was imposed upon Israel, and sustained by Christ. This burden was imposed upon all the Roman Empire, even when it came to Nero who would have Paul killed. How foolish is it, therefore, for any Latter-day Saint to be critical of the General Authorities of The Church of Jesus Christ of Latter-day Saints. How much better are these men than those wicked men whom the Lord sustained! How much better than the Roman rulers who Paul sustained! How little reason we have to complain. How great the reason we have to rejoice. For in the restoration we have again authority to minister in the ordinances of the Gospel! The Prophet of the restoration could hardly contain the joy we ought to feel at what we have been given:

> Now, what do we hear in the gospel which we have received? A voice of gladness! A voice of mercy from heaven; and a voice of truth out of the earth; glad tidings for the dead; a voice of gladness for the living and the dead; glad tidings of great joy. How beautiful upon the mountains are the feet of those that bring glad tidings of good things, and that say unto Zion: Behold, thy God reigneth! As the dews of Carmel, so shall the knowledge of God descend upon them! And again, what do we hear? Glad tidings from Cumorah! Moroni, an angel from heaven, declaring the fulfilment of the prophets--the book to be revealed. A voice of the Lord in the wilderness of Fayette, Seneca county, declaring the three witnesses to bear record of the book! The voice of Michael on the banks of the Susquehanna, detecting the devil when he appeared as an angel of light! The voice of Peter, James, and John in the wilderness between Harmony, Susquehanna county, and Colesville, Broome

> county, on the Susquehanna river, declaring themselves as possessing the keys of the kingdom, and of the dispensation of the fulness of times! And again, the voice of God in the chamber of old Father Whitmer, in Fayette, Seneca county, and at sundry times, and in divers places through all the travels and tribulations of this Church of Jesus Christ of Latter-day Saints! And the voice of Michael, the archangel; the voice of Gabriel, and of Raphael, and of divers angels, from Michael or Adam down to the present time, all declaring their dispensation, their rights, their keys, their honors, their majesty and glory, and the power of their priesthood; giving line upon line, precept upon precept; here a little, and there a little; giving us consolation by holding forth that which is to come, confirming our hope! (D&C 128: 19-21.)

Joseph could hardly rejoice enough. I can hardly thank the Lord enough. It is through The Church of Jesus Christ of Latter-day Saints I have come to know Christ. I have received His ordinances through this Church. I have been given promises, covenants, blessings, cleansing, healing, understanding, and joy through the hope which comes from the Gospel preached by The Church of Jesus Christ of Latter-day Saints. Therefore it would be profoundly ungrateful for me to not end my testimony of Jesus Christ without also expressing my gratitude for the ancient order of things which He restored through Joseph Smith.

Let us all be joyfully subject to the powers which be; and still press on to become a son or daughter of God. Let all of us come to the point where we can universally cry: "Abba! Father!" in a joyous refrain of worship, knowing we have a perfect brightness of hope for the world to come![108]

The Atonement of Christ is an ongoing and incomplete work. He has "finished His preparations" for us, but we are not complete.[109] We will not be complete until after we have become like Him. That process requires us to change, leave behind our defects, and develop faith, hope and charity. As we have seen, the kind of love Christ has is charity. It returns forgiveness for offenses. It suffers and forgives. It intercedes for the wrongdoer and asks for him to be forgiven even while the offender is deliberately harming. It shows itself in Stephen's life when he asks God to forgive his murderers while they are in the very act of killing him.[110] I use Stephen instead of Christ because he is one of us. He is a follower, and not the Master. But he became like the Master, and so must we.

There has been no offense I have suffered, no insult received, no wound inflicted which has not made me better. It is in that which disappoints us, dashes our hopes and inflicts suffering that

---

[108] I use the word "hope" here as defined in Chapter 4 of *Eighteen Verses*, pages 60-77.

[109] "For behold, I, God, have suffered these things for all, that they might not suffer if they would repent; But if they would not repent they must suffer even as I; Which suffering caused myself, even God, the greatest of all, to tremble because of pain, and to bleed at every pore, and to suffer both body and spirit--and would that I might not drink the bitter cup, and shrink-- Nevertheless, glory be to the Father, and I partook and finished my preparations unto the children of men." (D&C 19: 16-19.)

[110] "And they stoned Stephen, calling upon God, and saying, Lord Jesus, receive my spirit. And he kneeled down, and cried with a loud voice, Lord, lay not this sin to their charge. And when he had said this, he fell asleep." (Acts 7: 59-60.)

allows us to understand the Lord. Our mortal victories are meaningless. But our failings, our walk into the valley of the shadow of death, our dark and oppressive burdens, these are the things that enable us understand and even know Him. All Joseph's triumphs were of less value to him than the months in Liberty Jail. It was there the Lord taught him:

> If thou art accused with all manner of false accusations; if thine enemies fall upon thee; if they tear thee from the society of thy father and mother and brethren and sisters; and if with a drawn sword thine enemies tear thee from the bosom of thy wife, and of thine offspring, ..., and thou be dragged to prison, and thine enemies prowl around thee like wolves for the blood of the lamb; And if thou shouldst be cast into the pit, or into the hands of murderers, and the sentence of death passed upon thee; if thou be cast into the deep; if the billowing surge conspire against thee; if fierce winds become thine enemy; if the heavens gather blackness, and all the elements combine to hedge up the way; and above all, if the very jaws of hell shall gape open the mouth wide after thee, know thou, my son, that **all these things shall give thee experience, and shall be for thy good. The Son of Man hath descended below them all. Art thou greater than he?** (D&C 121: 6-8, emphasis added.)

More than through the First Vision, Joseph Smith learned to know God by the bitter suffering in Liberty Jail. For it was there his mind came to understand the meaning of the saying: "As many as I love, I rebuke and chasten[.]" (Rev. 3: 19.)

If you want the Atonement to work in your life, forgive others. Forgive even deliberate offenses. Lay them down, carry them no longer. Make intercession for those who have done evil and charity will develop. The same charity that Christ possessed. Find the freedom which comes from that kind of charity alone. Then you will know Him, because you are like Him. Then you will understand John's teaching: "when he shall appear, we shall be like him[.]" (1 John 3: 2.)

THE END

Bibliography

Backman, Milton V., Jr. *Joseph Smith's First Vision*, Second Edition. Salt Lake City: Bookcraft, 1971.

Burton, Theodore M. *Neither Cryptic Nor Hidden, Ensign.* May 1977, beginning at p. 28.

Burton, Theodore M. *The Power of Elijah*, *Ensign.* May 1974, beginning at p. 61.

Bushman, Richard L. *Rough Stone Rolling.* New York: Alfred A. Knopf, 2005.

Carroll, James Carroll. *Constantine's Sword.* New York: Houghton Mifflin Company, 2001.

Clark, J. Reuben. *Our Lord of the Gospels.* Salt Lake City: Deseret Book Company, 1954.

Edershiem, Alfred. *The Temple, Its Ministry and Services.* Massachusetts: Hendrickson Publishers, 1994.

Ehat, Andrew F. and Cook, Lyndon W. *Words of Joseph Smith.* Salt Lake City: Bookcraft, 1981.

John Wesley's Works. 7 vols. Grand Rapids: Baker Publishing, 1996.

Journal of Discourses, 26 vols. London: Latter-day Saints' Book Depot, 1854-1886.

Kimball, Spencer W. *CR*, *Ensign.* October 1959, Afternoon Meeting.

Lee, Harold B., *CR*, *Ensign.* October 1965, Afternoon Meeting.

McConkie, Bruce R. *Doctrinal New Testament Commentary*, *3 Vols.* Salt Lake City: Bookcraft, 1965..

Nelson, Russell M. *The Spirit of Elijah, Ensign.* November 1994, beginning at p. 84.

Nibley, Hugh. *Abraham in Egypt.* Salt Lake City: Deseret Book, 1981.

_____.*An Approach to the Book of Abraham.* Deseret Book, Salt Lake City, 2009.

_____.*Eloquent Witness: Nibley on Himself, Others and the Temple.* Salt Lake City: Deseret Book, 2008.

_____.*Mormonism and Early Christianity*,. Edited by Todd M. Compton and Stephen D. Ricks. Salt Lake City: Deseret Book, 1987.

_____.*Nibley on the Timely and the Timeless.* Religious Studies Center: BYU, 1978.

_____.*The Message of the Joseph Smith Papyri: An Egyptian Endowment.* Salt Lake City: Deseret Book, 1975.

_____.*The World and the Prophets.* Edited by John W. Welch, Gary P. Gillum, and Don E. Norton. Salt Lake City: Deseret Book Company, 1987.

Our Most Distinguishing Feature. Jeffrey R. Holland. Conference Report, April 2005.

Pratt, John. *Meridian Magazine.* 17 November 2004.

Smith, Joseph Fielding. *Doctrines of Salvation.* Edited by Bruce R. McConkie. 3 volumes. Salt Lake City: Bookcraft, 1956.

Smith, Joseph Fielding. *Answers to Gospel Questions, Volume 4. 5 Volumes.* Salt Lake City: Deseret Book, 1963.

Snuffer, Denver C., Jr. *Beloved Enos.* Mill Creek Press: Salt Lake City, 2009.

_____. *Eighteen Verses.* Mill Creek Press: Salt Lake City, 2007.

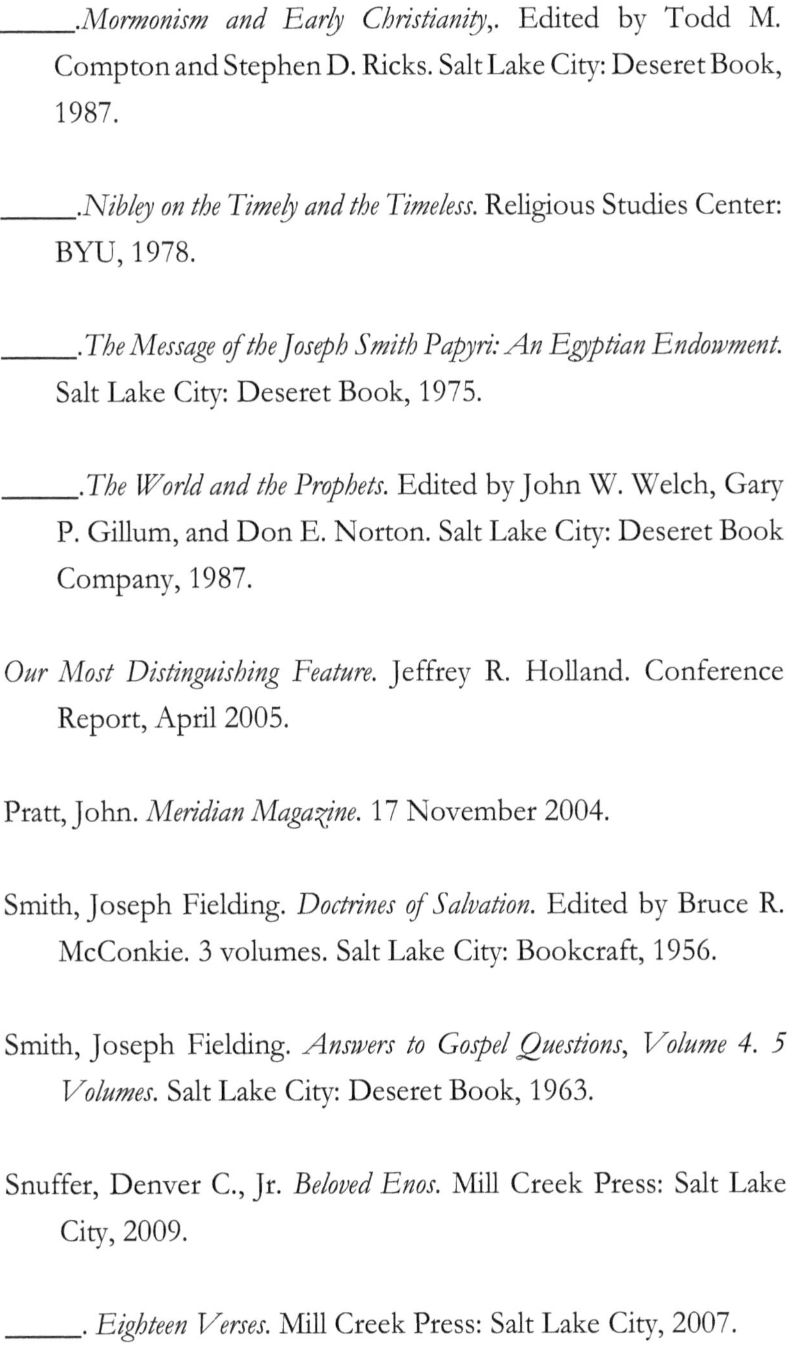

_____. *Nephi's Isaiah.* Mill Creek Press: Salt Lake, 2006.

_____.*Ten Parables.* Mill Creek Press: Salt Lake City, 2008.

_____.*The Second Comforter: Conversing With the Lord Through the Veil,* Second Edition. Mill Creek Press: Salt Lake, 2008.

Sorenson, John L. *Religious Groups and Movements Among the Nephites, 200-1B.C.* found in *The Disciple as Scholar: Essays on Scripture and the Ancient World in Honor of Richard Lloyd Anderson.* Edited by Steven D. Ricks, Donald W. Parry, and Andrew H. Hedges. Provo: FARMS, 2000.

Talmage, James E. *Jesus the Christ.* Salt Lake City: Deseret Book, 1983.

Teachings of the Prophet Joseph Smith. Arranged by Joseph Fielding Smith. Salt Lake City: Deseret Book Company, 1972.

Teachings of Spencer W. Kimball, The. Edited by Edward L Kimball. Salt Lake City: Deseret Book, 1982.

The Worlds of Joseph Smith: A Bicentennial Conference at the Library of Congress. Edited by John W. Welch. Provo: Brigham Young University Press, 2006.

Whitney, Orson F. *Life of Heber C. Kimball.* Salt Lake City: Bookcraft, 1945.

Young, Brigham. *Discourses of Brigham Young.* Selected and arranged by John A. Widstoe. Salt Lake City: Deseret Book Company, 1973.

Index

B

F

G

H

I

J

K

N

O

P

T

U

V

W

Y

Z

A Note About The Author

DENVER C. SNUFFER, JR. is an attorney living in Sandy, Utah. He has an Associates of Arts degree from Daniel Webster Jr. College, Bachelors of Business Administration from McMurry University, and Juris Doctor from the J. Reuben Clark Law School at Brigham Young University. He was admitted to practice law in 1980 in Utah, and has been a practicing attorney since then. A convert to the LDS faith in 1973 when 19 years old, he has now been a member of the LDS Church for over thirty-two years. He has served as a member of the Stake High Council in the Sandy Crescent Stake. Previously he has taught Gospel Doctrine and Priesthood classes for twenty-one years in Wards in Pleasant Grove, Alpine and Sandy, Utah. He has instructed Graduate Institute classes at the University of Utah College of Law for two years, and instructed at the BYU Education Week for three years. He also taught a weekly class on the Book of Mormon for eight years. He is the author of five earlier books, *The Second Comforter: Conversing With the Lord Through the Veil*, published by Mill Creek Press in 2006, second edition in 2008, *Nephi's Isaiah*, also published by Mill Creek Press in 2006, *Eighteen Verses*, published by Mill Creek Press in 2007, *Ten Parables*, published by Mill Creek Press in 2008, and *Beloved Enos,* published by Mill Creek Press in 2009.

A Note On The Type

This book was set in Garamond. The fonts are based on the fonts first cut by Claude Garamond (c. 1480-1561). Garamond was a pupil of Geoffroy Tory and is believed to have followed the Venetian models, although he introduced a number of important differences, and it is to him that we owe the letter we now know as "old style." He gave to his letters a certain elegance and feeling of movement that won their creator an immediate reputation and the patronage of Francis I of France.

Designed by Mill Creek Press
Cover by Arisman Design Studio
Essex, Massachusetts
Printed and bound by BookSurge Publishing
Charleston, South Carolina

www.ingramcontent.com/pod-product-compliance
Lightning Source LLC
Chambersburg PA
CBHW060454090426
42735CB00011B/1981
* 9 7 8 0 9 7 9 8 4 5 5 3 6 *